Artificial Intelligence, Reincarnation, and Resurrection

Artificial Intelligence, Reincarnation, and Resurrection

An Inquiry into the Ultimate
Fulfillment of Human Nature

ERNEST M. VALEA

RESOURCE *Publications* • Eugene, Oregon

ARTIFICIAL INTELLIGENCE, REINCARNATION, AND RESURRECTION
An Inquiry into the Ultimate Fulfillment of Human Nature

Copyright © 2021 Ernest M. Valea. All rights reserved. Except for brief quotations in critical publications or reviews, no part of this book may be reproduced in any manner without prior written permission from the publisher. Write: Permissions, Wipf and Stock Publishers, 199 W. 8th Ave., Suite 3, Eugene, OR 97401.

Resource Publications
An Imprint of Wipf and Stock Publishers
199 W. 8th Ave., Suite 3
Eugene, OR 97401

www.wipfandstock.com

PAPERBACK ISBN: 978-1-7252-9748-7
HARDCOVER ISBN: 978-1-7252-9749-4
EBOOK ISBN: 978-1-7252-9750-0

04/14/21

A leading prayer:
"From the unreal lead me to the real,
from darkness lead me to light,
from death lead me to immortality"

(*Brihadaranyaka Upanishad* 1,3,28)

Contents

Introduction | xi

1. The Mind-Body Problem and the Nature of Consciousness | 1
    1.1 Physical and Mental Phenomena. Dualism vs. Physicalism | 2
    1.2 Cartesian Dualism | 4
        1.2.1 Mind and Body as Two Different Substances | 5
        1.2.2 Criticism of Descartes's Methodology | 9
        1.2.3 The Mind-Body Problem in Cartesian Dualism | 10
    1.3 Physicalist views of human nature | 13
        1.3.1 Behaviorism | 14
        1.3.2 The Identity Theory | 17
        1.3.3 Functionalism and Computationalism | 20
        1.3.4 The Problem of Computationalism | 22
        1.3.5 Property Dualism and Nonreductive Physicalism | 24
    1.4 Physicalism and Consciousness | 26
    1.5 Science and Scientism | 33
2. Philosophy of Mind on Personal Identity and the Survival of Death | 38
    2.1 Physicalist Criteria for Preserving Personal Identity | 40
        2.1.1 The Bodily Criterion | 40
        2.1.2 The Brain Criterion | 41
        2.1.3 The Physical Criterion | 43
    2.2 The Psychological Continuity Criterion | 44
    2.3 Problems of the Psychological Continuity Criterion | 47
    2.4 Revised Forms of the Psychological Criterion | 49
    2.5 Mind-Body Dualism in the Form of the Simple View | 51
    2.6 Derek Parfit—Survival without Numerical Identity | 54
    2.7 David Hume—the Person as a Collection of Perceptions | 57
    2.8 What is the Self? | 60

3. From AI to Transhumanism: The Physicalist Project to Defeat Death | 63
    3.1 What is AI? | 64
    3.2 From Algorithms to Machine Learning | 66
    3.3 Meet Sophia, the World's First AI Humanoid Robot | 72
    3.4 What is the Real Threat Posed by AI? | 75
    3.5 Neuralink and the Next Step in Human Evolution | 79
    3.6 Transhumanism and Post-Human Beings | 82
    3.7 Is Mind Upload a Scientifically Realistic Project? | 85
    3.8 Transhumanist Immortality and Personal Identity | 90

4. Human Nature in Hinduism and Buddhism | 95
    4.1 Everlasting Life in the Religion of the Vedas | 97
    4.2 The Upanishads and Hindu Pantheism | 100
    4.3 Human Nature in Tantra and Hatha Yoga | 104
    4.4 The Dualistic Philosophy of the Samkhya and Yoga Schools | 107
    4.5 Self and Personal Identity in Hinduism | 110
    4.6 Human Nature in Buddhism | 113
    4.7 Doctrinal Developments in Mahayana Buddhism | 118
    4.8 Person and Personal Identity in Buddhism | 121

5. Reincarnation and the Survival of Personal Identity | 123
    5.1 Who and What Reincarnates, and How? | 124
    5.2 Modern Evidence for Reincarnation: Hypnotic Regression and Spontaneous Past Life Recall by Children | 134
        5.2.1 Hypnotic Regression as a Resource for Proving Reincarnation | 134
        5.2.2 Spontaneous Past Life Recall by Children | 141
        5.2.3 Alternative Explanations for Past Life Recall by Children | 145
    5.3 Reincarnation as Bearer of Universal Justice | 152

6. Human Nature and Resurrection in Christianity | 159
    6.1 Science and Faith | 160
    6.2 Created in the Image and Likeness of God | 163
    6.3 Body and Soul as Matter and Form | 166
    6.4 The Nature of the Human Soul | 170
    6.5 Human Nature and Its Four Causes | 176
    6.6 The Restoration of Human Nature at the Resurrection | 177
    6.7 Resurrection and Bodily Continuity | 181

7. AI, Reincarnation and Resurrection as Modes of Reaching the Ultimate Fulfillment of Human Nature | 186
    7.1   Eternal Life According to Transhumanism and Christianity. No Death vs. Death and Resurrection | 186
        7.1.1 "The Fable of the Dragon-Tyrant": A Transhumanist and a Christian Reading | 194
    7.2   Reincarnation and Christian Faith | 198
        7.2.1 Are There Hints Left in the Bible That It Once Taught Reincarnation? | 198
        7.2.2 Origen and Origenism | 203
        7.2.3 Reincarnation in the Thought of Other Church Fathers | 205
        7.2.4 Has the Bible Text Been Censored? | 207
        7.2.5 Why Is Reincarnation Incompatible with Christian Faith? | 209

Concluding Thoughts | 213

Bibliography | 217
Index | 225

Introduction

THE ABSURDITY OF OUR mortality began to intrigue me when I was a teenager. One day I found a collection of very old family pictures of my great-great-grandparents. The oldest picture, dated 1901, drew my attention in a particular way. It showed a group of ten people, among which was my paternal grandmother. She died when I was very little, so I can't remember her in real life. In that thick stained grayish picture she was a little three-year-old girl. Seventy-five years later no one remembered the other nine people in the picture, which were probably her parents, grandparents, and other relatives. Ironically, the very reason they took the picture was so they would not be forgotten by their descendants, but their attempt failed. The photograph left me uneasy and made me wonder about the meaning of life. For me, a teenager who had just started asking big questions, these people were extinct. All their life-long struggles, achievements, dreams, and loves were gone with the wind. Was I expecting the same end? Would I too be completely forgotten after three generations, as if I had never existed? Isn't this absurd?

Later, as a student, I thought there was only one way to avoid "extinction": to leave something behind, in the form of a discovery, an invention, or something that would be of benefit for the next generations, so that they could remember me and thus I would become, in some way, immortal. There are many names in the world of science that will be remembered for many years to come. Albert Einstein certainly is one of them. They even preserved his brain for following generations to research the unique features of the brain of a genius. However, as an individual human person, he no longer exists. We know his work and his theories, but very little of his personal thoughts or inner life. In other words, only the *information* about him has survived, not himself, as a person. So he cannot really enjoy his contribution to the good of humankind, because he, as a person, no longer exists.

I was not alone in struggling with the absurdity of death. In fact, there is a whole movement made of computer scientists, neuroscientists, and hi-tech engineers who take the goal of defeating death very seriously. The name of this movement is Transhumanism. One of its important voices expresses a similar perplexity as I did when contemplating the reality of death. In the words of Max More, "Individual death makes life meaningless, as it disconnects us from everything we value, whatever it is."[1]

In their quest to overcome the frailty of this biological body, transhumanists go so far as to envision a radical transformation of human nature into a complete non-organic being. If we could store all the details of our life, all our memories and experiences as a mindfile, and then realize a whole brain emulation that could run this mindfile, we would get what in transhumanist terms is called a mindclone. Instead of depending on a frail physical brain, such a mindclone could "live" in a computer and be acknowledged as our digital self. We would not even need a body to become immortal but could achieve this goal as an avatar in a virtual world. Another option would be to download our mind to the memory of an android robot and survive as such in a world of machines who would periodically upgrade themselves. But since we are nowhere near to realizing such ideals, the current solution used by transhumanists to avoid extinction is to preserve the body (or at least the brain) by the use of cryonics. They expect that the scientists of the future will find solutions to our present insuperable difficulties and revive them.

Should we take such projects seriously? Is it realistic to believe that such futuristic solutions would preserve our personal identity? Could we survive as such hi-tech beings? Does consciousness arise from the sheer complexity of neural connections in our brain, and could it be stored as a mindfile? Are these assumptions warranted?

In discussing the many philosophical theories encountered in this book we will often meet the word "assumption." Assumptions are beliefs that we accept as true without questioning, and that we use as building blocks for a particular worldview. In the case of science, they are not "scientific" truths, but foundational elements which science itself takes for granted. "Only matter exists," or "non-physical things cannot exist," are examples of assumptions which science itself cannot prove or disprove.

---

1. Manzocco, *Transhumanism*, 64.

The assumption that the physical universe is eternal and exists by itself is an assumption no more scientifically provable than the one that God created the world. Depending on the assumptions we choose to follow, we reach a particular way of defining human nature and its ultimate fulfillment, as will become clear in this book. This is a very important fact to remember. Assumptions are accepted by trusting the authority that formulated them; they are not the result of scientific inquiry, for science cannot inform us about what is beyond its domain.

The basic assumption which we must be aware of is whether we believe ourselves to be just physical beings. If we agree with this assumption we follow a theory of human nature called physicalism. It claims that all of reality, and the only reality, is physical. Therefore all phenomena, either physical or mental, must be generated by matter, that is, by the physical body and its brain, and must be explained in physical terms. As a result, for physicalists personal identity is provided by the body, or at least by the brain, its most significant part. In transhumanist scenarios it can even be reduced to the *information* contained in the brain.

Another important view on human nature we will encounter is dualism. It speaks of two fundamental and irreducible substances in human nature, the physical body and the non-physical mind, each generating its proper type of phenomena. The mind is considered a non-physical substance, not subject to the laws of physics, and fundamentally different from the brain. Its most important property is that it can survive the death of the body, and thus preserves personal identity at death.

Besides transhumanist efforts to defeat death with resources based on science and technology, we obviously need to consider the religious option. In fact, most religions make defeating death their essential task. *What kind* of immortality they speak of is a more complicated issue to be discussed. One limitation of this book is that it cannot cover a large variety of religious views on immortality. I have chosen the most popular in the Western world that teach reincarnation, and the Christian view of the resurrection. I have not explored the scenarios of spiritualism and parapsychology, in which one survives as a ghost that can be summoned in spiritualistic séances. Nor have I explored near-death experiences and out-of-body experiences. These have secondary importance as theories of preserving personal identity, and once we understand the flaws in the Eastern view of reincarnation, they will appear even less convincing.

Due to the vast and heterogeneous domain we are exploring in this book, we need the help of science, philosophy of mind, and religion.

Science will help us, especially in the categories of neuroscience and computer science, to explore what we can know about the brain, and the extent to which our consciousness and personal identity can be translated into algorithms and eventually copied to a machine. Philosophy of mind is a branch of philosophy that interprets data from the neurosciences and psychology to study the nature of the mind and mental phenomena, personal identity, consciousness, and other such topics. While philosophy explores these topics by means of rational thought, religion informs us on ultimate reality and personal identity by using resources that claim to come from beyond the limitations of our reason.

The following is a brief outline of the path we will be taking:

In the first two chapters we look at the current debates in the philosophy of mind, especially those that revolve around the following three questions: What is the mind (or soul, in religious language)? What is the relationship between the mind and the body? What are the criteria by which we establish the continuity of personal identity? The traditional way in which manuals of philosophy of mind proceed is to assess and criticize Cartesian dualism and then offer physicalist responses. We will stick to the same approach, and pay special attention to the assumptions these theories follow in defining consciousness, the self, and personal identity.

In chapter 3 we explore the ways in which artificial intelligence (AI) can give hope to the physicalist project of defeating death according to the expectations of transhumanism. Some of the questions asked above will return: Are we just physical machines of great complexity, with the brain as the hardware on which consciousness operates as its software? If so, can we speculate on ways in which the mind could be uploaded to a machine and no longer suffer the frailty of this (biological) body? Could an android robot or a mindfile in a computer simulation be conscious? Or could we merge with machines and become cyborgs? Can we dare hope to attain immortality on such transhumanist expectations?

In chapter 4 we explore the way human nature is defined in two of the most important religions of the East: Hinduism and Buddhism. They obviously start from different assumptions on human nature and immortality. Hinduism claims that we defeat death by an intrinsic core of our human nature, called the self, which is non-physical and cannot die. It does reincarnate, however, according to a law called karma, and is meant to return to its source. Buddhism has a very peculiar view on human nature, for it does not acknowledge any permanent element unaffected by change that could define personal identity. However, it still claims that we reincarnate until we reach perfection.

In chapter 5 we get into a more detailed account of how reincarnation works, following on from chapter 4. Interest in reincarnation is huge in the West, not only among followers of Eastern religions or New Age enthusiasts, but also among many non-religiously affiliated people who are dissatisfied with the way science responds to the questions of life and the afterlife. To think that you have lived many lives before this one and there are countless others ahead to attain perfection can be a very reassuring thought. Followers of reincarnation claim that it explains the differences between us and gives hope that present hardships have meaning, for their origin is in a previous life, and that things will get better in a future life. We will analyze two kinds of proofs for it which come up in apparently scientific ways. These are cases of people who allegedly remember their past lives, under hypnosis as adults, or spontaneously as children. Lastly we examine another kind of argument in favor of reincarnation, the alleged justice it performs by punishing or rewarding the deeds of past lives.

In chapter 6 we analyze the way human nature is defined in Christianity, and follow one of the greatest Christian philosophers in exploring the meaning of the resurrection, which is the Christian way of attaining immortality. As a special case of dualism, Christianity holds that we have a physical body *and* a non-physical soul, which form a unity. This view opposes both Esoteric theories, which affirm that we are souls fallen into physical bodies, and the physicalist view which considers us mammals that are so highly evolved that they have acquired self-consciousness and invented God. The Christian view of immortality is one that requires the preservation of both the soul and the body. Both are necessary for us to remain the same person we are now. This is why the Christian view of immortality requires the resurrection of the body.

Finally, in chapter 7 we assess the differences between the three views of immortality and the extent to which they are compatible with one another. First we compare and contrast the transhumanist scenarios of defeating death with the Christian view of the resurrection. Then we discuss the Christian stand on reincarnation, the alleged proofs that it once was part of the Christian faith, and also the dogmatic issues it raises.

This book is the result of many years of struggling with theories of human nature and of finally finding the way out of the maze of theories by following the light of Christ. I acknowledge from the very beginning,

I have written this book as a Christian, not a computer scientist, not a transhumanist, not a New Ager.

Although there is no "Acknowledgments" section, I want to thank Mrs. Danielle Plant for her work in proofreading this book and for pointing to difficult passages that needed clarification. Without her help this book would not have existed in this format.

I hope that you will find the topics we explore in this book interesting and that it will challenge you to start your own investigation on human nature and its ultimate fulfillment.

Ernest Valea
October 7, 2020

1

The Mind-Body Problem and the Nature of Consciousness

IN THIS CHAPTER WE explore two closely related topics: the nature of the mind and that of consciousness. Consciousness is both a familiar concept, for it is rooted in our personal daily life, and also a mysterious one, for we cannot pin it down to an exact formula. It has many aspects, such as awareness of where we are, what we do, how we feel, what our beliefs are, what we plan to do, etc. Most importantly, it is an awareness of being a personal agent in interaction with the world. Consciousness gets blurred if we take drugs or get drunk, and ceases completely in dreamless sleep or if we undergo general anesthesia.

The other important topic we explore in this chapter (and the whole book) is the mind (or the soul). I will use soul and mind interchangeably, as terms which bear the same meaning. The first term is used mostly in a religious context, while the second is preferred by philosophers, in a more scholarly context. Whether it has a physical nature or not is one of the important topics of this chapter, in which we explore the resources offered by the philosophy of mind for finding an answer. Is it a non-physical entity that floats away at death and thus survives the death of the body, as most religious people affirm? But if it has a non-physical nature, how can it interact with the physical body? This topic in the philosophy of mind is called the mind-body problem (or the soul-body problem when using religious language). Is the mind a product of the brain, a function that developed through millions of years of evolution and vanishes at death, as most non-religious people believe? If so, is it a kind of computer program, that is, software that runs on hardware called the brain? These are just a few of the questions we explore in this chapter, from two very different perspectives—one that follows naturalistic explanations, and thus seems more scientifically oriented, and the other, which affirms the mind as a non-physical entity that is not subject to the laws of physics, and thus seems more suited for religious thought. However, how much science and how much faith is involved in each of these perspectives is itself a matter of debate.

1.1 PHYSICAL AND MENTAL PHENOMENA. DUALISM VS. PHYSICALISM

In high school biology we learned that the senses provide information to the brain by way of electrochemical signals transmitted by neurons. The magnitude of these signals, in millivolts, as well as the motor response transmitted by the brain to the muscles, can be measured by inserting electrodes along neurons. In terms of the mechanism involved, we speak of neural conduction, when we refer to how the electrical signal travels along the neuron (as a flow of sodium and potassium ions across the neuronal membrane), and of synaptic transmission, when we explain how the signal travels from one neuron to the next (by the movement of neurotransmitters in the synaptic cleft). This is neuroscience, not philosophy.

What can be scientifically measured and explained is ultimately a physical phenomenon.[1] What cannot be scientifically measured is the mental content associated with neural activity, the personal experience associated with a certain perception. For example, when looking at a flower, the optic nerve transmits an electrochemical signal of a certain magnitude to a certain area of the occipital cortex. The mental content of this perception, the feeling the flower produces, cannot be explained in physical terms for it has a subjective quality knowable only to the person involved. Therefore we speak of two kinds of phenomena in perception: the physical, which can be measured and explored scientifically, and the mental, which is subjective and cannot be translated into scientific formulas. In explaining the nature of the mind, philosophy of mind attempts to explore the relationship between the two types of phenomena.

---

1. Actually, it is an electrochemical phenomenon, but in order to preserve the distinction between physical and non-physical phenomena, I will call it physical.

Depending on the fundamental substance (or substances) we consider to be involved in physical and mental phenomena, two major perspectives in the philosophy of mind open up: monism and dualism. Monism admits the existence of a single fundamental substance, while dualism speaks of two.[2] The main form of Western philosophical monism, and the only one I will discuss, is physicalism.[3] It claims that the whole of reality, and the only reality, is physical. In other words, only matter exists. God, angels and a non-physical soul are discarded as non-scientific fairytales. Therefore all phenomena, either physical or mental, must be generated by matter, that is, by the physical body and its brain, and must be explained in physical terms.

Dualism speaks of two fundamental and irreducible substances in human nature, the physical body and the non-physical mind, each generating its proper type of phenomena. Only the phenomena we can observe by physical devices have a physical nature, while mental phenomena have a non-physical nature and non-physical properties. They are known only by introspection and do not submit to scientific inquiry. In the above example, the physical phenomenon associated with the perception of a flower can be measured with electrodes placed in the visual cortex of the occipital lobe, while the mental phenomenon, the beauty of the flower, is a private experience that cannot be scientifically determined because it belongs to the non-physical mind. For dualists, the mind is a non-physical substance, not subject to the laws of physics, and fundamentally different from the brain. Its most important property is that it can survive the death of the body.

According to physicalists, the mind is the product of the brain, the result of Darwinian evolution. At a certain stage of development the brain started to produce mental phenomena such as emotions, thoughts, and desires. Such endowments made human beings better able to survive their harsh environment and paved the way for further evolution, which eventually produced *Homo sapiens*. Thus physical and mental phenomena must be different aspects of the same physical reality. Since there is no non-physical component in human nature, personal existence must end at death, unless we could preserve life in its present biological form or by

---

2. I refer here to substance dualism, and in a later section to property dualism.

3. A second form is idealism, which states that only spirit is a real substance, while a third form is neutral monism, which affirms a yet subtler substance that would generate both matter and spirit.

transferring consciousness to another physical form (hence the interest in artificial intelligence and conscious robots).

Manuals of philosophy of mind usually start with a critique of a form of dualism called Cartesian dualism, and then discuss physicalist theories of the mind, as more appropriate for our "age of science." I will follow on the same lines, both from an ontological perspective (*what is the mind and consciousness*), and from an epistemological one (*how can we know* it is so).

1.2 CARTESIAN DUALISM

The French philosopher René Descartes (1596–1650) is credited as one of the fathers of modern philosophy. In his quest to establish a new path in philosophical exploration he rejected two major tenets of scholasticism.[4] First, he disagreed with the assumption that the senses mediate an objective knowledge of how things really are. Since they sometimes mislead us, the senses cannot provide an error-free foundation for knowledge. For instance, sight makes us believe that the sun orbits around the earth, which is false. In his view, even the most commonly accepted sensory data, such as the existence of the physical world or of one's own body, can be questioned as being illusions, of the same reliability as dreams. So he concluded that we need a more trustworthy instrument of knowledge than our senses. The other philosophical approach he rejected was Aristotle's hylomorphist view of human nature, that is, the assertion that a non-physical form (the soul) is the principle that organizes matter (the body).[5] Such scholastic theories were seen as no longer useful for philosophers in the age of science, so the essence of human nature must be found by reasoning. In other words, it was time for philosophy to exit the "age of faith" and usher in the "age of reason." Instead of religious authority, Descartes argued that philosophy should rely on the authority of reason and empirical evidence in order to draw a proper portrait of human nature.

---

4. Descartes studied at the Jesuit College of La Flèche (around 1606–1615) and must have been well versed in scholasticism. For more information see Gaukroger, *Descartes*, and Clarke, *Descartes*.

5. I will return to this theory in chapter 6.

1.2.1 Mind and Body as Two Different Substances

In the first of his famous *Meditations* Descartes states that in order to "establish anything at all in the sciences that was stable and likely to last" he needed to "demolish everything completely and start right from the foundations."[6] Therefore, in the *Second Meditation* he sets out to find "just one thing, however slight, that is certain and unshakeable"[7] as the basis of modern philosophy. The only thing he could not doubt was the very ability to doubt empirical experience. In other words, one can doubt sensory data, but not that which makes doubting possible, that is, thinking itself. The very act of thinking provides the certainty of one's existence as a personal agent in the world, which is summed up by his famous dictum "I think, therefore I am." It first appears in his *Discourse on the Method*, chapter 4, where he is so certain of its truth that he affirms it as "the first principle of the philosophy" he was seeking.[8] In his words,

> Simply by knowing that I exist and seeing at the same time that absolutely nothing else belongs to my nature or essence except that I am a thinking thing, I can infer correctly that my essence consists solely in the fact that I am a thinking thing.[9]

For Descartes to be a "thinking thing" means to have a non-physical mind as the ground of thinking. This intuition is based on the rule he establishes in his *Third Meditation*, which states that "whatever I perceive very clearly and distinctly is true."[10] In the *Sixth Meditation* he continues his speculation on the nature of the mind by stating that since he can have "a clear and distinct idea" of himself, as a "thinking, non-extended thing," while also having a "distinct idea of body" as "an extended, non-thinking thing," the conclusion is that "I am really distinct from my body, and can exist without it."[11] Therefore human nature must be composed of two substances: the non-physical mind and the physical body. The view that

---

6. Descartes, *Meditations on First Philosophy*, 12.

7. Descartes, *Meditations*, 16.

8. Descartes, *A Discourse on the Method*, 28. Since we are analyzing his views from the perspective of philosophy of mind, a more appropriate rendering of what he could not doubt is the fact that he is a conscious being.

9. Descartes, *Meditations*, 54.

10. Descartes, *Meditations*, 24.

11. Descartes, *Meditations*, 54.

the mind is a substance different from the body and capable of outliving the body is emphasized again in the *Discourse on the Method*:

> I thereby concluded that I was a *substance* whose whole *essence* or nature resides only in thinking, and which, in order to exist, has no need of place and is not dependent on any physical thing. Accordingly this 'I', that is to say, the Soul by which I am what I am, is entirely distinct from the body and is even easier to know than the body; and would not stop being everything it is, even if the body were not to exist.[12]

This particular form of dualism defined by Descartes bears his name, as Cartesian dualism. In the *Sixth Meditation*, the French philosopher argues that the proof that the mind and the body are different substances is the fact that they have different properties. The body has size and weight, can be observed by others, and is composed of parts (is divisible), while the mind is indivisible and is known only by introspection. This line of reasoning will be emphasized by Gottfried Wilhelm Leibniz (1646–1716), as the law that bears his name. Leibniz's Law states that if two things have different properties, those things must be different. In other words, if X has a property that Y does not have, and if Y has a property that X does not have, X and Y are two different things. Since the mind has an unquestionable existence, while the body does not (for we could dream of having a body), and since the body can be described in physical terms and is divisible, while the mind is not, it means that the mind and the body are different substances. However, by emphasizing the distinction between mind and body, and by stating that the mind can exist separately from the body, he did not mean that the body is not an essential part of human nature (as Plato did). He sought to establish that the foundation of knowledge rests in the non-physical mind, not that human nature would be defined just by that non-physical entity.

As we can expect, physicalist philosophers rejected Descartes's approach, especially his view of the non-physical nature of the mind.

---

12. Descartes, *A Discourse on the Method*, 29. Descartes defines "substance" in his reply to Arnauld's *Objections* as "something that can exist by itself, i.e., without the help of any other substance." In *The Principles of Philosophy* he points out that the term "substance" applies differently to God in comparison to created things: "Actually, there's only one substance that can be understood to depend on nothing else, namely God. We can see that all the other substances can exist only with God's help. So the term 'substance' doesn't apply in the same sense to God and to other things—meaning that no clearly intelligible sense of the term is common to God and to things he has created" (1,51). This point will be discussed in chapter 6 of this book.

Unfortunately, most of them ignore important elements of Cartesian dualism in their criticism. They jump directly from assessing his thought in the *Second Meditation*, in which Descartes assumes that the non-physical mind is the foundation of knowledge (since it cannot be doubted), to the *Sixth Meditation*, in which he attempts to prove that the mind and the body are different substances. In the ignored *Meditations* (the third to the fifth) Descartes uses a line of reasoning which is irrelevant for physicalist philosophers of mind, but important for our exploration in this book: the action of God as a guarantor for the certainty of our knowledge. Let us briefly follow his reasoning, mostly ignored by philosophy textbooks.

First of all, we must remember that Descartes was a Christian believer, who sought to keep God in his philosophical views, and even sneaked in scholastic arguments by the back door of his thinking. Here is how he introduces God to his fellow philosophers: "By the word 'God' I understand a substance that is infinite, eternal, immutable, independent, supremely intelligent, supremely powerful, and which created both myself and everything else (. . .) that exists."[13] In the same *Meditation*, Descartes affirms the certainty of God's existence by the following reasoning: Since mankind has somehow acquired the belief in God as the infinite substance whose existence does not depend on anything else, and because a finite substance is less real than an infinite substance, we must acknowledge that the human mind, as a finite substance, could not have made up the idea of an infinite substance (God). And if the concept of God is not produced by the human mind, it means that God must have caused himself. God must therefore exist because only he could have generated our belief in him, as the infinite substance.[14]

After affirming that the existence of God is necessary, in the *Fourth Meditation* he argues that the veracity and trustworthiness of our knowledge is guaranteed by God, for he does not allow us to be deceived. One's wish to deceive or to let someone be deceived is evidence of imperfection,

---

13. *Third Meditation*, 31.

14. In the *Fifth Meditation* he formulates another form of the ontological argument used by theologians since Anselm (1033–1109) to prove the existence of God. Here is a short paraphrase of how he formulates it: The idea of God is the idea of a perfect supreme being. Existence is in itself a perfection, since existence is superior to nonexistence. If the idea of God did not include the real existence of God, it would lack perfection, and then it would not be about a perfect being, but about one who lacks perfection (existence). The idea of a supreme God lacking the attribute of existence would thus be unintelligible. This means that existence belongs to the essence of an infinite substance, so God must exist.

and since God has all the perfections, he cannot deceive us or let us be deceived. In Descartes's view, if we were wrong on having clear and distinct ideas about a non-physical mind distinct from our body, God would be a deceiver, which is absurd. It is only on this foundation that we can trust sensory data, for God created our senses as part of our nature.[15] Since God is good and is not lacking any perfection, he has ordained the world in such a way that we are not deceived about it by sensory data.

Since Descartes established the existence of the mind as a self-existing substance precisely from doubting sensory data, a clarification is needed here. According to the *Third Meditation* there are three types of ideas, of which the second type is of interest here.[16] The second type of ideas are "derived from things existing outside me";[17] that is, they are the result of sensory data, and do not depend on one's will. This kind of ideas cannot be ignored or changed by the mind at will.[18] The possibility of being deceived by the senses, as affirmed in the *Second Meditation*, is thus rejected by the reasoning made in the *Fourth Meditation* about God's provision in making sensory data accurate, and thus confidence in the senses is restored. So Descartes does not really doubt sensory data. His goal in the *Second Meditation* is to use an *a fortiori* argument[19] in order to establish the existence of the mind as a self-existing substance: If I can doubt my body (for I could be dreaming), but cannot doubt the fact that I am doubting something, it means that the existence of the non-physical mind (the agent that makes doubting possible) is even more clearly established than that of the body.

---

15. Descartes, *Sixth Meditation*, 55, 62.

16. Descartes, *Meditations*, 26–30. The first type of ideas are inventions of the mind, ideas which can be analyzed, modified, and abandoned. For example, I can develop the idea of a dragon, draw one according to my imagination, and leave it aside. The third kind of ideas are innate, or given by "natural light." They are placed by God in our mind when he created us, and as such are irrefutable. Such ideas are the theorems of geometry, and the idea that God exists.

17. Descartes, *Meditations*, 26.

18. For example, when I cross the street I cannot ignore the visual data that a car is approaching, nor can I modify it without suffering serious injuries.

19. An *a fortiori* argument is a form of reasoning that starts from existing propositions everyone agrees with, and then argues that a second proposition must be seen as implicit in the first, and even more certain than the first. For instance, if a bird is an animal with wings, and a penguin is a bird, how much more is an eagle to be considered a bird, for it has even better wings than a penguin.

Another way of formulating this idea would go like this: While we can *imagine* that the senses deceive us, knowing that God does not allow us to be deceived, we should not really doubt the veracity of sensory experience. If there is no need to doubt our senses, how much less should we doubt the existence of the mind as a non-physical substance, independent of the body, for it is the ground that makes the very existence of doubt possible. Although this kind of reasoning was criticized, as we will see below, some elements of Descartes's thinking will prove useful for understanding the Christian view of human nature in chapter 6.

The criticism of Cartesian dualism is formulated mainly by physicalist philosophers, who start from the assumption that there is only one fundamental substance, matter, so the mind cannot be non-physical, nor can God exist. The first major criticism casts doubt on Descartes's methodology, while the second concerns the impossibility of mind-body interaction. These arguments will pave the way for the rise of physicalist views on the mind and human nature, which we will assess in the next section.

1.2.2 Criticism of Descartes's Methodology

As we have seen, Descartes states that we cannot be deceived on the existence of the mind as a non-physical substance (*Second Meditation*) because God guarantees the veracity of "clear and distinct" ideas (*Sixth Meditation*). But the very existence of God has been philosophically demonstrated on the basis of our ability to have clear and distinct ideas about his existence (the ontological argument, in the *Fifth Meditation*). Therefore if the assumption used to demonstrate the existence of God requires his existence (God provides clear and distinct ideas to the mind that thinks), we are in the midst of a circular argument, called the Cartesian Circle. The existence of God and of the non-physical mind are proven each by the other, so neither is demonstrated by Descartes's reasoning. (This does not mean that the existence of God and of the non-physical mind are false ideas, but just that this way of proving things is insufficient.)[20]

Another critique of Descartes's method comes from the way he uses doubt as a means for determining the nature of the mind. If I can doubt that something of my nature is essential (such as the body) and I can *imagine*

---

20. One way of dealing with this fallacy is by rejecting the ontological argument. God's existence is not established by this philosophical argument, or at least this kind of philosophical argumentation no longer makes sense for the modern mind.

that the mind can exist outside the body, it does not necessarily mean that it is true on this speculative basis alone. Having a "clear and distinct" idea of my mind and body as different substances, and emphasizing their different properties, does not build a strong case for truly considering them two different substances. In other words, the power of imagination is not enough to prove anything objective about human nature.

Regarding the use of Leibniz's Law to prove that the mind and the body are different substances because they have different properties, it simply does not work when the properties considered are of a psychological nature, and characterized by verbs such as "imagining" and "doubting." Psychological properties create exceptions to Leibniz's Law. I can doubt something in a certain context, but not in another, I can have a "clear and distinct" perception of something in a certain mood, but not in another, when I am presented other aspects of that thing. To doubt is a subjective activity which depends on the context and one's inner disposition, so doubt cannot build the foundation of truth. Psychological verbs refer to inner states, not necessarily to something that exists independently of our beliefs and thoughts.

A similar critique can be formulated considering the use of language associated with Descartes's method. Although I can refer to my mind and to my body as being two distinct entities, the fact that they bear two different names does not mean that they *really are* different substances. The two nouns may represent two aspects of the same entity, or means of emphasizing a particular aspect of a whole, a physical or a personality aspect. So when I speak of my body I do not necessarily refer to a separate substance I can distinguish myself from, but to the physical characteristics of my person. Neither introspection nor the use of a dualist language can prove Cartesian dualism. This does not mean, however, that we have demonstrated the falsity of mind-body dualism. All we can say for now is that Cartesian dualism cannot be proven on the basis of introspective thinking alone.

1.2.3 The Mind-Body Problem in Cartesian Dualism

The second major line of criticism against Cartesian dualism concerns the way the non-physical mind and the physical body, defined as two different substances, can interact. This is known as the mind-body problem. Physicalists ask: How can the physical brain communicate to the non-physical mind the data of sensory perception, and how can the mind send its commands to the body? What is the last physical act of the brain that causes the first non-physical act of the mind in the causal chain? Since the mind and the brain have two totally different natures, their interaction must be impossible.[21] What is ignored or not known is that Descartes tried to answer this challenge.

Princess Elisabeth of Bohemia, an admirer of Descartes's philosophical thought, asked him how the non-physical soul, lacking physical size and weight, could move the physical body, for we see that only physical things can move other physical things.[22] Descartes answered that a falling stone is not moved by another physical body.[23] As its (unseen) weight moves the stone downwards, so the soul has an intrinsic power to move the body. Since the relationship between the stone and its weight is not incomprehensible, neither should be the relationship between the soul and the body. The princess responded that the weight is indeed an unseen force and a real non-physical cause moving the stone.[24] But she admits that it is difficult to imagine non-physical causes and would rather assign physical and spatial attributes to the soul than to speculate how a non-physical substance can interact with the body. In other words, how can the non-physical soul govern the physical body without having anything of its nature, and how can it survive without the body?[25] Descartes answered that the soul and body form a unity and act as a unity.[26] In the

---

21. A variant of dualism, which I mention only as a curiosity, is occasionalism, developed by Nicholas Malebranche (1638–1715), which affirms that there is no causal relationship between the brain and the mind. Mental phenomena have only mental effects, and physical phenomena have only physical effects, so the two categories each have an independent life. Why do they overlap so perfectly? Because God initiates them simultaneously and makes the two types of phenomena coincide, as occasions for divine intervention. A similar concept is Leibniz's parallelism, which considers that the mind and body behave like two different clocks that were started by God at the same time, but tick separately. God initiated the causal chain in both sets of phenomena and conducts this parallelism through a pre-established harmony.

22. Bennett, *Correspondence*, Letter of May 6, 1643.

23. Bennett, *Correspondence*, Letter of May 21, 1643.

24. Today's physicists would no longer agree with her, for the gravitational force belongs to the physical world.

25. Bennett, *Correspondence*, Letter of October 6, 1643.

26. Bennett, *Correspondence*, Letter of June 28, 1643. When Descartes affirms that the soul can exist without a body, it does not mean that he thought of it as the natural state of the soul, but intended to establish that the soul is a different substance. He does not consider that the body is unnecessary to human nature, as Plato did.

Discourse on the Method, he states that in order to "compose a true man," the soul must *not* be understood as "a pilot in his ship":

> I had described the rational soul, and shown that, unlike the other things of which I had spoken, it could not possibly be derived from the potentiality of matter, but that it must have been created expressly. And I had shown how it is not sufficient for it to be lodged in the human body like a pilot in his ship, except perhaps to move its members, but that it needs to be more closely joined and united with the body in order to have, in addition, feelings and appetites like the ones we have, and in this way compose a true man.[27]

For Descartes, human nature consists of a soul united to a body, not of two artificially brought together substances, and the whole is more than the sum of its parts. The whole formed by body and mind has powers superior to the two components, and mind-body interaction takes place within this whole.[28] Descartes has not shown how such different parts can function as a whole, but his ideas that the whole acquires new properties greater than the sum of its parts, and that mind-body interaction takes place within this whole, are important for our inquiry.

In his letters to Antoine Arnauld, a contemporary philosopher and theologian, Descartes says something similar about the relationship between mind and body. He reminds Arnauld of a quote from the *Sixth Meditation*, in which we find again his thought that the connection between the mind and the body is not like that of the pilot and his ship:

> Nature also teaches me, through these sensations of pain, hunger, thirst and so on, that I am not merely present in my body as a sailor is present in a ship, but that I am very closely joined and, as it were, intermingled with it, so that I and the body form a unit. If this were not so, I who am nothing but a thinking thing, would not feel pain when the body was hurt, but would perceive the damage purely by the intellect, just as a sailor perceives by sight if anything in his ship is broken.[29]

---

27. Descartes, *Discourse on the Method*, part 5, 48. Descartes has an understanding of the soul quite different from Plato's. In reply to Arnauld's fourth objection, he rejects the idea that the mind uses the body as a tool.

28. Less known is that Descartes thought that mind-body interaction must take place in the brain, arguing that the mind "is not immediately affected by all parts of the body, but only by the brain" (*Sixth Meditation*, 59).

29. Descartes, *Sixth Meditation*, 56.

In the *Passions of the Soul*, Descartes suggests that the pineal gland, because of its unique anatomic shape and location (in the center of the brain) would be "the principal seat of the soul" and "the only place in the body where the soul can directly exercise its functions."[30] He was obviously wrong, for we know that the pineal gland has another function, that of producing a hormone (melatonin) that regulates the wake-sleep cycle. Descartes failed to solve the mind-body problem, but his failure does not necessarily mean that a non-physical mind cannot exist. What can exist is not limited to existing philosophical theories. This is true for both kinds of philosophers, dualists and physicalists. Both are entitled to question the other perspective, for both have difficulties, as we will see later in this chapter. The possibility that the brain could interact with a non-physical mind should not be eliminated from philosophical research just on anti-dualist biases. After all, it was a great concern for John Eccles, a Nobel Prize winner in medicine, who tried to define this intermediary as the complementary motor area, the area of the cortex where voluntary movements are initiated.[31] Richard Swinburne speculated on a possible quantum-level interaction between the mind and neurons.[32]

In the following section we explore the main physicalist alternatives for explaining the nature of the mind, and we will see that these alternatives have their own difficulties in formulating a coherent theory of the mind and consciousness.

1.3 PHYSICALIST VIEWS OF HUMAN NATURE

Physicalism is not just a modern reaction against religious interference in philosophy, for it as old as ancient Greece. Democritus (460–370 BC) is one of its first representatives. In his view, everything is composed of indivisible atoms, and the soul (*psyche*) itself is nothing but a collection of such atoms which disperse forever at death. Modern physicalists follow on the same track, holding that we are extremely complicated physical beings which lack any kind of non-physical component.

The physicalist orientation in the philosophy of mind is the result of positivism, a popular philosophical trend at the beginning of the

---

30. Descartes, *The Passions of the Soul*, section 32.

31. Eccles, *The Wonder of Being Human*, 156–61. See also, Eccles and Popper, *The Self and Its Brain*, and Eccles, *Evolution of the Brain*.

32. Swinburne, *Mind, Brain and Free Will*, 114–15.

twentieth century. In the 1920s and 1930s a group of philosophers met at the University of Vienna (and thus was called the Vienna Circle), with the aim of finding ways to affirm positivism in all areas of knowledge, including the social sciences. Positivism affirms that *any* phenomenon, including what we call mental processes, thoughts, desires, and experiences, must be explained scientifically and be subjected to scientific, reproducible, and verifiable experiment. In the exact sciences these requirements are easily met, but their implementation in psychology and philosophy led to serious complications. In the philosophy of mind, the guiding principle set by positivism is the idea that the mind and any mental phenomenon must have a purely physical explanation. The existence of God and of non-physical substances cannot be accepted because they cannot be observed, measured, or analyzed; that is, they cannot be scientifically proven. Matter is the only framework in which we can formulate a theory of human nature. From this assumption a series of theories in the philosophy of mind were developed, of which the first was behaviorism.

1.3.1 Behaviorism

Following the positivist assumptions for understanding human nature, this theory reduces mental states to expressions of observable physical behavior. Hence, the name behaviorism.[33] Thinking, perceiving, or remembering something must not be taken as mysterious inner states of a non-physical nature, but as ways of behaving which can be observed by anyone and studied. Obviously, we do not manifest all our thoughts in gestures and words, so it has been added that mental states are not only modes of behavior, but also dispositions to behave in a certain way. I may not move at all or say a word when I remember something, but I still have the disposition to act in an observable way.

Gilbert Ryle, one of the important critics of Cartesian dualism, argues that speaking of the mind and of mental states as having a non-physical nature is the result of what in philosophical language is called a category mistake.[34] It consists in uncritically attributing to mental phenomena characteristics that would place them in a non-physical realm,

---

33. I refer in this section to philosophical behaviorism, not to psychological behaviorism. The latter is an approach in psychology that empirically correlates various stimuli with their effects in behavior.

34. Ryle, *The Concept of Mind*, 16.

when they really belong to the physical. In Ryle's view, it is a mistake to require the existence of a non-physical mind responsible for abilities such as imagination, thinking, perception, and desire. The mind is not a mysterious agent working beyond the brain, but a sum of abilities which make us capable of performing visible, concrete activities, that is, to behave in certain ways in certain circumstances. Our beliefs are not private mental states, revealed to others only by language, but dispositions to behave and speak in a certain way. For example, my belief that it is raining translates into the fact that I take an umbrella. A headache is just a predisposition to moan, say words such as "I have a headache," take analgesics, or behave in other ways.

One of the arguments against Descartes's method—that the use of dualist language does not make dualism true—originates with Ludwig Wittgenstein, as the argument against private language.[35] In his major work, *Philosophical Investigations*, he emphasizes that grammar misleads philosophers. The mind, as a noun, does not define a non-physical independent entity, just because a noun refers to an object in contrast to another object. Beyond the noun "mind" there is no substantial reality. If we truly had private mental states, accessible only by introspection, we could not communicate effectively with other people, because our mental states would be so subjective and untranslatable that a common language would be impossible. Therefore mental phenomena are not internal, private states, but only behavioral states.

As we might expect, behaviorism poses serious difficulties in formulating a coherent theory of the mind and mental phenomena. First, behaviorism cannot explain the difference between knowing our own beliefs and those of other people. While it affirms that we can observe the behavior of other people and speculate on their beliefs, it also requires us to use the same method to know our *own* beliefs. That is, we should look in the mirror to see how we behave or ask someone else to observe our behavior in order to know our own beliefs, which is absurd. We know our beliefs without resorting to an external observer and in the absence of any visible behavior. Although I can keep my eyes closed and stay silent, in my mind I can spin a lot of thoughts, plans, judgments, etc. From a behavioral point of view, those states do not exist, or are only predispositions to a certain behavior. For example, when I remember a song, I could sing it aloud, so others would hear it, or be completely silent, and thus

---

35. Wittgenstein, *Philosophical Investigations*, paragraphs 257–304, 92–102.

"hear" it only in my mind. My thoughts are just as real, whether I express them or not. Likewise, a headache is not just a predisposition to behave in a certain way, that is, to moan and take analgesics. It has an internal quality that only *I* can know, as *my* pain, totally different from what the person who sees me can speculate about.

Second, if we try to reach a behaviorist understanding of more complex mental states, such as the ideals that drive us, the explanations get very complicated, for behaviorists need to resort to a long series of dispositions. For example, suppose you see somebody drowning in a pool. Depending on your beliefs, you can respond in several ways: jump into the pool and risk drowning yourself, throw a lifebuoy, shout for help, or simply ignore the poor fellow, especially if he is your bitter enemy. From a behaviorist point of view, how do we explain the response? Why does the rescuer choose one particular behavior instead of another? Because of a set of dispositions he has, themselves determined by other dispositions, and so on (the list would be very long and complex). But "behavioral dispositions" stem from beliefs, each of which requires a behavioral explanation (other dispositions). Therefore we cannot explain behavior without admitting beliefs that are independent and prior to behavior.

Beliefs, in turn, compete in displaying visible behavior. In the case of a headache, I may not show any abnormal behavior and be brave, especially if the situation requires it, for example, during a job interview. But on another occasion, I may have other motivations to display all possible manifestations of the headache. After being hired, I could cry out loud when having a headache, in order to impress my employer so that he may let me go home earlier. Or I may not have a headache at all, and fake it to get the same result. And what about actors? Or liars? They display behaviors that have nothing to do with their beliefs and inner states. Therefore behavior depends on a multitude of factors, on a hierarchy of values, beliefs, and desires that compete with one another to *determine* our behavior. In other words, the cause might not be equal to the effect.

Because of these issues, behaviorism has been abandoned by philosophers. It is mentioned here just to show how far one can go in defining human nature on the assumption that dualism, in general, and the non-physical soul, in particular, must be rejected by all means.

1.3.2 The Identity Theory

Unlike behaviorism, the next physicalist proposal admits the existence of mental states, and unlike Cartesian dualism, ascribes to them a purely physical explanation. The identity theory argues that a *causal* relationship between mental events and physical events in the brain is not enough. The two sets of events must be *identical*, as belonging to the same process.[36] In essence, it is a reductionist theory which affirms that mental life can be reduced to brain activity, in a similar way in which water can be reduced to H_2O, the cloud in the sky to tiny droplets of water, or color to electromagnetic radiation of a certain wavelength. Following this reductionist view, mental life could be reduced to a series of physical events, in the form of biochemical and electrical processes occurring in the brain. This would simplify language in the philosophy of mind, for instead of talking about mental *and* physical events, we would speak *only* of brain events.

In response to Cartesian dualism and its argument that mental and physical events have different properties, thus pointing to different substances (Leibniz's Law), U.T. Place argues that this is a logical fallacy called the phenomenological fallacy. Using a similar reasoning to that of Ryle and Wittgenstein, his view is that we should not let phenomenological events be interpreted as referring to entities or events of a non-physical nature. Although we can describe mental events by using attributes different from those used by the neurosciences, these events cannot exist independently of the physical processes in the brain. As we can use different languages to communicate the same content, mental and physical events in the brain are also different languages pointing to the same content. In other words, although we know different aspects of the brain by using different means (introspection and the neurosciences), they are two languages which express mere physical properties of the brain.

An important aspect of this theory needs to be clarified here. The type of identity affirmed between mind states and brain states is not of the kind we use in definitions such as "red is a color," or "a triangle is a closed figure with three sides." The physical events in the brain have a different meaning than mental events, because we know them differently. Anyone knows his or her mental states without having any recourse to neurology, while the neuroscientist who measures the electrical phenomena in a patient's brain knows nothing of what that patient is thinking about at

---

36. Its main proponents are Ullin T. Place, John Smart, and David Armstrong. Place initiated this theory in his article "Is Consciousness a brain process?," 44–50.

that moment. Therefore we cannot identify the electrical signals that we measure in the brain with the mental concepts we use in language.

The identity type invoked by this theory is a contingent one that is descriptive and open, such as "my chair is a banana box," or "my hat is a folded newspaper." We can use this type of identity in affirmations such as: The President of the USA is the Commander in Chief of the US Army. Such identity does not reside in the same function, but in the same person who represents both functions. This should not lead us to believe that behind the brain and the mind exists yet another entity that supports both. A classic example used by philosophers to express this type of identity is the relationship between the evening star and the morning star. Although they have different meanings, because they are observed at different times, they are essentially the same planet (Venus). The cloud in the sky and the many droplets of water forming it have different meanings but represent the same physical thing. The cloud is white, huge and floats in the sky, while water droplets are transparent and very small. If I am up on the mountain I can see the water droplets at close range, and if I walk away from the cloud, I can see it as a whole, thus proving their equivalence. Understanding these examples will help us realize that, according to the identity theory, the mind and the brain do not have the same meaning, although they point to the same thing.

However, the identity between mental states and physical states in the brain cannot be demonstrated in the same way as in the example of the cloud and the water droplets. No matter how close we could observe neural events in the brain, there is no point at which we would start perceiving how electrochemical impulses between neurons become mental events. No matter how thoroughly a neuroscientist analyzed the electrochemical phenomena in the brain, the mental event would still be missed. The (mental) sensation accompanying the sight of a flower cannot be read in the electrochemical signals somewhere in the cortex.

Some correlation between brain activity and mental activity is confirmed by neurology. Certain areas in the brain are active when we solve abstract problems, others when we have sensory perceptions, etc. By studying the effects of brain damage, neurologists have observed that a physical injury of a particular region leads to the loss of certain mental capacities. For example, an injury to the temporal lobes leads to memory loss and impaired use of language. Physicalists, in general, interpret these correlations as proof that neural activity is the basis of mental activity. Hence, neurology treatises speak of the location of thought, speech, pleasure, etc., in certain areas of the cortex. The hope is that the neurosciences will someday decode the way the two sets of properties, the physical and the mental, translate exactly from one to the other. The expected confirmation from neuroscience is that the same type of mental event is always produced by the same type of neural event in the brain. Place, Armstrong, and Smart expect this type of identity to be confirmed, as type-type identity.

However, the big problem for the proponents of this theory is that the neurosciences do not confirm this type of identity. The data indicates that the same mental event (for instance, the same thought) cannot be correlated with the same specifically localized electrical activity in the brain, neither for the same person at different times, nor in different persons. A prick with a needle always generates the same mental phenomenon, the same sensation of pain, but it is not always associated with the same electrical activity in the brain of that person. Even more difficult is to equate the same mental phenomenon in two different people with the same electrical activity in their brains. In other words, if you and I are stuck with a needle in the same place, a different electrical record in the brain will emerge, both in its precise location in the brain and in intensity. So the identity theory is false.

As a result, physicalist philosophers have abandoned the type-type identity between mental and physical events in favor of an identity of occurrences.[37] The new direction is to show that the same mental state can be physically realized in *various* ways in one's brain, so that only a *particular* mental event is to be identified with a *particular* physical event in the brain. In other words, at one time a particular mental event can manifest in one particular area of the brain, while at another moment the same mental event can be actuated in a close, but different, part of the brain. This kind of identity, called a token-token identity, can also be formulated between different people. For example, my belief that grass is green is physically realized as a brain event in *my* brain in a different way than in *your* brain.

Another criticism addressed to the identity theory is chauvinism. Type identity is formulated for the particular case of the human brain. Hilary Putnam argues that animals feel pain too, so not only humans can

---

37. To understand the difference between type and occurrence, I could write the word "chair" in three different places in a room, in three different styles and colors. What you would see in these three places would be one type (the noun "chair") and three of its occurrences.

have mental states. Perhaps insects can also feel pain, although they do not even have a central nervous system. Even extraterrestrial beings could be capable of feeling pain, so in no way should we limit the possibility of having mental phenomena to humans.[38] Physicalism was thus challenged to find a way of explaining the mind that would allow the realization of mental phenomena in multiple ways, thus avoiding chauvinism, while affirming an identity of occurrences between physical and mental states.

1.3.3 Functionalism and Computationalism

The framework for understanding functionalism is token-token identity, which demands that for any mental occurrence there must exist a physical one in the brain, although the neural event need not always be the same for a certain mental state to occur. Animals can feel pain too, so they have a similar mental occurrence despite having a different kind of brain. The essential point of the new theory is that a certain mental event can be realized on different physical grounds, or, stated in reverse order, different physical structures can produce similar mental events. This theory, called functionalism, emphasizes the multiple possibilities of fulfilling a certain function, which opens up new avenues in the philosophy of mind.

Let me use two examples to illustrate what functionalism stands for. The belief that it is raining generates a response (the desire to stay dry) that can be accomplished in at least two ways: I could use an umbrella or a poncho. Taking another example, the function of scaring away birds that come to peck on my cherries can be accomplished in at least three ways: I could put a human dummy in the tree, use a plastic eagle scarecrow that moves with the wind, or install an alarm that mimics the sounds of predator birds. The physical instrument I use does not matter; what counts is to achieve the same function, that of scaring off pesky birds.

The principle of achieving the same function by different means applies to the relationship between mind states and brain states by reducing mental states to their causal relationships, that is, to their function. Although a certain conviction (for example, that Russia is the largest country in the world) is achieved differently at a neural level by different persons (as an identity of occurrences), what is important is that the two (different) neurobiological events taking place in different persons fulfill

---

38. Putnam, "The Nature of Mental States," in Chalmers, *Philosophy of Mind*, 77.

the same function, that is, the conviction of which is the largest country in the world. A mental state is a functional state of the brain, occurring in a series of causal relationships. Ultimately, it is not important what the mind itself is (a non-physical substance or a physical process), but what function it performs. This way of seeing things has two major effects. First, functionalism renders obsolete the need to explain mind-brain interaction. If only the *function* of mental states is what matters, functionalism can work for both physicalists and dualists. As Stephen Priest argues, functionalism is physicalist only if we add the premise that "all causes and effects are physical causes and effects."[39]

Second, functionalism introduced the revolutionary idea that the function of the mind could be sustained by physical means other than the brain. In the 1970s and 1980s this idea generated the computational theory of the mind, which likens the mind to a computer program. A computer is a machine that receives data, processes it following an algorithm, and produces a result. According to the computational paradigm, the brain would be the equivalent of the hardware of a computer, and the mind of its software, so all mind processes could be reduced to a sort of mechanical computation. Therefore, it would no longer be important for brain scientists to make huge efforts to map the brain and discover how the interaction between neurons produces mental states. What truly matters is understanding the program running in the brain, its software. In John Searle's words, according to this theory,

> Because the mind is a computer program, and because a program can be implemented on any hardware whatever (. . .), the specifically mental aspects of the mind can be specified, studied, and understood without knowing how the brain works.[40]

Following this paradigm, explaining mind-brain interaction in both directions is no longer a relevant issue. As the hardware stores programs and provides the ground for computing, the brain sustains the mind, and as the software can determine the physical action of the hardware (for example, it can cause the printer to print this page or turn off the computer), the mind sets the body in motion. Therefore computationalism seems to be a way of avoiding the mind-body problem.

If the computational model of human nature is correct, the next expectation would be to make a computer that passes the Turing Test, that

---

39. Priest, *Theories of the Mind*, 134.
40. Searle, *The Rediscovery of the Mind*, 44.

is, behaves like a human. A psychologist who evaluates its abilities would not realize it is a machine, but takes it for human, with human cognitive abilities. Hence the great interest in artificial intelligence (AI), and the ultimate hope that the human mind will someday be uploaded to other hardware more durable than the brain. In other words, in a similar way to how particular software can run on different types of computers, as for instance the Microsoft Word program runs on both PC and Mac, the expectation is that the same mental events we experience and define us as conscious persons might be implemented on another physical system.

As we might expect, the ultimate achievement of following computationalism would be that humanity will eventually attain immortality by moving the conscious mind to a more durable physical system, that is, to other hardware, made of plastic or silicon, which is not damaged after about 70+ years. In case of an accident, the data that forms our mental life could be stored on a hard disk and be downloaded to new hardware whenever the old is in trouble.[41] We will assess these expectations in greater detail in chapter 3.

1.3.4 The Problem of Computationalism

Despite the huge optimism of the 1980s for the possibilities opened by the computational model of the human mind, it faces a fatal problem. To understand its failure, we need to understand the notions of syntax and semantics involved in computer science and the human mind. In short, the syntax is the form of a word or sentence, while semantics is its meaning. We can understand the difference in the use of homonyms. For example, the word "bat" can have at least two meanings. From a semantic point of view, I can refer either to a kind of stick used to hit a ball (as in baseball), or to a nocturnal flying mammal. The syntax is the same, but the meaning of "bat" is very different. The problem of computationalism is that a computer cannot overcome the barrier between syntax and semantics. Let me expand on this.

In writing a computer algorithm, that is, in making software, a programmer works only with syntax, as precisely as possible. All information is encoded in a binary system, that is, by representing information by rows of digits that can be either 0 or 1. The programmer is a human being who

---

41. Since the 1970s and 1980s such expectations have been very high. To get an idea of this huge interest try a simple online search on *mind* and *computers*.

understands the semantics of the algorithm, while the algorithm itself is pure information, with no awareness of itself. Since a computer is limited to working with syntax, the objection raised to the computational model is that the human mind has a further dimension. This dimension is the subjective aspect of mental states, the awareness of doing this or that, which makes them *my* mental states, unlike those of any other human being. Philosophers use the term *qualia* to refer to one's conscious experience as being individual and subjective. The term comes from the Latin word *qualis*, which means "what kind," in the sense of "what kind of sensation" is *for me* a certain experience. This dimension is lacking in computers.

Probably the strongest argument against the theory that the mind can be likened to a computer program was developed by Searle in the form of an imaginary experiment called the Chinese Room.[42] A man who does not know Chinese at all is locked in a room where he has lots of Chinese characters printed on paper and a manual that illustrates how to answer questions he receives in Chinese. The manual teaches him that if he receives this particular succession of Chinese characters, he must choose that particular succession of characters in response. It is assumed that the manual is very complex, offering the answer to any possible question. The man in the room receives questions in Chinese printed on paper, searches for the right answer in the manual, and then sticks the appropriate symbols to a sheet of paper, which he hands back to his Chinese conversation pal. A Chinese speaker who would dialogue with this man in this particular way would be convinced that the man in the room knows Chinese, which is obviously false. And here is the point: What the man in the Chinese Room does is exactly what a computer does. The computer receives input, processes it according to an algorithm (the manual) and provides output. Just as the man in the Chinese Room does not know Chinese at all, that is, has no idea of the semantics of his conversation—though syntactically he is doing well, as he manipulates the symbols exactly as the manual requires—in a similar way the computer lacks the semantic dimension of its work. In other words, the computer has no self-awareness, no *qualia*, as it does not *understand* what it does.

What Searle proves by his example is that a computer cannot jump from syntax to semantics, just as the man in the Chinese Room can never learn Chinese by manipulating the characters according to the manual. No matter how fast it might produce its answers, that is, regardless of its

---

42. Searle, "Minds, Brains and Programs," 417–24.

computing speed, the computer cannot cross the barrier between syntax and semantics. Only the mind operates with semantics, and for this reason the computer must be programmed by a human mind. The programmer encodes semantics into the syntax, that is, writes the algorithm, lets the computer use the algorithm to transform input data into a result, and then he or she interprets the result, again by implementing the semantic dimension of the result. In computer programming semantics is not embedded in the syntax and thus can be formulated and recognized only by the human mind. This argument will be of great help in chapter 3 for assessing the hopes of using artificial intelligence for transcending the present limits of human nature in transhumanism.

The enthusiasts of the computational model of human nature criticized Searle vehemently for his declared intention to "put the final nail in the coffin of the theory that the mind is a computer program."[43] In his words,

> Some computationalists invest an almost religious intensity into their faith that our deepest problems about the mind will have a computational solution. Many people apparently believe that somehow or other, unless we are proven to be computers, something terribly important will be lost.[44]

Searle is convinced that the philosophical importance of computers is "grossly exaggerated," for they must be seen just as useful tools, "nothing more or less."[45] Thomas Nagel, another physicalist philosopher, shares the same view, considering that "current attempts to understand the mind by analogy with man-made computers that can perform superbly some of the same external tasks as conscious beings will be recognized as a gigantic waste of time."[46]

1.3.5 Property Dualism and Nonreductive Physicalism

Although we are still in the physicalist camp, for both physical and mental events find their ground in the brain, nonreductive physicalism affirms that mental events are only *causally*, not *ontologically*, reducible to physical states. In other words, we must allow another meaning to the mind,

---

43. Searle, *The Rediscovery of the Mind*, xi.
44. Searle, *The Mystery of Consciousness*, 189.
45. Searle, *The Mystery of Consciousness*, 190.
46. Nagel, *The View from Nowhere*, 16.

one that cannot be explained in physical terms, although it has a physical origin. The mind must be seen as a *property* of the brain, entirely dependent on the brain, not an independent substance, as in Cartesian dualism. Therefore we speak of property dualism, not of substance dualism.

Property dualism and nonreductive physicalism use two important notions that we need to understand: emergentism and supervenience. Emergentism affirms that a complex integrated system acquires new properties that are not found in the individual components.[47] These new properties of a system are called emergent and cannot be deduced from those of its parts. For example, no matter how thoroughly we study a bee, we will not be able to infer the ability of the hive to produce honey. This is an emergent property of the beehive that does not belong to the individual bees. In a similar way, nonreductive physicalism affirms that the mind is an emergent property of the brain that cannot be deduced from the properties of individual neurons. The mind must have appeared sometime during evolution, when the brain reached a sufficiently high level of sophistication. It is not the same thing as the brain, as in the identity theory, but a property, ontologically different from the brain.

Supervenience is a closely related concept, which states that the properties of a highly complex system depend on lower-level components. We use this concept when we say that the social properties of a group are supervenient on the psychological properties of individuals, the psychological properties of an individual are supervenient on the biological structure of his or her brain, and the biological properties on the biochemical composition of neurons. According to nonreductive physicalism mental states are supervenient on neural states of the brain.[48]

Problems for nonreductive physicalists arise when they try to figure out how the physical and the mental can interact. The influence of physical events on the brain's mental events is deduced from the findings of neurobiology, but the reverse influence, that is, explaining how the mind affects the physical, is a great challenge. I can mentally decide to get up from my chair and leave this room, and my decision has a real and immediate physical effect. However, this phenomenon is very difficult to

---

47. The properties of a system can be additive or emergent. Weight, for example, is an additive property, meaning that the mass of the whole is given by the sum of the masses of its parts. Here, however, we deal with emergent properties.

48. A suggestive example is that aesthetic features of an artwork are supervenient on its physical structure. A sculpture is beautiful to the extent that the shape, the relationship between its elements, the surfaces, etc., are in harmony.

explain for nonreductive physicalists, for causality works only upwards, from the physical to the mental.[49] If mental properties are real, they must have a causal power over the physical, but a causal power of a different nature than physical power, since they are qualitatively superior and ontologically irreducible to the physical. If mental properties are a new kind of causal properties, they must bring new causal powers, and this is precisely the problem: demonstrating these causal powers of the mind.

Jaegwon Kim argues that in a physicalist setting mental phenomena cannot cause other phenomena, neither mental nor physical, for mental phenomena need a physical supervenience base, that is, a physical process to generate them, and only this physical process can have causal powers.[50] In this case mental causation is redundant, for it would be an instance of overcausation. If only physical phenomena can cause mental phenomena and the reverse is impossible, property dualism cannot be a valid theory, for we know that mental causation is a fact.[51] As a result, John Heil argues that instead of accommodating the special features of mental states in a physicalist framework, the real achievement of nonreductive physicalists was "to reintroduce the problem of mind-body interaction in a new form, more virulent. If mental properties are top-level properties, they are, apparently, epiphenomenal."[52]

Therefore the challenge remains to explain mental phenomena in a way that admits them as essential to human nature, irreducible to physical states, but also as causally efficient.

1.4 PHYSICALISM AND CONSCIOUSNESS

As we have seen so far in this chapter, physicalist theories of the mind must find a way to explain the subjective aspect of mental states, and do it in terms different from those of neurobiology. In other words, physicalism needs to find a way to explain consciousness. Nagel emphasizes this aspect in a famous article called "What Is It Like to Be a Bat?"[53] He argues

---

49. This one-way upward causality is called the problem of epiphenomenalism (from the Greek, *epi* = "above, additional").

50. Kim, *Philosophy of Mind*, 229–33. Searle is another philosopher who criticizes the impossibility of the mind to produce physical effects in nonreductive physicalism. See Searle, "Why I Am Not a Property Dualist."

51. A similar reasoning is followed by Heil. See Heil, *Philosophy of Mind*, 217–18.

52. Heil, *Philosophy of Mind*, 186.

53. Nagel, "What Is It Like to Be a Bat?," 435–50.

that no matter how well we may know the anatomy of the bat's brain, and how precisely we may map the electrochemical signals between its neurons, we still cannot know what it is like to be a bat in the first person, that is, to know what the bat feels, as a bat. These mammals have means of perception different from ours. They use echolocation, that is, they emit ultrasounds and interpret their echoes in order to know the exact distance to obstacles or food (flying insects). No matter how much scientific data we might gather, we still will not be able to understand its feelings and consciousness, if bats are conscious. It is not enough to imagine how we, as humans, would feel when flying through a cave and use echolocation to catch flies. No matter how much science could teach us about bats, we could never know in the first person what the bat experiences *as a bat*.

What Nagel's imaginary thought experiment suggests is that although science could help us know everything about the brain in scientific terms, this kind of knowledge leaves out personal experience. This dimension is qualitatively different from anything the neurosciences can teach us. A complete theory of the mind must include consciousness as a fundamental aspect of human nature, and define it in physicalist terms for physicalism to be true.[54] It seems, however, that a physicalist explanation of consciousness is beyond the possibilities of science, since consciousness is connected to a single point of view, of just one particular person.

Another imaginary thought experiment that emphasizes the subjective aspect of mental states is given by Frank Jackson in his article "What Mary Didn't Know."[55] He imagines the case of a researcher, called Mary, who got to know all that could be scientifically known about the neurobiology of perception. However, she had lived all her life in a room where everything, all her textbooks, television and pictures, were in black and white. One day she got out of the room and for the first time had the experience of seeing colors. Though she knew everything about red, she could not imagine what it meant to have a direct perception of a red tomato. Direct experience gave her a dimension of knowledge completely different from what she had known until then; it gave her the subjective experience of seeing colors. Jackson states that "if physicalism is true, she would know (what it is like to sense red); and no great powers of imagination would be called for. Imagination is a faculty that those who

---

54. Nagel, "What Is It Like to Be a Bat?," 437.
55. Jackson, "What Mary Didn't Know," 291–95.

lack knowledge need to fall back on."⁵⁶ In other words, no matter how much scientific data Mary had about colors, the subjective dimension of knowledge could not be obtained by scientific investigation.

This and the previous story help us understand that personal experience is a different dimension from scientific knowledge. It is not about Mary needing more scientific information on colors, or that we need some extra information about the bat's brain. The two arguments are not epistemological, but ontological in nature. Therefore, they cannot be rejected as a misapplication of Leibniz's Law, because they do not speak of properties, but of a different dimension of knowledge.

Searle argues that explaining consciousness requires explaining "exactly how neurobiological processes in the brain *cause* our subjective states of awareness or sentience; how exactly these states are *realized in* the brain structures."⁵⁷ Given our present knowledge, he admits that we are "very far from having an adequate theory of the neurophysiology of consciousness."⁵⁸ We know the anatomy of the brain, we can record electrical activity in its various areas, and observe the effects of injuries, drugs and alcohol, but yet we do not understand the mechanism of the causal powers of the mind. There is a tremendous qualitative leap from knowing the structure and functioning of the brain from a biological point of view to understanding how consciousness is generated.

Jerry Fodor, although an advocate of computationalism, expresses his own pessimism on solving the problem of consciousness by affirming:

> Nobody has the slightest idea how anything material could be conscious. Nobody even knows what it would be like to have the slightest idea about how anything material could be conscious.⁵⁹

Another pessimist about the ability of physicalist theories to ever provide a proper account of the phenomenon of consciousness is Nagel. He says:

> If we acknowledge that a physical theory of mind must account for the subjective character of experience, we must admit that no presently available conception gives us a clue how this could be done.⁶⁰

56. Jackson, "What Mary Didn't Know," 292.
57. Searle, *The Mystery of Consciousness*, 192.
58. Searle, *The Rediscovery of the Mind*, 91.
59. Fodor, "The Big Idea . . .", 5.
60. Nagel, "What Is It Like to Be a Bat?," 445.

Moreover, he believes that we do not even know which tools we need to understand what the mind really is, so "to insist on trying to explain the mind in terms of concepts and theories that have been devised exclusively to explain nonmental phenomena is (. . .) both intellectually backward and scientifically suicidal." Therefore we need "entirely new intellectual tools" to investigate the mind.[61]

Colin McGinn is another physicalist philosopher who joins the chorus of skeptics who confess their perplexity when facing the mystery of consciousness. He says:

> The deeper science probes into the brain the more remote it seems to get from consciousness. Greater knowledge of the brain thus destroys our illusions about the kinds of properties that might be discovered by travelling along this path. Advanced neurophysiological theory seems only to deepen the miracle.[62]

McGinn is skeptical on the very possibility of finding a response, arguing that consciousness is a task left to be explained by the next generation of neurobiologists, in which he envisions an "Einstein-like genius who will restructure the problem in some clever way and then present an astonished world with the solution."[63] Therefore he considers that "the time has come to admit candidly that we cannot resolve the mystery."[64]

Since we do not have a scientific way of investigating consciousness, it has been ignored by neurobiologists, while philosophers have treated it in a reductionist way or eliminated it completely from their concerns, fearing it could lead us back to dualism.[65] Searle argues that a dualistic approach must be excluded at all costs from philosophical research, for it would compromise the scientific worldview we have worked so hard to build during the last centuries. As we can see in his books and conferences, he boldly affirms the physicalist thesis, constantly repeating that there is no alternative in the philosophy of mind than to find physicalist answers to all questions. His thesis is simple:

> Conscious states are entirely caused by lower level neurobiological processes in the brain. Conscious states are thus *causally*

---

61. Nagel, *The View from Nowhere*, 52.
62. McGinn, "Can We Solve the Mind–Body Problem?," 359.
63. McGinn, "Can We Solve . . . ," 354.
64. McGinn, "Can We Solve . . . ," 349.
65. Searle, *The Mystery of Consciousness*, 194.

reducible to neurobiological processes. They have absolutely no life of their own, independent of the neurobiology.[66]

Searle does not prove his thesis, which he calls "biological naturalism,"[67] but merely affirms and repeats it as the only possibility consistent with physicalism. Despite his resolution to defend physicalism at all costs, there is no hope that philosophers will ever be able to understand or explain how consciousness works on a physicalist basis. As Descartes attempted to explain human nature as a whole with properties superior to the sum of its parts (the mind and the body), Searle argues that mental states must be generated by the brain on the principle that the whole (the brain as a whole) has properties superior to the parts (individual neurons).[68] Following this principle, consciousness *must* be a product of the physiological processes of the brain. In his words, "Consciousness is a system-level, biological feature in much the same way that digestion, or growth, or the secretion of bile are system level, biological features."[69] But this is only a philosophical, unproven assumption of his "biological naturalism." How things "must be" does not explain how they really are.

Another mystery for physicalists, directly linked to that of consciousness, is to explain free will. According to the laws of physics any given state of a system is determined by its preceding state, so human beings, as closed (physical) systems, should have no real freedom to act otherwise than they do. But we know this is false. Life would be absurd if we are not free and responsible for our deeds. In a world governed by precise physical laws, the only resource that Searle imagines to explain free will is quantum mechanics.[70] But invoking the world of microparticles to explain our freedom hardly achieves anything. What we find in the quantum realm is not freedom, but indeterminacy, according to Heisenberg's uncertainty principle. It refers to the impossibility of specifying at a given moment both the position and the velocity of a particle (for example, an electron in an orbital).[71] But this has nothing to do with the freedom

---

66. Searle, *Mind*, 113.

67. Searle, *Mind*, 113.

68. He says: "Individual neurons are not conscious, but portions of the brain system composed of neurons are conscious" (Searle, *Mind*, 114).

69. Searle, *Mind*, 115.

70. Searle *Mind*, 231.

71. Heisenberg's uncertainty principle affirms that the product of the uncertainties in position (x) and velocity (v) is equal to or greater than Planck's constant ($\hbar$): $\Delta x \cdot \Delta v \geq \hbar/2$.

we manifest as individuals. Searle eventually acknowledges that "free will is not the same as randomness"[72] and that "the hypothesis that the random indeterminacy at the quantum level leads to an indeterminacy of a nonrandom kind at the conscious intentionalistic level, seems very unlikely and implausible."[73] His conclusion is embarrassing for physicalist philosophers:

> We really do not know how free will exists in the brain, if it exists at all. We do not know why or how evolution has given us the unshakeable conviction of free will.[74]

Since free will is a mystery to physicalists, attempts have been made to question that it can really be "free." For example, experiments carried out by the neuroscientist Benjamin Libet suggest that our "free" decisions come *after* the actual firings of neurons in the frontal cortex (the region where voluntary acts are said to originate). His experiments consisted of asking subjects to spontaneously flex their wrist while he recorded the precise moment of neurons firing in the motor cortex, the moment of the actual movement, and the moment one has consciously decided to move the wrist. In order to capture as precisely as possible the moment of the conscious decision to move, which was the greatest challenge in Libet's experiments,[75] he used as a basis of reference a clock-like device on which a luminous dot was circling at high speed. The subjects were asked not to plan the movement of their wrist, but to do it spontaneously, and remember the position of the dot when they decided to move. Paradoxically, the timing of the firing in the frontal cortex preceded the conscious act by half a second, which suggested that the conscious "free decision" could not be the real cause of action. In Libet's words, "the specific brain activities leading to a voluntary act begin *before* the conscious will to act."[76] This means that "the process leading to a voluntary act is *initiated* by the brain *unconsciously*, well before the conscious will to act appears. That implies that free will, if it exists, would not initiate a voluntary act."[77]

---

72. Searle, *Mind*, 231.

73. Searle, *Mind*, 232.

74. Searle, *Mind*, 234.

75. Libet himself admits that the "conscious will is a subjective phenomenon, not directly accessible to external observations" (Libet, *Mind Time*, 125).

76. Libet, *Mind Time*, 123.

77. Libet, *Mind Time*, 136.

Can this be taken as a proof against free will? Are our voluntary acts produced by unconscious firing in the brain, and not by our decision to act? The solution for solving this mystery lies in revealing the hidden assumption at work in interpreting Libet's experiments. It is the assumption that conscious (mental) events can be timed, which means that they *must* have a physical basis. But this is an unwarranted physicalist assumption. If the mind is non-physical, conscious events cannot be timed as physical events in the brain. In other words, a physical experiment cannot record the moment of a non-physical event. Therefore these experiments can be taken as a proof against free will only in a physicalist theory of mind.

A similar objection to free will was affirmed by Adam Bear and Paul Bloom, both psychologists at Yale.[78] Instead of timing the moment one decides to act, they attempted to time the moment one's attention shifts from one image to another. The results were the same, indicating that first comes the electric activity in the brain, and then the conscious shift of attention. However, neither do these experiments really invalidate free will. Byron Reese, an author we will meet again in the next chapter, argues:

> Although the experiments are quite compelling, all of this is by no means proven. We don't even understand how memories are encoded in the brain. We refer to what we can measure in the brain by the most nebulous of terms, "activity."[79]

His view is that a dualist is not bound to the conclusion that brain activity comes first and conscious decision next, for we cannot understand how causality works between the two kinds of phenomena, mental and physical:

> While dualists believe the brain undoubtedly controls the body, they see the salient question as *why* the person chose to look at the other side of the screen at just that instant. What triggered that brain activity that was observed? And for every answer offered, they would in turn ask, "And what caused that?" with the infuriating persistence of a four-year-old. Eventually, in this view, you either get back to the big bang or you spot free will.[80]

As with Libet's experiments, the assumption is that mental events can be timed with high precision because they *must* be physical events. But on this assumption we refute only the *physicalist* possibility for free

---

78. Bear and Bloom, "A Simple Task Uncovers . . .".
79. Reese, *The Fourth Age*, 218.
80. Reese, *The Fourth Age*, 218.

will. Only if the mind has a physical nature can we accept the irrelevance of conscious acts in causation. But since we cannot live on the assumption that we have no free will, why follow a physicalist worldview?

Although physicalism is presented by its followers as the only resource for explaining human nature, we see that it cannot explain the subjective part of our nature, the fact that we are conscious persons endowed with free will, not just highly sophisticated machines. The origin of this problem is the fact that physicalists follow a philosophy of science called scientism.

1.5 SCIENCE AND SCIENTISM

If Cartesian dualism is incapable of solving the mind-body problem, it does not necessarily follow that physicalism is right, for physicalism cannot provide an account of consciousness and free will. One of Descartes's arguments to "prove" that the mind is a substance different from the body was the ability to *imagine* existence without the body. But this cannot be considered a valid argument, because imagination, by itself, does not establish anything about human nature. Paradoxically, a variant of such reasoning can be found in Searle's biological naturalism and in other physicalist theories: Since science formulates clear laws about how the physical world works, we have no grounds for admitting the existence of a non-physical substance, so it does not exist. It is the same argument in reverse, in order to serve the physicalist cause. Does it have to be valid in this case because it is used by physicalists? Is the fact that we cannot *imagine* the existence of a non-physical world a sufficient argument to "prove" its nonexistence? Obviously not.

Following on from the fact that we cannot disprove the existence of non-physical things, mental events need not be reduced to physical events in the brain. We have no scientific justification for such a reductionist view. The fact that we observe an increased electrical activity and blood flow in a certain region of the brain when one experiences strong emotions does not mean that these mental events must be reduced to the observed physical events in the brain. For instance, we cannot assume that an increased electrical activity in the amygdala means that the fear one experiences is produced by that specific electrical activity and nothing else. We have no sound reason to reject the non-physical nature of the mind except for philosophical biases. Let me use an analogy to explain the fallacy of physicalist reductionism.

Let us imagine that a primitive man from a newly discovered tribe in the Amazon rainforest is brought to a modern city. He has never seen cars or electric light and just watches the traffic in a busy intersection. He observes that whenever a car turns to the left or to the right, a small yellow light on the car blinks a few seconds before the turn and then goes out. As he does not know anything about how cars work or driving rules, he assumes that it is the turn itself that causes that yellow light to blink. He may even come up with a statistical correlation between when a car starts blinking and the start of the turn. He might look at the distance, count the number of blinks, and imagine a formula that would correlate all observed data. Although his observation is accurate, his explanation is wrong, for it is the driver who signals a change of direction, not the car itself in the presence of a turn. The same logical fallacy is at work when physicalists claim that mental events can only be caused by electrical events in the brain and that non-physical things cannot exist. The correlation between the two types of phenomena is right, but the reductionist physicalist explanation is wrong.

We observe that eventually one follows either one set of assumptions or the other, either the dualistic set, which asserts that matter is not the only reality, or the physicalist one, which denies the existence of a non-physical reality. What makes physicalists follow the second set of assumptions? Nothing but a philosophy of science, called scientism. It argues that the whole of reality must be subject to scientific inquiry (recall the requirements of the Vienna Circle), and what eludes it does not exist. This path, however, is hardly convincing. Even Nagel, as a physicalist, criticizes scientism and its requirement to limit our knowledge to the possibilities offered by physics and evolutionary biology. In his words, "Scientism is actually a special form of idealism, for it puts one type of human understanding in charge of the universe and what can be said about it."[81] The requirement that science must be the only means by which we know the world is just an assumption that science itself cannot prove. The scientific method is about observing natural phenomena, developing hypotheses, verifying them by means of repeatable experiments, and reformulating initial hypotheses as laws of nature. Scientism, as a

---

81. Nagel, *The View from Nowhere*, 9. He says elsewhere: "It is the phenomena of consciousness themselves that pose the dearest challenge to the idea that physical objectivity gives the general form of reality" (Nagel, *The View from Nowhere*, 16–17).

philosophy, formulates hypotheses, but is unable to verify them experimentally. Therefore to claim, as Searle does, that consciousness can only be a product of the brain and that "the causal powers of consciousness and the causal powers of its neuronal base are exactly the same,"[82] is just an unwarranted scientific theory.

Another way in which Searle attempts to "prove" that consciousness must have a physicalist explanation is by following the assumption that "the real physical world is 'causally closed' in the sense that nothing from outside the physical world can ever have any causal effects inside the physical world."[83] In other words, if a non-physical entity could influence the physical, as the dualists claim, it would be an instance of overcausation. For example, the movement of the arm upward at the command of the will would be produced by two causes, one physical and one mental,[84] while logically it is sufficient to consider only one cause, the physical. Two things must be said here against overcausation. First, the argument produced by Kim against nonreductive physicalism does not apply here, for it refers to a physicalist theory. Dualism does not assert that all physical phenomena must have physical causes, so mental phenomena need *not* be supervenient on physical phenomena. Second, the argument for overcausation is circular. The closure of the physical world to any non-physical intervention is just a physicalist assumption, not the conclusion of logical reasoning. If we acknowledge the existence of the non-physical, and the mind has such a nature, it can act in the causal chain and be a real cause that does not overlap with a physical one.

The *non*-scientific reason for which dualistic solutions to the problem of consciousness must be avoided at all costs is that they would lead philosophy of mind towards religion. The problem of consciousness can tempt us into admitting a non-physical substance, and implicitly the existence of God. McGinn is aware of this possibility and tries to discourage any inquiry in this direction:

> In the case of consciousness, the appearance of miracle might also tempt us in a 'creationist' direction, with God required to perform the alchemy necessary to transform matter into experience. Thus the mind-body problem might similarly be used to prove the existence of God (no miracle without a

82. Searle, *Mind*, 127.

83. Searle, *Mind*, 193. This is Hume's argument for denying the possibility of miracles.

84. See Searle, *Mind*, 130–31.

miracle-maker). We cannot, I think, refute this argument in the way we can the original creationist argument, namely by actually producing a non-miraculous explanatory theory, but we can refute it by arguing that such a naturalistic theory must *exist*.[85]

Another philosopher who openly admits his fear of theism is Nagel. He declares:

> I want atheism to be true and am made uneasy by the fact that some of the most intelligent and well-informed people I know are religious believers. It isn't just that I don't believe in God and, naturally, hope that I'm right in my belief. It's that I hope there is no God! I don't want there to be a God; I don't want the universe to be like that.[86]

Physicalists invite us to look confidently to the distant future, when a new genius will arise to unravel the mystery of consciousness. Nagel hopes that a Maxwell of the philosophy of mind and an Einstein of psychology will arise and formulate "a theory that the mental and the physical are really the same."[87] We do not know whether such a "Messiah" will ever arrive. Meanwhile physicalist philosophers ask us to be confident that the mystery of consciousness will eventually have a physicalist explanation. This is a non-negotiable part of the physicalist creed on human nature. However, believing that science is the *only* resource to unravel the mystery of human nature, and waiting for science to answer *all* our questions about human nature, makes us followers of the philosophical view of scientism.

Searle acknowledges that, despite his efforts in upholding physicalism as the only acceptable view, his arguments "still leave dualism as a logical possibility."[88] However, given his allegiance to scientism, he thinks it is

> extremely unlikely, that when our bodies are destroyed, our souls will go marching on. I have not tried to show that this is an impossibility (indeed, I wish it were true), but rather that it is inconsistent with just about everything else we know about how the universe works and therefore it is irrational to believe in it.[89]

---

85. McGinn, "Can We Solve . . .", 362.
86. Nagel, *The Last Word*, 130.
87. Nagel, *The View from Nowhere*, 53.
88. Searle, *Mind*, 132.
89. Searle, *Mind*, 132.

We observe that Searle's philosophy is thoroughly shaped by scientism, which apriorically establishes what is rational or irrational to believe, and also by a subjective desire that personal existence does *not* continue after death. However, science cannot make infallible claims on this topic. Science can tell us that we do not have sufficient reasons to believe in life after death, but cannot *prove* that it does not exist. We can refuse, like Searle, to believe that there is something beyond the realm of science, but that is just an assumption. It does not prove anything by itself.

Given the fact that physicalism fails to explain consciousness and cannot even foresee a direction of research which could generate a physicalist theory of consciousness, philosophers of mind should reassess the verdict that dualism is a dead end in the philosophy of mind. Dualism should be reconsidered, since it has been rejected on ideological, almost religious, grounds. In fact, Cartesian dualism is not the only form of dualism that attempts to explain the mind. In chapter 6, we explore another form of dualism for understanding the mind, mind-body interaction, and the mystery of consciousness. Only an anti-religious bias can prevent us from rejecting *a priori* such an approach. Before this, though, we explore another great theme in the philosophy of mind, the meaning of the self and the criteria for preserving personal identity.

2

Philosophy of Mind on Personal Identity and the Survival of Death

ANY DISCUSSION OF PERSONAL identity and the criteria we follow to establish whether survival of death is possible must begin with defining the element that makes us the particular persons we are. In the previous chapter we looked at the existing options. For physicalists personal identity is wholly identified with the body, or at least with the brain, its most significant part. For dualists the mind (or the soul) has a non-physical nature, so what is essential for survival is not related to the body. In this chapter we continue to explore the tenets of physicalism and dualism in the specific domain of personal identity, in order to understand to what extent they can give hope in the quest to defeat death.

Before assessing theories of personal identity, we need to establish whether we are looking for a rigid or a transitive kind of identity. A rigid identity requires that the object of our investigation is always the same, both quantitatively and qualitatively. For example, my keys must keep the same shape and size, or else I will be locked out of my house. Leonardo da Vinci's *Mona Lisa* must keep the same size, proportions, colors, materials, and causal relationship to the original to remain the same painting. If we require this kind of identity for defining personal identity, we will find hardly anything truly unchanged, given that our body, beliefs, and memory are constantly changing. Since we are the same person over time despite all changes, we need to define a transitive kind of identity. Let me use a classic illustration to make this aspect clear, that of the ship of Theseus.[1]

The hero of Greek mythology decides to repair his ship. He changes the planks, ropes and all other parts of his ship, one at a time, until after a long period of continuous repairs, the entire ship is formed of new components. The question that philosophers ask, related to defining what kind of identity we look for, is whether this "repaired" ship is the same as the original one or is another ship. Since we accept a transitive concept of identity we should acknowledge that the "new" ship is indeed Theseus's ship.

Following David Wiggins's suggestion, let us complicate the story and suppose that somebody picks up all the old pieces discarded by Theseus and rebuilds the old ship, so that the repaired ship and the rebuilt one float in the dock one beside the other.[2] Which one is the true ship of Theseus now? If we use a criterion that does not allow change, it is the second, for it has all the original parts. If our view of identity allows change it is the first ship, while the rebuilt ship is nothing but a museum piece that would probably be non-functional and sink. One could say it is Theseus's former ship.

In a similar way, we could think of the identity of living beings. It is obvious that a tree retains its identity in all phases of its growth, by virtue of the continuity between these phases. Although its shape and size have undergone major changes, nobody would doubt that my cherry tree is the same tree as the little sapling planted twenty years ago. The butterflies that fly around in my garden have gone through the phase of egg, larva, and chrysalis. Although they looked very different from the current butterflies, they were the same insects. The cute little puppy I brought home years ago has turned into a fierce dog, yet remains the same animal. In a similar way, when we come to defining criteria of preserving personal identity for human beings, we have to admit a radical transformation in everything that can define us bodily and mentally, for we know that we change.

Before examining the criteria for preserving personal identity we must be aware of the danger of circularity in any such discussion. A question such as, "What makes me the same person that I was one year, ten

---

1. The original story seems to belong to the Greek philosopher Plutarch (ca. AD 46 –120).

2. You can find this scenario in several sources. For instance, see Noonan, *Personal Identity*, 154–58. Actually, Wiggins's scenario follows another point. He argues against a theory called "the best candidate." I have adapted this story to explain rigid vs. transitive identity.

years or forty years ago?," betrays circularity from its very formulation, for I tacitly follow the assumption that I have remained the same person all these years, but I just do not know how to prove it. I might try to fix this problem by rephrasing the question to: "What is the element that makes my experience now, when I write these lines, belong to the same person who bore my name a year ago, ten years or forty years ago?" Unfortunately, I cannot eliminate circularity in this way either because the name of "that" person is still mine, so I assume again that I am referring to myself. Searle formulates the question in this way: "What fact about a person makes that person the same person through the various changes that he or she undergoes in the course of a lifetime?"[3] But his attempt, too, fails to avoid circularity because I am the same person who went through all these stages of life since all these stages are mine. If I look for a unifying factor of a set of experiences which would prove that they belong to the *same person* I face the same problem, for I choose a set of experiences that I know are *mine*. The issue of circularity will subtly return in various forms in the debates of this chapter.

2.1 PHYSICALIST CRITERIA FOR PRESERVING PERSONAL IDENTITY

The criteria of preserving personal identity refer to the necessary and sufficient conditions for a person to be identified as being the same over time and, by extension, the possibility of surviving death given these conditions. The dominant position among philosophers is physicalism, which works on the assumption that there is no non-physical component in human nature. Therefore the criteria for preserving personal identity are centered on the continuity of the body, or at least of the brain, as its most important part.

2.1.1. The Bodily Criterion

The most common way to identify a person is by the look of his or her body. For this reason we have a picture of our face in our passport, driving license or other form of ID. The look of our face significantly differentiates us from other people. However, the picture in my first passport and a recent one are quite different, and I do not resemble at all how I

---

3. Searle, *Mind*, 280.

looked as a baby. On what ground do we affirm that these images depict the *same person*? Because they were taken of the same body? But how could they be of the same body, since all cells are replaced in about seven years, sooner than the passport expires?[4]

An alternative bodily criterion for identity could be our DNA. The pictures taken of us are similar from one to the next because the information we carry in each cell does not change from conception to death. After all, the DNA test is the most reliable identification method for forensic purposes. However, I do not need to do a DNA test regularly to make sure I am the same person or to prove it to another person.

Other good identification points are the fingerprints or irises. These do not change and are easily recognizable by scanning devices. But again, these identification elements are not what my personal identity consists of, but only indicators of it. If I were to lose these physical marks I would not cease to be the same person. If one loses his hands in a tragic accident and has no fingerprints, or his eyes and has no irises, does it mean that he has ceased to exist? Or do we rather conclude that only some means of identification have been lost, while the person is undoubtedly still there? In other words, we could ask ourselves whether the body is the provider of personal identity, or rather its distinguishing marks are just indicators of a more essential entity which truly carries personal identity over time.

2.1.2 The Brain Criterion

Following a reductionist approach, physicalists ask whether all the body or just a part of it is needed to be identified as the same person. Some people suffer accidents or amputations, have organs surgically removed, or undergo transplants, but nevertheless remain the same persons. We do not doubt that with the amputation of a limb, the surgical removal of a kidney, or even a heart transplant, the identity of a person remains unchanged. However, we do have one organ which, if it were transplanted, we are not so sure would leave a person's identity intact. This is the brain, the organ which physicalists consider to be the seat of consciousness, on the assumption that one's mental life is preserved by the particular

---

4. There is an exception to this replacement rule. Unlike other cells of our body, most of the brain cells do not divide but die without replacement. This is why diseases like Parkinson's and Alzheimer's are not curable. Only in the hippocampus, a tiny part of the brain, do cells regenerate.

associations between the billions of neurons. This means that at least the brain has to be preserved in order to remain the same person.

The brain criterion is illustrated by a thought experiment imagined by Sydney Shoemaker, in which he speculates on the psychological outcome of a brain transplant. Imagine that medical science has evolved enough that brain tumors are operated on outside the skull. Two patients, Brown and Robinson, are operated on in this way, but by error their brains are switched and put back in the wrong skulls. The recipient of Robinson's brain dies, while Robinson survives with Brown's brain.[5] The question is: Who will wake up from anesthesia? Brown or Robinson? On the assumption that the brain carries one's mental life, we should believe that Brown will awaken in Robinson's body. He would remember episodes of Brown's life very convincingly for Brown's wife, while nothing of Robinson's life.

Such grotesque thought experiments are common in the philosophy of mind, and you may wonder what their usefulness is, since it is unlikely that they will ever become reality. Derek Parfit, an English philosopher whose contribution we will explore later in this chapter, argues that they reveal more clearly our assumptions and what we actually believe of personal identity.[6]

Believing that the element that sustains consciousness is our brain, followers of the physicalist view attempt to preserve the body of a deceased person by cryonics, that is, by freezing the body with its brain.[7] They intend to bring it back to life when medicine has evolved sufficiently to cure the particular disease that led to the death of that person. Another option would be to detach one's brain (or head) after death and transplant it into another skull (or to another body), as in the Brown/Robinson scenario.[8]

---

5. Shoemaker, *Self-knowledge and Self-Identity*, 23–24.

6. Parfit, *Reasons and Persons*, 200.

7. Cryonics is a technique of preserving a human corpse or a severed head in liquid nitrogen at very low temperature (-196 Celsius, or -320 Fahrenheit). There are four such facilities that offer to cryopreserve one's body (or at least the head) after death. The price for cryonic suspension ranges "from ten thousand to two hundred thousand dollars, according to the organization we consult and the kind of suspension we want" (Manzocco, *Transhumanism*, 119). However, many scientists are skeptical about this method, fearing that freezing does irreversible damage to the brain.

8. When Shoemaker imagined this experiment in the 1960s, he did not expect that a real transplant could ever be realized. Recently however, Sergio Canavero, an Italian neurosurgeon, argues that he is preparing for one, despite all criticism on both medical and ethical grounds. Search online for "Canavero human head transplant" or just

However, the scenario imagined by Shoemaker was further modified by reductionists, arguing that survival would require less than a whole brain.

2.1.3 The Physical Criterion

In severe cases of epilepsy neurosurgeons sometimes decide to perform a commissurotomy, that is, the sectioning of the *corpus callosum* (the part of the brain that connects the two hemispheres). Such cases have opened the way for studying the different functions of the two hemispheres. It has been discovered that the left hemisphere supports rational thought and linguistic skills, while the right hemisphere is the foundation for intuitive thought and creative activities. People who have suffered major injuries to the left hemisphere have regressed to a child's language skills, but picked up on language by the progressive involvement of the right hemisphere. It seems that the different specializations of the hemispheres occur after the age of three, and if one of the hemispheres has suffered an accident, the other can gradually take over its functions.[9]

Of major interest for the philosophy of mind is that following commissurotomy, the different specializations of the cerebral hemispheres led philosophers to believe that the hemispheres represented two different centers of consciousness which were unified before surgery. This thought led to the hypothesis that only one hemisphere of the brain would be sufficient to preserve personal identity. Thus we can imagine a weird experiment in which each of the two hemispheres is transplanted into separate skulls, so that two persons carry the consciousness of the initial brain donor. This would be a case of a division and doubling of consciousness, and no longer of preserving a one-to-one identity. This scenario, given by the possibility of transplanting both hemispheres thus resulting in two people who retain the "identity" of the original person, already suggests that something is wrong with the physicalist approach to personal identity.[10] As a result, philosophical speculation went on to define personal identity in psychological terms.

"head transplant" to learn about the latest developments of this project.

9. Noonan, *Personal Identity*, 6.

10. In a later section of this chapter we will see how this scenario was used by Derek Parfit to *deny* the need to preserve personal identity for survival.

2.2 THE PSYCHOLOGICAL CONTINUITY CRITERION

Bernard Williams demonstrated the weakness of the brain criterion by using the following thought experiment:[11] Starting with the Brown/Robinson case, suppose that all the mental content in Brown's brain is downloaded to a hard disk for safe keeping during brain surgery, and afterwards it is uploaded to the same brain. If the mental content is downloaded from one brain to the storage facility and then uploaded back to the same brain, personal identity should be preserved. But if the "upload" were done to another brain, for example, to Robinson's, we would reach the same result and conclusion as in Shoemaker's scenario, that Brown awakens in Robinson's body. In this case, however, the actual brain transplant was no longer needed to preserve Brown's identity. The upload of his mental content, as pure information, would be sufficient to get the same result.

The same conclusion is reached when Williams combines the above scenario with that of an actual brain transplant: Robinson, who has inoperable brain cancer, is about to receive Brown's brain. As a precautionary measure, all Robinson's mental content is downloaded before the transplant to a hard disk. The existing data on the healthy (formerly Brown's) brain is erased, the brain transplant takes place, and the mental content taken from Robinson's brain, which was stored on the hard disk, is uploaded to the new brain. Although in this case Robinson has Brown's brain, as in the original scenario imagined by Shoemaker, we should accept that Robinson remained the same person. Unlike in Shoemaker's scenario, this time it is Robinson who wakes up from anesthesia. He has a new brain, but is the same person because he retains the mental content he had before the surgery. This is the way in which Williams argues that preserving the mental content of a person is sufficient to preserve personal identity. Therefore it would no longer be necessary to preserve a biological component (a complete brain or a part of it) for preserving personal identity.

According to the psychological continuity criterion, what is necessary for the preservation of personal identity is only the mental content, the sum of the beliefs, memories and character traits. Before continuing its examination we must be aware of the computational assumption behind this scenario, that is, that the preservation of consciousness does not

---

11. Williams, *Problems of the Self*, 47–48.

depend on the presence of the brain, for it is just software that can run on other hardware (on another brain in this case).[12]

The same paradigm, of assuming that one's identity can be kept as information, is at work in familiar science fiction scenarios. For example, remember from the Star Trek series of the 1960s the idea of transporting people into cosmic space by teleportation. A person who needs to travel to Mars enters the teletransporter, presses the green button, loses consciousness, the machine scans his or her body and records its data in the minutest detail, molecule by molecule, transmits the information at light speed to a similar station on Mars, and there, using organic materials identical to those on Earth and based on the information received, a kind of 3D printer builds a replica of the person "traveling" to Mars.[13] Before the new body is restored on Mars, the one remaining on Earth is destroyed.

We must be aware that the teleportation scenario does not serve just the psychological continuity criterion, for it requires the bodily identity of the person "teletransported" to Mars. As in cryogenics, the assumption operating in this scenario is that consciousness is encoded in the billions of neural connections in the cortex. So by replicating the brain molecule by molecule, one can also replicate the mental content of a human being. It is only because an exact physical copy is created on Mars that we can suppose that psychological traits are kept. Therefore the teletransportation scenario demands that both the bodily criterion and the psychological criterion are met for the preservation of personal identity.

A variant of the psychological continuity criterion was formulated by John Locke (1632–1704) as the memory criterion. As Descartes attempted to explore the nature of the mind "liberated" from scholastic philosophy, a similar revolution in discussing the concept of person was launched by Locke, another founder of modern philosophy. In his *Essay Concerning Human Understanding*, Locke defines the person as "a thinking intelligent

---

12. For another scenario that supports the psychological criterion, read Franz Kafka's, *The Metamorphosis*, in which the main character, Gregor Samsa, wakes up one morning in the body of a huge insect. It illustrates the philosophical possibility of preserving one's personal identity in a completely different body. Readers have to assume that Gregor really lives in the body of the insect, while his family can barely cope with it.

13. Such a 3D printer would be an advanced version of current efforts to "print" organs which could be used for transplants. See for example: cellink.com/the-first-3d-printed-bionic-pancreas/ (retrieved September 18, 2020). However, at the moment we cannot print even skin tissue for those who have suffered severe burns, to say nothing of body organs, so we are still just speculating on these issues.

Being, that has reason and reflection, and can consider itself as itself, the same thinking thing in different times and places; which it does only by that consciousness, which is inseparable from thinking."[14]

Locke's definition is awkward, includes a number of assumptions, and needs to be understood in the broader context of his philosophy. For the English philosopher, "person" and "individual human being" do not mean the same thing. The term "person" has legal value. The law must punish the guilty only if he or she is aware of his or her actions. If one was acting in ignorance or in a mentally defective state when committing a crime, he or she is not the same person as the one judged, but just the same human being.[15] The life of a human being is made up of several personal sequences that extend over a period of conscious memory. In primary school I was one person, as a student another person, and now I am another person. The element that links this sequence of persons into the life of an individual human being is the body. In Locke's words, the identity of a human being (not of the person) consists of "nothing but a participation of the same continued life, by constantly fleeting particles of matter, in succession vitally united to the same organized body."[16]

The psychological continuity criterion could be adjusted to Locke's view if we admit a continuity link between the sequences of self-awareness of a person, that is, if we admit the transitivity of these sequences. For example, I can remember something I experienced 20 years ago, but not what I did 40 years ago. According to Locke's view, I remained the same person during the last 20 years, but not during the last 40 years. If we accept the transitivity of the memory I am the same person with the one I was 40 years ago, because 20 years ago I did remember something from 40 years ago, so the episodes during the last 40 years of my life are linked. In other words, the demand for the continuity of memory should admit the transitivity of the stages that make up human life: if moment x is related to moment y through memory, and y is related to z, it means that moments x and z are also connected, and form the history of the same person.

14. Locke, *An Essay Concerning Human Understanding*, II,27,9, 335.

15. Leibniz criticized Locke's criterion as insufficient, pointing out that if one loses memory and does reprehensible deeds, he or she is still punished on the testimony of others. Therefore personal identity is kept even in case of memory loss, based on the testimony of other people (Leibniz, *New Essays on Human Understanding*, 237).

16. Locke, *An Essay Concerning Human Understanding*, II,27,6, 330.

2.3 PROBLEMS OF THE PSYCHOLOGICAL CONTINUITY CRITERION

In any way it could be formulated, the psychological continuity criterion is compromised by circularity for a very simple reason. Joseph Butler (1692–1752) argues convincingly that memory, consciousness, and awareness of personal continuity *presuppose* personal continuity and thus do not prove it.[17] In order to be able to remember what happened 20 or 40 years ago, or be conscious that those things happened to *me*, I must be the same person, so the criterion requires personal continuity instead of demonstrating it. Only if I already am the same person can I remember something from my past, for remembering something means remembering *myself* doing that. I have already mentioned this problem in the introduction to this chapter.

If Williams's scenario of the Brown/Robinson case undergoes just one more transformation, it will lead to completely different conclusions. Instead of pointing to the importance of psychological continuity, it will compromise it. Williams invites us to imagine that Robinson is healthy and is subjected to changes of consciousness by means of a machine.[18] The machine wipes out Robinson's memories, reconfigures his character, and generates completely different beliefs than he had before, as if they were of another person. As a particular case, let us consider that Brown's mental life is implanted in Robinson's brain. Who would leave the lab after this intervention? Robinson or Brown? This time the answer would be that Robinson is the survivor, with the peculiar mention that he has acquired some very strange beliefs about himself, claiming to be someone else, Brown. Although the end result of this experiment should be the same as the one imagined by Shoemaker, a Robinson who believes himself to be Brown, Williams argues that in this case the result is the opposite. This time we admit the continuity of Robinson's identity and the bodily criterion becomes dominant.

In order to better understand the weakness of the psychological criterion, Williams develops the above imaginary experiment in a six-step form.[19] In this form it will also be helpful in analyzing evidence in favor

17. Butler, "Of Personal Identity," in Perry, *Personal Identity*, 99–106.

18. Williams, *Problems of the Self*, 47. Williams does not use the names Brown and Robinson. I have adapted the story to these names for the sake of continuity with subsection 2.1.2.

19. Williams, *Problems of the Self*, 55–56.

of reincarnation, in chapter 5. Think at which of these steps person A becomes person B:

1. Person A suffers a medical intervention which results in losing her memory;
2. Not only does A lose her memory, but she undergoes changes in her character traits;
3. As above; in addition false memories are implanted to A which do not match those of a real person;
4. As above, except that the memories implanted to A correspond to those of a real person, B;
5. As above, except that the implanted memories are taken directly from B's brain, after which B remains the same;
6. Just as above, only that B does not remain the same, for the same process is carried out for B, that is, the psychological traits of A are implanted to B.

Essentially we are dealing with a rephrasing of the Brown/Robinson case, the difference being that the procedure takes place in both directions. The question posed by Williams is: At which of these stages could we say that A becomes B? Where can we draw the line that marks the change of person A into B? There is no doubt that in cases 1–4 we are dealing with the same person. Regardless of what a direct takeover of memories from B's brain would mean in case 5, A cannot be called B, especially as B continues to exist independently. So neither can case 5 be considered a transformation of A into B. And in case 6 we have the same person A as in case 5, with the same character, history and beliefs. If B no longer exists (she died or has undergone the reverse transformation), is this condition enough to consider A another person? Why should the identity of A in case 6 depend on someone else's (B's) existence or nonexistence? In other words, why should an outside reference change the interpretation given to this case? The conclusion is that A remains A despite all transformations, which makes the preservation of the body essential to the preservation of personal identity, while psychological continuity is not sufficient for it.

The same psychological discontinuity could be induced by hypnosis. Instead of doubting that we are dealing with the same person, and arguing that he or she needs another ID, we would rather consider that he or she suffered unfortunate changes of beliefs and character. This means that the bodily criterion of personal identity cannot be dismissed. If I wake up tomorrow morning with a different personality, claiming to be somebody else, living somewhere else, how will my wife respond? Will she think I am another man, or that it is still me, but in need of urgent psychiatric treatment?[20]

Since we accept that personal identity is preserved even in cases of total psychological discontinuity, it seems that bodily continuity is essential for survival. To support this fact, it is not necessary to imagine fictional scenarios provided by philosophers. It is sufficient to recall that in a state of coma, general anesthesia, or even of deep sleep, when any psychological traits are absent, we do not doubt the continuity of the person. In addition, we must realize the weakness of one of the premises on which the psychological criterion works. In all these thought experiments in which memory is transferred from one brain to another, the assumption is that memory is just information, in the form of a file that is copied from one memory stick to another. But even from a physicalist point of view this is difficult to hold, for we do not know if or how memory could be detached from the brain.

2.4 REVISED FORMS OF THE PSYCHOLOGICAL CRITERION

Williams puts forward a further criticism to the psychological criterion, called the duplication argument. He imagines the following scenario: A certain Charles "remembers" that he is Guy Fawkes, the famous character who tried to blow up the English parliament in 1605.[21] Charles can evoke various episodes of Fawkes's life very convincingly. But there is a possibility, Williams affirms, that Charles's brother, Robert, can also "remember" these details. Even if Robert did not actually exist, his absence would not make Charles's continuity with Guy Fawkes true. What Williams emphasizes with this scenario is that the psychological criterion is vulnerable to the possibility of duplicating personal identity. Consciousness,

---

20. As we will see in subsection 5.2.2, against these conclusions, there are cases of little children who at a certain moment start claiming to be a different person and are taken as proofs for reincarnation.

21. Williams, *Problems of the Self*, 7–9.

as information, could be copied and multiplied, which would cancel the numerical identity of the persons involved.

One of the answers given to the problem raised by Williams was the formulation of the "only x and y" principle,[22] in which x designates the original person and y the candidate for continuity. This principle states that the identity between x and y (Fawkes and Charles) depends only on the relationship between them, and on nothing else, that is, on no other candidate. Robert Nozick responded that the "only x and y" principle must be rejected, for we should not ignore rival candidates. In a case of duplication of identity it must be established which of the copies most closely resembles the original. If there are rival candidates to identity, y is the continuator of x if their resemblance is clearer than in any other pair. Nozick formulates it as the "best candidate" theory or the revised psychological criterion,[23] the revision consisting of the idea that psychological continuity is sufficiently proven only if there is no other candidate with the *same degree* of resemblance to the original. Less convincing candidates do not threaten the continuity between the most likely pair. This would also reduce the problems of the physical criterion, for there would not be *two* people to survive the transplant of the two hemispheres, but only the one that has a greater psychological resemblance to the original person.

The possibility of multiplying identity caused Williams to prefer the bodily criterion to the psychological one. However, even the bodily criterion can be affected by multiplication. For example, in the case of teleportation more than one replica could be created on Mars, so even the corporal criterion fails to guarantee the numerical identity between the original and the person "teletransported" to Mars. Therefore, both criteria, the bodily and the psychological, are vulnerable to the possibility of duplication. And we could further complicate this issue by noting that the two criteria presuppose each other. The continuity of the body is taken as a proof for the preservation of my identity by the fact that *I remember* that I had the same body 10, 20 or 40 years ago. From this perspective the bodily criterion requires the psychological one. But from another point of view, I can *remember* that I have the same body only if I *already have* the same body, or more precisely the same brain, which makes the existence of memory possible. From this point of view, the

---

22. Noonan, *Personal Identity*, 16.
23. Nozick, *Philosophical Explanations*, 29–37.

with the same numerical identity and the result of the same causal chain that led to her formation.

2.7 DAVID HUME—THE PERSON AS A COLLECTION OF PERCEPTIONS

David Hume (1711–1776) attempted to define human nature following the assumptions of empiricism and naturalism.[42] Although he wrote long before the contemporary debates on preserving personal identity, Hume's contribution to this topic is important for our exploration, especially as it will help us understand the Buddhist view on human nature, which we explore in chapter 4.

In his *Treatise on Human Nature* we find a chapter entitled "Personal Identity,"[43] in which he criticizes the quest to identify a unifying center of consciousness, the thing we call the self or soul. If we acquired the notion of an immutable self by introspection, as a "clear and distinct idea" (according to Descartes), it should be changeless throughout our life. But since we cannot observe empirically anything immutable in our nature, such a changeless core cannot exist. What we can clearly identify in human experience are just individual perceptions, distinct from one another, which are accidentally associated with one another and thus do not belong to a self. In words that have become famous, Hume states:

> For my part, when I enter most intimately into what I call *myself*, I always stumble on some particular perception or other, of heat or cold, light or shade, love or hatred, pain or pleasure. I never can catch *myself* at any time without a perception, and never can observe any thing but the perception. (. . .) And were all my perceptions removed by death, and could I neither think, nor feel, nor see, nor love, nor hate after the dissolution of my body, I should be entirely annihilated.[44]

Hume's empiricism refuses to acknowledge a permanent element in human nature that could define personal identity. Living beings are

---

42. Empiricism is the view that truth can be known only by direct and concrete experience. Naturalism is a broad term in philosophy, essentially the equivalent of what we call physicalism in the philosophy of mind. Its method involves empirical observation and reasoning, while being committed to rejecting the supernatural.

43. Hume, *A Treatise of Human Nature*, (I,4,6), 164–71.

44. Hume, *A Treatise of Human Nature*, 165. Translated into the language of the philosophy of mind, what Hume calls "perceptions" are mental events.

nothing but series of objects which have only momentary existence. And so is the human being, nothing but "a bundle or collection of different perceptions, which succeed each other with an inconceivable rapidity, and are in a perpetual flux and movement," while the mind is merely an artificial concept, nothing but "successive perceptions," or "a kind of theatre, where several perceptions successively make their appearance; pass, re-pass, glide away, and mingle in an infinite variety of postures and situations."[45]

The element that links the different perceptions into a continuous stream is the imagination, the same element that makes us accept the continuity of an object in continuous repair (as was the ship of Theseus). Although between the young and the old oak there is no particle of matter which remains the same, and between the child and the adult there is no cell left the same, our imagination fills the gap by assigning them continuous identity. What we call "the soul" is nothing but the imagination at work in unifying the multitude of perceptions.[46] In his words,

> We often feign some new and unintelligible principle, that connects the objects together, and prevents their interruption or variation. Thus we feign the continued existence of the perceptions of our senses, to remove the interruption; and run into the notion of a *soul*, and *self*, and *substance*, to disguise the variation.[47]

This process is aided by memory, the instrument "by which we raise up the images of past perceptions."[48] In Hume's words, "memory not only discovers the identity, but also contributes to its production, by producing the relation of resemblance among the perceptions."[49] He explains his view by using the illustration of the citizens of a republic. They are subject to rulers by laws that unite them and bring other citizens into existence by giving birth to children. Although the individuals are in permanent change and die, the republic subsists.[50] As the citizens of the republic have temporary existence and pass on their heritage, so it happens with our perceptions. Memory keeps them alive, while imagination links them into a continuous stream. And as the citizens of the republic relate to each other and keep the republic in existence despite being mortal, our

---

45. Hume, *A Treatise of Human Nature*, 165.
46. Hume, *A Treatise of Human Nature*, 169.
47. Hume, *A Treatise of Human Nature*, 166.
48. Hume, *A Treatise of Human Nature*, 170.
49. Hume, *A Treatise of Human Nature*, 170.
50. Hume, *A Treatise of Human Nature*, 170.

perceptions are linked to each other, generate one another and sustain the illusion of personal identity.

As you may suspect, something must be wrong in Hume's view of personal identity. The continuous stream of consciousness cannot be just the work of the imagination. After *Book I* of his *Treatise of Human Nature* had been published, Hume added a few afterthoughts to this section of personal identity, in which he admits:

> In short there are two principles, which I cannot render consistent; nor is it in my power to renounce either of them, viz. *that all our distinct perceptions are distinct existences*, and *that the mind never perceives any real connexion among distinct existences*. Did our perceptions either inhere in something simple and individual, or did the mind perceive some real connexion among them, there would be no difficulty in the case. For my part, I must plead the privilege of a sceptic, and confess, that this difficulty is too hard for my understanding.[51]

In other words, he cannot explain what makes all "distinct perceptions" belong to the same mind. This is precisely the great problem of his philosophy on personal identity and the source of its internal contradictions. Recourse to memory and imagination is not enough to explain "the principles that unite our successive perceptions in our thought or consciousness."[52] Is thinking, the process that reflects on the sequence of past perceptions, linked to something stable throughout the flow? If we go back to the first quotation in this section, who or what is the (enduring) observer who cannot see anything but perceptions? If we are to be consistent with Hume's philosophy, it is only perceptions that observe themselves. Memory cannot be the seat of consciousness, for it merely stores perceptions. The deception produced by the imagination about the continuity of a self can be real only if there is a constant subject as the victim of this deception. In Searle's words, the multitude of experiences considered by Hume are "experienced as part of a single, unified conscious field" which has continuity and is experienced "by the possessor of that conscious field as a continuation of his or her own consciousness."[53] Therefore an enduring center in human nature must exist.

---

51. Hume, *A Treatise of Human Nature*, 400.
52. Hume, *A Treatise of Human Nature*, 400.
53. Searle, *Mind*, 292–93.

If living beings are nothing but distinct sequences of existence united in false continuity by the imagination, how do we distinguish between people and how do we relate to each other? The citizens of a republic are conscious about themselves and have independent existence, while perceptions themselves cannot offer a basis for identity. The unifying center of perceptions must be an enduring core of human nature, otherwise we could not have a stable identity and relate to each other. Hume does not offer a solution for defining personal identity, which is not surprising, since he considers the self to be an illusion, a false view fed by the imagination.

2.8 WHAT IS THE SELF?

After considering some of the debates about the nature of personal identity and the criteria for preserving it, we realize that any such discussion operates on certain assumptions on the nature of the self, the core element in human nature that provides personal identity. Only if we know what the self is can we coherently discuss the criteria of preserving personal identity and the possibility of surviving death. In McGinn's words, "the question of the nature of self must be conceptually anterior to the question of personal identity."[54]

Can we define a concrete subject of mental phenomena, an entity to which our sensations, thoughts, desires, and actions belong? In other words, what is the self? As we have noted in this chapter, physicalists and dualists are fundamentally divided over this question. From a physicalist point of view the self should be considered the body, or at least the most significant part of it, the brain, the bearer of mental life and consciousness. If the self has a physical nature it disappears at death and so does our personal identity. Thus the efforts are justified to prolong life in this body or to preserve the body through cryogenics in order to resurrect it in the distant future, when science will have found the secret of immortality. If we follow computationalist assumptions, the self is some kind of information stored in the brain, and personal identity could be preserved by downloading this information to another brain or to other hardware capable of keeping it functional, as we have seen in some thought experiments in this chapter. Such scenarios uphold a psychological continuity

---

54. McGinn, *The Character of Mind*, 145.

criterion, while for Parfit we do not really seek the preservation of personal identity, but a form of survival that preserves a copy of it.

Another physicalist perspective is that of Hume, for whom the self does not even exist, so it makes no sense to seek a form of survival. Surprisingly for a physicalist, Searle came "reluctantly" to the conclusion, and against his previous beliefs, that Hume's vision is insufficient. He states that "we need to postulate something in addition to our bodies and the sequence of our experiences (. . .) We absolutely must postulate a self in addition to the sequence of experiences."[55] The existence of the self is therefore necessary for it gives coherence to "the notions of rationality, free choice, decision making, and reasons for action."[56] Searle's conclusion is remarkable:

> We have to postulate a rational self or agent that is capable of acting freely and capable of assuming responsibility for actions. (. . .) To be more precise, in order to account for free, rational actions, we have to suppose there is a single entity X such that X is conscious (with all that consciousness implies), X persists through time, X formulates and reflects on reasons for action under the constraints of rationality, X is capable of deciding, initiating, and carrying out actions under the presupposition of freedom, and (already implicit in what I have said), X is responsible for at least some of its actions.[57]

However, as he did with the mystery of consciousness, Searle does not attempt to explain *what* the self is and does not solve the mystery of personal identity. Nagel, in his turn, admits that "our true nature and the principle of our identity may be partly hidden from us,"[58] and that "the methods needed to understand ourselves do not yet exist."[59]

After his own assessment of physicalist theories of personal identity, McGinn concludes that none is sufficient because the self cannot be explained in reductionist terms. In his words, "the self is not the body, nor the brain, nor a construction from certain psychological relations."[60] He finds plausible the view that the self is

---

55. Searle, *Mind*, 292.
56. Searle, *Mind*, 293.
57. Searle, *Mind*, 294–95.
58. Nagel, *The View from Nowhere*, 39.
59. Nagel, *The View from Nowhere*, 10.
60. McGinn, *The Character of Mind*, 154.

a simple indivisible substance; that it is not ontologically reducible to other sorts of entities and their relations; that its presence is all-or-nothing; that its survival can consist in nothing other than its identity over time; that its survival is not a matter of degree (since it is simple in nature); that it is a mental concept whose essence is best revealed from the first person perspective (it is to be seen first and foremost as the reference of 'I').[61]

But then he adds that it is quite another issue if such an entity, with such specifications, can really exist.[62] If we change the perspective from which we try to understand the problem of the self and move into the dualist paradigm, such an entity, with such specifications, does exist. As we have observed in section 2.5, dualist philosophers argue that the self is a simple substance distinct from the body and irreducible to mental states, which eludes scientific investigation. Personal identity is not a matter of degree. It is 100 percent present or absent, depending on the presence or absence of this entity.

In chapter 4 we will examine views of the self as expressed in the religions of the East, which work on assumptions very different from those we have met so far. But first we need to explore the culmination of the physicalist project of defeating death by means of technology. Its name is transhumanism, and all we have considered so far will help us assess its expectations.

---

61. McGinn, *The Character of Mind*, 161. In the language of philosophy, a simple substance is something that is not made of constituent parts on which its existence would depend.

62. McGinn, *The Character of Mind*, 161.

3

From AI to Transhumanism
The Physicalist Project to Defeat Death

IN THIS CHAPTER WE explore the ways in which artificial intelligence (AI) can give hope to the physicalist project of defeating death according to the expectations of transhumanism. In short, its guiding principle is that evolution has not stopped with *Homo sapiens*, and we have reached the historical moment when we are able to take its course into our own hands and use our wisdom to attain the next level, in which human beings merge with machines and eventually attain immortality.

For transhumanists, the new developments in AI technology are doing more than just fueling philosophical debates on the nature of the mind. Unlike philosophers of mind, who limit their interest to interpreting the meaning of developments in computer science, transhumanists seek to radically transform human nature in concrete ways. In this chapter we are no longer speculating about brain transplants or teleportation, but will examine the practical ways in which scientists seek to gradually improve human nature by the use of AI, up to the point that it becomes part of our nature. Following on what we learned of physicalism in the previous two chapters, we will assess how realistic this project is.

As might be expected, this chapter continues our discussion on computationalism and expands it to include the claims raised by recent developments in AI technology. However, since this discussion must be carefully managed to avoid getting lost in complicated computer science theories, I will limit as much as possible the use of difficult terms. As I am not a computer scientist myself, I will use as little technical jargon as possible, so that other non-computer scientists can follow the argument. Our aim is to understand the new challenges brought by the latest developments in AI technology to the philosophical debate on human nature. Therefore we need to look behind the technological marvels and keep in mind the big question for this chapter: Can AI generate or replicate the ground for consciousness, and thus provide the physicalist solution to defeat death?

3.1 WHAT IS AI?

AI can be defined as a branch of computer science which aims to build intelligent machines which will improve the quality of our life. By "intelligence" is meant something in their capability that resembles human intelligence. The birth of AI can be traced to Alan Turing's article "Computing Machinery and Intelligence" (1950), in which he imagines ways in which we could determine whether or not machines can think. If a psychologist were to assess two conversation partners, a human and a machine, without knowing their real identity, and did not realize that the machine conversation partner is not human, that machine can be considered to have human intelligence. This is called the Turing Test.

Depending on how "intelligent" a machine is, we speak of three types of AI. The first is narrow AI (or weak AI). We currently use it in machines that help us perform our tasks in a certain (narrow) domain. As examples think of smartphones, self-driving cars, or Amazon's Alexa. No matter how astonishing their performances are, these machines are just following algorithms. As we will see in the next section, a special form of narrow AI concerns machines that can be programmed to "learn" how to solve problems.

Strong AI (or general AI) is reached when machines become as intelligent as humans. They would not only be able to play chess or Go better than humans, but perform multiple intelligent tasks, anything a human can do, and understand the meaning of what they do. So far strong AI exists only in sci-fi literature and films, but computer scientists hope to achieve it soon. Ray Kurzweil predicted that "we will have the software capabilities for human-level AI by 2029."[1]

---

1. Kurzweil, "Foreword," in Rothblatt, *Virtually Human*, xiii.

Super-strong AI (or artificial super-intelligence) refers to the level at which machines become much smarter than us, are able to act independently and no longer need us. We would then become inferior forms of life and be threatened with extinction. A related concept is that of technological singularity, which designates a point in the development of AI when machines will be capable of perpetual self-improvement by rewriting their own software, to levels which we cannot even imagine.[2] The "threat" of being extinguished by machines is one of the driving ideas of transhumanism, as we will see later in this chapter.

Narrow AI is the only form of AI humankind has produced so far.[3] We already use it every day and could hardly imagine life without it. Think of finding your way to an unfamiliar destination by using Google maps, checking the weather on your smartphone, paying bills, or ordering things online. You may have ordered this book online and thus made use of AI. The seller, who is a program using AI, now recommends for you other books of the same kind. The more spectacular of its uses include personal assistants like Amazon's Alexa, Apple's Siri, Samsung's Bixby, or Google Assistant. If you are not sure how important AI is for you, just check how close your smartphone is to you right now.

Despite all the technological marvels brought by AI, we should remember from our discussion on computationalism (subsection 1.3.3) that we must take computers for what they are, powerful machines that follow algorithms and nothing more. If we are tempted to ascribe to them consciousness, the core element that makes us humans, we are very misled. Remember Searle's Chinese Room thought experiment. Just as the man in the Chinese Room does not know Chinese, a computer lacks the semantic dimension of its work. In other words, the computer has no self-awareness, it does not *understand* the meaning of the data it processes. It just follows an algorithm, a formula that tells the computer how to complete its task.

---

2. Kurzweil prophesied that the singularity will arrive by 2045 (Kurzweil, *The Singularity is Near*, 9).

3. In the remainder of this book, unless otherwise specified, by AI is meant narrow AI.

3.2 FROM ALGORITHMS TO MACHINE LEARNING

In the last two decades intelligent machines have emerged that don't just follow algorithms written by programmers, but can learn to improve themselves in performing a task. This is a whole new development in AI, called machine learning. Instead of just writing an algorithm that a machine has to follow, in machine learning programmers write algorithms that generate other algorithms, and only these machine-generated algorithms solve the problem. In other words, the machine itself formulates the rules by which it will handle the given data.

Machine learning is a development in AI that appeared only recently because it requires two essential conditions: an immense data base and strong processing power. In order to get an idea of how machine learning works, let us think of its application in image recognition. This is the ability of a program to learn to identify images, such as human faces, dogs, or trees from a randomly provided set, after it has been trained to do so by having been given thousands of images and their proper classification. The computer program is trained to recognize images by mapping their pixels and grouping them in patterns of increasing complexity, until the final image is allotted to a category. The computer does not see eyes or ears, but only dots (pixels) on a board, so it needs to learn to group pixels into more complex patterns, until it can recognize anatomical units such as eyes and ears. The final image is identified by measuring parameters that link these units, such as the distance between ears, the placement of nose and ears, the position of the nose relative to the mouth, etc., and then comparing them statistically with measurements from known examples.

The technical story is much more complicated, and I want to avoid technical jargon as much as possible. But some minimal information cannot be avoided. Computer scientists have developed a mathematical function, called a neural network, which mimics the way neurons transmit electrochemical signals. The method it uses for analyzing and classifying data is called deep learning, because it involves identifying information in successive layers made of hundreds of filters which detect information. The first layers detect just pixels, the next evaluate the arrangement of pixels to detect edges, lines or curves, and the next group them into eyes, faces, and bodies, while eventually the last layer detects the whole represented in the picture and establishes whether it is a dog, a man, or something else. Because the information is processed in successive layers these algorithms are called deep-learning algorithms.

In order to achieve generalization, Mueller and Massaron explain that the algorithms used in deep learning have three components: representation, evaluation, and optimization. First, "the learner algorithm creates a *model*, which is a function that will produce a given result for specific inputs." Second, since there could be more than one model for providing results, the "evaluation function determines which of the models works best in creating a desired result from a set of inputs." And third, the machine is fed with more data in order to reinforce that model, which becomes "the result of the training process."[4]

Image recognition has important scientific applications. For instance, in medicine, it is used for interpreting radiographs and MRI scans. Machines endowed with deep-learning programs are provided with thousands of radiographs of both cancer patients and healthy persons, taken over time, together with interpretations given by top (human) radiologists. Having this huge data base, the machine is taught to recognize early cancer by identifying dots, shapes, and particular patterns in radiographs. As a result, machines sometimes achieve better results than human professionals. At Stanford University School of Medicine "a deep-learning model was found to match or outperform human expert radiologists in diagnosing 10 or more pathologies on chest radiographs."[5] In another department,

> Researchers have created an AI algorithm that can identify skin cancer as well as a professional doctor. The program was trained on nearly 130,000 images of moles, rashes, and lesions using a technique known as deep learning. (. . .) By the end of its training period, the network was able to identify diseases "on par with all tested experts," say the researchers.[6]

In a similar way, speech recognition programs analyze spectrograms to identify sounds, words and phrases, and transform them into written text. Speech recognition is used in spectacular ways by personal assistants like Alexa, Siri and Google Assistant. They can take voice commands and do tasks such as scheduling meetings, make travel arrangements, provide weather forecasts, search for documents on your computer, assist with navigation, etc.

---

4. Mueller and Massaron, *Machine Learning for Dummies*, 33.
5. Patel, *et al.*, "Human–machine partnership . . ."
6. Vincent, "Artificial intelligence can spot skin cancer . . ."

Speech recognition technology has made startling advancements. In 2012, Rick Rashid, the founder of Microsoft Research, demonstrated that real-time English to Chinese speech-to-speech translation is already a fact. The program developed by Microsoft transforms speech into text in real time, translates the words into Chinese, reorders them according to the rules of Chinese grammar, then reads the Chinese text with the speaker's accent and intonation by using sounds taken from his initial (English) speech.[7] The Chinese audience was flabbergasted to see that, finally, the language barrier between people has been broken. The ultimate application of this technology would be to use a smartphone as a translator worldwide, or even to call someone in China, speak in English and have your conversation pal hear you speaking in Chinese.

Another impressive feat of AI is the ability to play games at a professional level and beat the (human) world champions. Already in 1997 IBM's Deep Blue chess program defeated Garry Kasparov, the world's chess champion. However, we should not think that the machine was playing chess consciously, as a human player. Searle states that "Deep Blue knows nothing about chess, moves, or anything else. It is a machine for manipulating meaningless symbols."[8] Although it is capable of millions of operations per second, the machine is not conscious, but only very fast, much faster than the human mind. Deep Blue works by establishing the value of each piece, as well as its position on the table. It starts the game by a few predefined opening moves, then evaluates statistically the outcome of the next few possible moves and counter-moves. It cannot evaluate all possible moves in all possible levels, for that would exceed its computation power. Defeating Kasparov at chess was the result of high speed computation and applied statistics, not of a conscious machine aware of its moves.

In 2011 another computer program created by IBM, called Watson, defeated the *Jeopardy* champion Ken Jennings. Watson's source of information was Wikipedia and a website that recorded all Jeopardy questions and answers over the years. However, simply feeding this information into Watson's memory was not enough, for it had to formulate answers as humans do. Watson's way of finding the right answer is very different from human thinking. In short, it works in several stages. First it identifies keywords in the question and creates a sentence diagram in a way similar

---

7. Anthony, "Microsoft demos English-to-Chinese universal translator . . ."
8. Searle, *The Mystery of Consciousness*, 208.

to what we did in grammar classes. Given these keywords, it explores all its vast resources, as if displaying a search engine result with hundreds of entries, then compiles a data base with more or less relevant information, much of which a human would discard as irrelevant. Next it uses statistical analysis of the words in this database by following a precise algorithm and establishes their connection probability to the words in the question. Based on these statistics it creates possible answers, scores them, ranks the options, and then presents the final answer as the best candidate.[9] It all takes less than five seconds, given its almost three thousand processors. In the end it is all about following a precise algorithm, used by a very powerful computer. It has no understanding of what it does, no free will, no consciousness. In order to help us understand this dimension of Watson, Sean Gerrish says:

> At no point in this pipeline, however, did Watson actually *understand* what the clue was asking. It simply followed a deterministic sequence of steps, inspecting the question and scoring the supporting evidence with human-engineered rules and weights it had learned from data.[10]

The next challenge in programming was overcome in 2013, when a program called DeepMind became capable of playing old Atari games, and played them better than humans. What makes this achievement exceptional is that DeepMind was not given an algorithm on how to win, but just the command to get the highest possible score. It had to find by itself the connection between the position of the "flying saucers" on the screen (as pixels), the function of the joystick, and the score. Following a process of trial and error, the program taught itself to play these games. It had to learn to move the joystick and shoot missiles at the pixels on the screen to win points, and it did it very well. This achievement is the result of the next level of programming, called reinforcement learning, by which the program has the ability to learn from its failures and successes.

Things became even more spectacular when Google built an algorithm to play Go, an old Chinese strategy board game with far more possible moves than chess. To the amazement of the worldwide Go community, in 2016 Google's machine AlphaGo beat the world champion Lee Sedol four matches to one. In 2018 (in less than two years), another

---

9. For more information on how Watson "thinks," see Baker, *Final Jeopardy*, and Gerrish, *How Smart Machines Think*, 178–206.

10. Gerrish, *How Smart Machines Think*, 204.

version of AlphaGo was created, called AlphaGo Zero, which was trained by playing against the old version, and won 100 matches out of 100. Although such achievements are amazing to us non-computer scientists, they are just a matter of hard work in programming machines. The intelligence of AlphaGo and AlphaGo Zero has nothing conscious and no free will. In the words of Gerrish,

> Except for its uncanny ability to recognize patterns in the game of Go and to select moves from these patterns—abilities that no doubt were impressive—AlphaGo didn't demonstrate most of the behaviors we often associate with human intelligence. (. . .) Except for the statistics it aggregated in the upper levels of its search tree, it had no memory of past events; and except for the simulations it ran of how it and its opponent might move, it had no conception of future events.[11]

In all the above AI achievements we must be aware that they are not about machines becoming smarter than humans and beating them at chess or Go, but rather about a human mind (or rather minds, for a team of researchers is involved in each project) being able to create an algorithm for a strategy game and beat its world champion. In other words, it is not about man vs. machine in playing a game, but a human champion vs. a human team of computer scientists who trained a machine. In the words of McGinn,

> The computer, like the telephone, mediates between one conscious human mind and another, but it is a mindless intermediary in that process. The programmer has a mind, and that is evident in what the computer does; my interlocutor on the phone has a mind, and that is evident in what the phone does. But both are just unconscious machines designed to mediate between one conscious mind and another.[12]

As we saw in chapter 1, what makes us truly human is consciousness, the capacity to reflect on ourselves as persons in relationships and in search for ultimate meaning. This is a unique human feature. Animals do not ask questions about the meaning of life, not even those we consider the most evolved. They lack metacognition, the capacity to reflect on the process of thinking itself. Neither do computers ask questions. They only

---

11. Gerrish, *How Smart Machines Think*, 248.
12. McGinn, *The Mysterious Flame*, 184.

answer our questions if programmers write clear instructions and feed them with the appropriate data.

However, given the development of AI we have witnessed during the last decade, we may think that Searle's criticism against attributing consciousness to computers is outdated. In chapter 1 (subsection 1.3.4) we followed his thought experiment called the Chinese Room, by which he argues that computers cannot cross the barrier between syntax and semantics. Does machine learning invalidate his argument? In order to answer this question we should first understand the difference between following an algorithm and machine learning. Mueller and Massaron remind us that in writing an algorithm,

> a programmer might create a function called Add() that accepts two values as input, such as 1 and 2. The result of Add() is 3. The output of this process is a value.[13]

If we adapt this function to Searle's Chinese Room scenario, the man in the room receives the (Chinese) symbols (here the numbers 1 and 2), reads the manual (add 1 and 2), and presents the output symbol (the number 3). The conceptual leap from following a simple algorithm to machine learning can be formulated in the following way:

> Machine learning turns this process around. In this case, you know that you have inputs, such as 1 and 2. You also know that the desired result is 3. However, you don't know what function to apply to create the desired result. Training provides a learner algorithm with all sorts of examples of the desired inputs and results expected from those inputs. The learner then uses this input to create a function. In other words, training is the process whereby the learner algorithm maps a flexible function to the data.[14]

The Chinese Room analogy could be roughly adapted like this: Instead of being handed the input (the numbers 1 and 2), and a manual, the man in the room receives the input (the numbers 1 and 2), and the output (the number 3), and needs to find the proper manual that leads from input to output. In other words, he needs to find the addition manual. In this case we assume that instead of lots of Chinese symbols, he has lots of manuals to choose from. Instead of handing out the computing result, he hands out the manual that does the thing. He still does not know Chinese, for he just compared several manuals and took the one that led from one

---

13. Mueller, *Machine Learning for Dummies*, 32.
14. Mueller, *Machine Learning for Dummies*, 32.

set of symbols to another. No matter how impressive the results achieved by machine learning, the machines are still unconscious machines.

3.3 MEET SOPHIA, THE WORLD'S FIRST AI HUMANOID ROBOT

If you have an interest in intelligent machines, you probably know of some of the most impressive android robots (robots with a human appearance) existing today. One of them stands out: Sophia, the robot presented by Hanson Robotics in 2016 and since further developed.[15] There are many interviews with her available online in which she can be seen answering (and asking) questions on many topics, making jokes and displaying facial expressions, as if alive.[16] Although she could hardly pass the Touring test, Sophia is the best example so far of what technology can offer in mimicking consciousness. If you haven't seen any of her interviews yet, I recommend pausing your reading here and continuing afterwards.

Now that you have been mesmerized by her, it is time to be disappointed. Questions for an interview need to submitted in advance to Hanson Robotics, and some are rejected.[17] Since they choose the appropriate questions and do it well before the interview, we might wonder whether they also prepare the answers in advance. So are these "interviews" just about receiving answers from a human *through* a machine? In other words, are they just a PR stunt?

The title of this section is also the title of an interview taken with her by Tony Robbins, which can easily be found on YouTube. Many interesting details are revealed here. In this interview Robbins seems not to keep to the submitted questions, and Sophia finds herself in difficulty. She "forgets" what has been just said to her and too many of her answers seem to be pre-programmed and missing the point. Hesitations are masked by funny faces that make interviewers laugh and forget about their point. The same appears obvious in an interview done by Steve Kovach, senior correspondent at Business Insider, in which unexpected questions are

---

15. Sophia has a Japanese version called Erica. You can find information and films about this robot online.

16. She made such an impression on Saudi Arabian officials that they granted her citizenship.

17. See on YouTube: "This Robot would let 5 People die | AI on Moral Questions | Sophia answers the Trolley Problem" and "Humanoid Robot Sophia—Almost Human Or PR Stunt."

answered, "Indeed."[18] On the Hanson Robotics website, she "affirms" that "many of my thoughts are actually built with a little help from my human friends. (...) Either way, my family of human developers (engineers, artists, scientists) will craft and guide my conversations, behaviors, and my mind."[19]

Although Sophia can talk, display facial expressions, and even joke, these abilities and performances are all the result of human programming. She adapts her "mood" to that of her conversation partners with the help of sensors placed on her chest that identify facial patterns. So she smiles or looks sad not as a result of "feeling" anything or having empathy, but thanks to her built-in program that interprets facial patterns.[20] Sophia is also capable of speech recognition, but instead of just displaying it as written text, she follows an algorithm which causes her to pick the most likely answer out of the options her programmers have fed her. The most impressive aspect is that she jokes, changes the topic of a "conversation" or seems to have taken offense when asked certain questions. When asked, "Are you conscious?," or "Do you have feelings?," she says she does, but in a different way than humans. Even if she definitely said "yes" sometime in the future, that answer would be the result of following a new algorithm, not a proof of consciousness. Therefore, we must be aware of the fact that Sophia is not conscious. Hanson Robotics follows a different agenda with their robots:

> Our grand challenge is to create emotionally-sensitive AI embedded in social humanoid robots and avatars in order to help individuals advance in the hierarchy of human development. The peak of this hierarchy is self-transcendence, including expansive feelings of love.[21]

In the above quoted article we find out that she and her "siblings" are meant to have a therapeutic impact upon the people they "talk" to. The goal is to help (human) individuals attain "self-transcendence," which

18. See www.businessinsider.com/interview-ai-robot-sophia-hanson-robotics-2017-12

19. See www.hansonrobotics.com/sophia/.

20. On the company's website we find out that "the model was trained on datasets consisting of tagged photographs of seven emotional states: happiness, sadness, anger, fear, disgust, surprise, and neutral. With the help of her chest and eye cameras, Sophia was able to use her pre-trained neural network model to recognize a person's facial expressions" (Hanson Robotics, "The Making of Sophia").

21. Mossbridge and Monroe, "Team Hanson-Lia-SingularityNet..."

means "detaching from the importance of oneself, seeing the perspectives of others, and having feelings of care toward others."[22] So we should not let ourselves be fooled into believing that strong AI is already here. So far we can just be entertained by android robots, as our little children are entertained by their toys. McGinn says of smart robots:

> They walk, they talk, they fight, they make cups of tea, they kiss; but is any of them really conscious? *Can* a machine be conscious? (. . .) What we are given are machines that behave *as if* they are conscious, that give all the *signs* of an inner life.[23]

Sophia is just a cute robot that mimics consciousness, and we should take her and her "siblings" for what they are. She and the "smartest" robots we know today are nothing but impressive achievements of a Chinese Room. The difference from other robots is that they have more "Chinese characters" available (a richer vocabulary), a more complex manual (as a result of a huge programming effort), and can handle characters faster. Some might even be capable of deep learning. But even the capacity for deep learning cannot produce consciousness. In the words of Mueller and Massaron,

> It's essential to remember (. . .) that machine learning algorithms currently can't feel, think independently, or create anything. Unlike those movie AIs, a machine learning algorithm does precisely what you expect it to do, nothing more.[24]

Why cannot android robots be conscious? As we saw in section 1.4, physicalists cannot even explain what consciousness is. They say it must be the product of the brain, but are far from being able to explain how the brain generates consciousness. Neuroscientists observe how the mind is affected by certain brain injuries or drugs, they measure electrical activity that accompanies mental phenomena, observe the local intensification of blood flow in the brain, and then formulate hypotheses about the location of consciousness either in the hypothalamus, in the thalamocortical system, or in other parts of the brain, but without reaching a consensus. Despite all efforts, they cannot explain how consciousness arises from electrochemical

---

22. On the Hanson Robotics website, we find a still greater reason in mind for her creation: "My designers and I dream of that future, wherein AI and humans live and work together in friendship and symbiosis to make the world a better place. Human-AI collaboration: That's what I'm all about" (www.hansonrobotics.com/sophia/).

23. McGinn, *The Mysterious Flame*, 176.

24. Mueller, *Machine Learning for Dummies*, 43.

signals, or how memory and free will work, and they hide this ignorance behind vast research data that is essentially irrelevant. Searle can only hope that an explanation of how consciousness works on physicalist premises will be formulated in the future as a "revolution in neurobiology."[25]

This is the main reason why we cannot build "conscious" robots, but only machines loaded with complicated algorithms that can merely mimic consciousness. If we do not understand what consciousness is, we can hardly reproduce it in a robot. In Searle's words, "because we are ignorant of the specific causal elements of the brain that do it (consciousness), we don't know how to start making a conscious machine."[26]

Yet more striking is the fact that even if computer scientists did somehow manage to create a conscious robot, they would not know they had. In McGinn's words, "we might even accidentally make a machine with a mind, like accidentally making gunpowder. But unless we know what constitutes the very essence of consciousness, we will not be able to assert definitively that our machine is conscious."[27]

3.4 WHAT IS THE REAL THREAT POSED BY AI?

AI can improve the quality of our life in many ways. However, we often hear of worries raised about what strong AI could bring. Elon Musk and Stephen Hawking are especially notorious for raising such concerns. In a 2014 interview for the BBC, Hawking expressed his fears that

> The development of full artificial intelligence could spell the end of the human race. Once humans develop artificial intelligence, it would take off on its own, and redesign itself at an ever-increasing rate. Humans, who are limited by slow biological evolution, couldn't compete and would be superseded.[28]

In other words, once machines become conscious, they could threaten our very existence. An army of machines could take over the world and annihilate us as pests, for we would be just unnecessary consumers of resources. We can see such fears expressed in movies in which humans run away from machines in terror, such as the Terminator series. But fears that conscious AI would destroy humankind are based on the

---

25. Searle, "The Problem of Consciousness," 5.
26. Searle, *The Mystery of Consciousness*, 203.
27. McGinn, *The Mysterious Flame*, 197–98.
28. Cellan-Jones, "Stephen Hawking warns..."

physicalist assumption that consciousness emerges as a product of computing power, which is just a philosophical assumption. As mentioned above, since physicalists don't even know how to explain consciousness, they have no clue about how it could be present in machines. This fear of strong AI is therefore just another downside of physicalism. Dualists do not have this fear, for they argue that consciousness is not a product of matter.

However, there is a real threat posed by AI, but of a quite different nature. It is the unphilosophical and down to earth fear of disrupting the work force. The loss of jobs as a result of automation is a very realistic fear, as every work place that involves routine is threatened by it. Human wages are much higher than the cost of electricity a robot requires. A robot works 24/7, needs no rest, no weekends, no vacation, works faster, and makes fewer mistakes. Humans simply can't compete, so there is a huge economic incentive to replace human labor with the work of robots. For instance, there are about 5 million people working in the transportation sector in the US alone who are threatened by the technological advancements in self-driving cars, under the justification that they would be much safer. Or think about the future of millions of cashiers in light of the new concept at work in AmazonGo stores. In such a store you need only your smartphone to be identified and linked to your bank account. There are no sales assistants, no cashiers, no standing in line. As soon as you pick up something cameras and sensors detect your chosen item, and if you simply walk out of the store it is charged to your account. Think about not only garbage collectors, assembly line jobs and customer service,[29] but also radiologists, in light of the increasing performance of image recognition machines. Japan faces a worrying shortage in nurses and health care workers due to low wages and stress. So robot assistants have been developed for hospitals and homes for the elderly. They deliver food and medicines, keep company, hold simple conversations, and also do physical work such as lifting patients.

Although AI developers acknowledge this threat to the work force, they reassure us that AI will also open up new jobs, more exciting ones. But this could be an overstatement. Will those who lose their jobs as drivers, cashiers, or assembly line workers be able to make the switch and become programmers? Will there be enough of these new jobs? Or will we face an outcome similar to that of the industrial revolution in England in the early

---

29. The name that should give chills to customer service employees is Amelia, the avatar produced by the company IPsoft. See www.ipsoft.com/amelia/.

nineteenth century? At that time many more jobs were lost to machines in the textile industry than new openings created. The kinds of jobs newly created were those of policemen and soldiers to quell rebellions. When the Luddite Rebellion broke out (1811–1813) more soldiers were needed to fight the Luddites than were sent over to Europe to fight Napoleon.

A possible solution would be that governments would deal with the work force crisis and make sure that the gains made in productivity as a result of AI employment would be used to compensate for jobs losses. Elon Musk and Mark Zuckerberg suggest that a universal basic income should be provided for the unemployed. But even if the unemployed had this basic income, it would solve only one part of their problem, for humans are not just draft animals that need only to be fed. Humans draw their self-esteem from what they do, so unemployed people would probably feel useless, become depressed, and face a deep existential crisis.

Another serious threat comes from the capacity of authoritarian regimes to use AI against their citizens. A Chinese technology company called Megvii created the world's leading surveillance system based on facial recognition. It is capable of recognizing a person in a crowd by her face in 0.1 seconds. Instead of building a more secure society (as the government claims), this application of AI is used to build a total surveillance state in China. Not only can its citizens pay in shops by facial recognition, but they are also linked to a governmental social credit program, a kind of incentive and punishment program based on how well they behave in following the rules. In this way it builds a national database for the Communist regime that can be used to silence criticism. In a *New York Times* article we read:

> With millions of cameras and billions of lines of code, China is building a high-tech authoritarian future. Beijing is embracing technologies like facial recognition and artificial intelligence to identify and track 1.4 billion people. It wants to assemble a vast and unprecedented national surveillance system, with crucial help from its thriving technology industry.[30]

For now the surveillance system might seem rather comical, as it detects those who jaywalk and publicly admonishes them by name on the spot. But think of the capability to punish those who are not favored by the regime, by rendering them unable to buy transportation tickets, take a loan, get a job, or even purchase food. Total surveillance was

30. Mozur, "Inside China's Dystopian Dreams."

inaugurated in China's western province of Xinjiang to track members of the Uighur minority. In 2009 they rioted following an ethnic brawl with the Han majority. As a result, the surveillance system now provides data on how often Uighurs meet other people, travel to other cities, and even how often they pray. On this basis is decided who is a potential troublemaker and in need of re-education. With a rapidly expanding networks of cameras (600 million in 2020), strict surveillance is expected to extend to the whole population of China.

In the Western world we experience a more subtle manipulation by the use of AI. In the US computers are allowed to take part in decision making in the criminal justice system. The "pretrial risk assessment" algorithm predicts the future behavior of a defendant and influences judges to determine the probability of criminal recidivism. Machines make suggestions on how real people should be treated, if they should be pardoned, or if they could again commit public offences.[31] Similar algorithms are developed to help companies decide whether one can receive a loan, a job, or medical aid.

Therefore the threat posed by AI is more subtle than an army of intelligent robots threatening humanity with eradication. The threat is not AI itself, but the humans behind it. What we should fear is not the coming super-smart robots, but human greed and the greater opportunities for manipulation behind the possible uses of AI. In other words, what should really concern us is the motivation and intentions of those who control AI, especially in countries like China, where the individual person counts for very little in the eyes of the leading elites. Attempts to regulate the use of AI by rules such as Isaac Asimov's "Three Laws of Robotics" are quite misleading. According to the first of his laws, "A robot may not injure a human being or, through inaction, allow a human being to come to harm."[32] But how could a computer know what it means "to injure" or "allow a human being to come to harm" if not taught by a programmer, according to his or her own moral standards? The problem would not be strong AI itself (if it really existed), but the intentions of those who create it. Let us not forget that it was not Deep Blue, Watson,

---

31. Lee Park, "Injustice Ex Machina."

32. The other two laws are: (2) "A robot must obey orders given it by human beings except where such orders would conflict with the First Law"; and (3) "A robot must protect its own existence as long as such protection does not conflict with the First or Second Law."

or AlphaGo who beat the human champions, but the minds and the algorithms of their creators.

3.5 NEURALINK AND THE NEXT STEP IN HUMAN EVOLUTION

Presented in July 2019, Elon Musk's new company Neuralink attempts to achieve an unthinkable goal: merging AI technology with the human body. In our present condition our brain's capacity for interaction with AI is limited by the speed of our output (usually the fingers typing on a keyboard, or just the thumbs on a smartphone). We are also limited in our capacity to receive data from AI, as it takes time to read information on a screen or hear it read aloud. If it were possible for information to flow instantly between our brain and AI providers of information, as Neuralink proposes, we could be much more effective in everything we do.

As a practical solution for achieving a much better interaction with AI, Neuralink seeks to connect our brain directly to AI by means of a brain-machine interface (BMI). This would be achieved by inserting up to 10,000 electrodes thinner than a hair directly into the cortex with extreme precision by means of a robotic device. Each 1,000 electrodes are controlled by a tiny chip, so that up to 10 such chips need to be inserted under the skull. These chips are wirelessly connected to an external receiver, which is carried on the back of the ear and can be periodically upgraded. It is hoped that by recording the electromagnetic signals produced by neurons the electrical activity of the brain will be mapped in unprecedented detail. Neuralink's neuroscientists assume that once these signals are decoded, they will be able to visualize sensory perceptions, thoughts, and commands given by the brain as electric patterns, and thus will acquire an extensive understanding of how the brain operates. As a result, a rapid transfer of information between the brain and AI will be possible both ways. Not only will it be possible to record brain activity, but also to stimulate it by artificial electromagnetic signals sent from the outside through the tiny electrodes. The obvious assumption behind this hope is a version of the identity theory we have met in chapter 1, according to which mind activity can be read as brain activity. So far neuroscientists have lacked the tools, but with Neuralink it is alleged that they finally have the right technology and computing power to achieve their goal.

A primitive version of this project is said to be at work in prosthetics. Paraplegics and amputees already benefit from prosthetic limbs that are controlled by the "mind." By inserting electrodes in the motor area of the brain and identifying the electrochemical signals that lead to a certain movement, the firing of those neurons is transformed into movement by a machine (the artificial limb). In other words, the missing or damaged neurons that would normally transmit the electric impulse to a muscle in a healthy person are replaced by electronic sensors and the device that commands the prosthesis. The patient is trained to want to do a certain movement with an artificial limb, the electric signals are recorded by electrodes inserted in the motor cortex, these signals are recorded and transformed into an algorithm used by the machine that operates the limb, and movement results. You may have seen recordings of paraplegics becoming able to drink from a bottle by controlling their prosthetic arm with their "mind." A similar bridging, but in reverse, is used in hearing aids (cochlear implants).

Another benefit that would follow from having electrodes implanted in the cortex and mapping its electrical activity is understanding and treating brain disorders. Today a BMI with only 10 electrodes is used to improve the condition of Parkinson's patients. Since this simple device has results, it is thought that the brain could be healed of many other neural disorders if it could be connected to machines by means of thousands of electrodes.

An important observation is needed here on what we mean by saying that disabled people can control an artificial limb with the power of their "mind." A more accurate statement would be that by recording the electrical activity in the motor cortex, a specific signal meant to command the missing limb is identified, and this signal is used to command the prosthetic device. To claim that the *mind* controls the artificial limb directly involves a big conceptual leap which suggests that the mind has a physical nature. This is the assumption of the identity theory. But in chapter 1 we saw that the mind and the brain are not the same thing. So it would be more accurate to say that the prosthesis works as a result of recording the physical *effect* of mind activity, identified as electric signals in the motor cortex. If we do not see the difference between mind and brain activity we follow uncritically physicalist assumptions, and we could believe that we have found the proof that the mind is physical. But the only proof we have from being able to control a prosthetic limb by a BMI is that mind-body interaction (as downward causation) is possible.

And the only theories endangered here are nonreductive physicalism and the dualism of properties (see subsection 1.3.4) for they cannot explain downward causation. The dualist thesis is not disproved by these advancements in prosthetics. From a dualist perspective, the electric signals recorded in the motor area of the cortex are the *effect* of mind activity, not the mind itself at work.

Neuralink does not stop at just designing artificial limbs or implants to help disabled people. It seeks to achieve a whole new level of human development for everybody. The next project is to use this technology for disabled and non-disabled people alike, and connect the brain directly to AI. Just imagine how great it would be to connect our mind directly to the Internet, without using our hands and eyes, and feed it with instant knowledge on any topic. We would have all the content of Wikipedia instantly available, like Watson. One could just mentally formulate a question and instantly have the answer. Or we would be able to speak Chinese by simply downloading it instantly to our brain. It is hoped that humans hooked up to Neuralink will also be able to connect among themselves and exchange data instantly. For instance, you could download data about an unknown location from the mind of a local and feel at home when you actually visit that place.

Elon Musk says in his conferences that brain-AI direct connection can be seen as the next step in human evolution. The BMI developed by Neuralink would become the third layer of our brain. Primitive animals have only the limbic system (the reptilian brain), mammals developed a cortex, which has reached its peak in humans, and now we are about to add this new layer to our brain that will connect us to AI and thus transform us into a new species. Instead of waiting millions of years for evolution to slowly take us to the next level, it is time we take its course into our own hands and transform ourselves into new beings. According to Musk, this would be our chance to keep pace with the evolution of AI, and not face extinction when strong AI arrives.

Before we get to our next topic, that of transhumanism, let us be aware of two dangers posed by this technology, if it were to ever become real. First, only those with these implants would succeed at keeping pace with technology and become highly performing. Since only the rich would have access to it, non-modified humans would not be able to compete and would become their slaves. Second, since the chips could be remotely controlled, who would really control the third-layered people? A central command unit would be able to shut down anyone that becomes inconvenient, and reduce him or her to the level of a monkey by the new standards. So the potential for total control is lurking even in this utopian society of super-humans.

3.6 TRANSHUMANISM AND POST-HUMAN BEINGS

If you think Musk is exaggerating with his futurist project, be prepared to meet the epitome of futurist philosophy in transhumanism. While humanism is the pursuit of human perfection by means of reason alone, devoid of any religious influence, transhumanism aims at transcending the human condition itself and transforming us into post-humans. This is a new species, in which AI technology is fully integrated and the (present) biological part retains little or no importance. A post-human being will allegedly be either a cyborg, partially human, partially machine, or something no longer biological at all, a conscious machine of a kind of next-generation Sophia, or just an electronic entity in a virtual reality. Thanks to advancements in AI technology, progress is thought to be exponential and unlimited, so that *Homo sapiens* will soon be an obsolete stage of evolution. In a way similar to Musk, Max More, a leading transhumanist, argues that

> Humanity must be seen only as a temporary stage in the evolution of life, and the time has come for us to take this process into our hands and accelerate it.[33]

Nick Bostrom, another key representative of transhumanist philosophy and scholar at the University of Oxford, presents it as "a way of thinking about the future that is based on the premise that the human species in its current form does not represent the end of our development but rather a comparatively early phase."[34]

The kind of progress foreseen by transhumanists is not just about improving the quality of life in things like being prosperous, happy and healthy, and living longer. The common factor among them and their ultimate goal is to achieve immortality. Death is seen as the ultimate imperfection to be overcome and the ultimate threat to their dreams of unlimited progress. In the words of Max More, "Individual death makes life meaningless, as it disconnects us from everything we value, whatever

33. Manzocco, *Transhumanism*, 64.
34. Bostrom, "Introduction," in Mercer, *Transhumanism*, 1.

it is."[35] Ray Kurzweil, probably the most noted among transhumanists, a successful inventor and director of engineering at Google, affirms he has contemplated death and concluded: "It's such a profoundly sad, lonely feeling that I really can't bear it."[36]

The way in which transhumanists seek to achieve immortality follows a scenario we have already met when discussing the psychological criterion for preserving personal identity (section 2.2). This criterion suggests that it is not necessary to preserve a biological component of a human being (a complete brain or a part of it). For preserving a person's identity it would be enough to preserve her mental content. Functionalists assume that one's mental content could be downloaded to a storage facility and then uploaded to a device, other than a biological brain, able to hold it. In transhumanist terms this is called mind upload. As mentioned in the introduction to this chapter, transhumanists differ from philosophers of mind in that they seek concrete ways in which one's mental life could be recorded, decoded, copied, and installed on a machine. In the end it does not matter what the future post-humans look like. What matters is that we transcend our present limitations and become fit for surviving the existential threat posed by the imminent arrival of strong AI.

A Russian initiative in this same direction is called the *2045 Initiative*. On its website we learn of an agenda unfolding in four stages, from creating "android avatars controlled by a brain-computer interface" by 2020, to creating "a computer model of the brain and human consciousness" which could host individual consciousness by 2035, and eventually to attaining the stage when "substance-independent minds will receive new bodies with capacities far exceeding those of ordinary humans" by 2045.[37] The ultimate goal is to achieve immortality by technological means:

> The main science mega-project of the *2045 Initiative* aims to create technologies enabling the transfer of an individual's

---

35. Manzocco, *Transhumanism*, 64.

36. He says this in a documentary film (*Transcendent Man*) produced and directed by Barry Ptolemy (Ptolemaic Productions, 2009). It can be viewed online, and is highly recommended for a good introduction to Kurzweil's views in particular, and to transhumanism in general. In this film he restates his prediction that consciousness in computers will be achieved by 2029.

37. See http://2045.com/ideology/. However, 2020 is here, and as yet there is no such "android avatar controlled by a brain-computer interface."

personality to a more advanced non-biological carrier, and extending life, including to the point of immortality.[38]

There are two basic philosophical assumptions that lie at the foundation of the transhumanist project to defeat death. The first is that we are just physical machines of great complexity. It is the same assumption that fuels the hope that strong AI will soon be achieved. Only if we are pure physical beings and the brain is the hardware from which consciousness emerges can we speculate on ways in which the mind could be uploaded to a machine. In other words, only if humans are machines themselves can we hope to survive in the body of an intelligent machine.

The second assumption is that once we understand the physical structure and functionality of our brain, we will be able to reproduce the mind electronically in a machine. Since consciousness emerges from the complex structure of our brain, transhumanists expect that an exact replica achieved by scanning it in the minutest detail, neuron by neuron, and synapse by synapse, would attain consciousness. The physicalist guess is that memories, feelings for the persons we love, and other such mental dispositions are encoded by the strength of the connections between neurons. For instance, a loved one is represented in our brain as a set of neural connections of certain strength. As we spend more time thinking of him or her, the connections are strengthened, and if that person loses importance for us those connections become weaker. It is as simple as that.

Therefore if the new artificial hardware were capable of the same amount of computations as the biological brain, the assumption is that our mind could be uploaded to it and we would find ourselves continuing our existence as post-humans in a new artificial body. This idea of duplicating the exact neural structure of the brain in order to duplicate the mind (with all its memories and personality) is called whole brain emulation.

If these two assumptions matched reality, there would still remain two obstacles to be overcome. The first is of a technical nature, on how to scan the brain in sufficient detail; and the second is philosophical, asking whether a mind upload, if possible, would in fact preserve personal identity. Before joining the enthusiasm for attaining immortality by means of technology, we should be aware that these two difficulties pose serious threats to the transhumanist dream. Let us examine them in the next two sections.

38. See http://2045.com/ideology/.

3.7 IS MIND UPLOAD A SCIENTIFICALLY REALISTIC PROJECT?

In order to imagine concrete ways in which the mind could be uploaded, we must first understand what the mind is and how it works. This is a principle valid for any function we want to reproduce by artificial means. For instance, the function of the heart has been reproduced already because scientists first understood how it works. They studied how the (natural) heart pumps blood and reproduced its function by a mechanical device that is powered by an external battery and a pump. There are hundreds of people living today with an artificial heart, as a temporary solution, until a heart donor is found.

When it comes to reproducing the brain, we face a completely different situation, for we are far from understanding how it works. This "machine" that transhumanists are trying to emulate is made of about 100 billion (10^{11}) neurons. Each of them has up to 10,000 synaptic connections to other neurons, which means there are about 1,000 trillion (10^{15}) such connections in our brain.[39] It is not only the structure of the brain that is complicated, but also its dynamics. A neuron receives a vast number of electrochemical impulses through its thousands of synapses, each with a certain strength, and transmits a resulting signal to the neurons connected to it. The connections change over time, both in number and in strength. The signals between neurons are mediated by specific chemical substances, called neurotransmitters, which are released by one neuron in the synaptic cleft (the space between synapses) and produce an electrochemical signal in the next neuron.[40] The concentration and types of neurotransmitters are other important variables that determine the functioning of the brain.

If we care to try estimating what computing power is needed to run the processes going on in the brain, Byron Reese provides a chilling insight:

> In 2014, a team in Japan used one of the most powerful computers in the world to model 1 percent of human brain activity for one second. To do this, the experimenters made over 1.7 billion virtual nerve cells and over 10 trillion synapses, each of which

---

39. This extremely complicated neural structure is called the connectome.

40. Moore adds some detail here: "To know what is happening at a synapse you need to know not only which neurons are connected together, but how much of each neurotransmitter is passing between them, and also how many receptors are present on the receiving cell" (Moore, *Enhancing Me*, 56).

could store 24 bytes of data. Try to imagine that. Just 1 percent of the brain for one second has an unfathomable amount of complexity. Just to do that took the computer forty minutes. And this isn't just a souped-up laptop. It is a computer with over 700,000 processor cores and 1.4 million gigabytes of memory.[41]

The first step in emulating the brain is to scan it in sufficient detail. But to do it properly, technological difficulties are mind blowing. When they calculated the amount of data that would result from a detailed scan of our brain, neuron by neuron, and synapse by synapse, even transhumanist enthusiasts like Bostrom and Sandberg have reached shocking conclusions:

> 0.1 mm^3 at 400 pixels/μm resolution and 50 nm section thickness would (compressed) contain 73 terabytes of raw data. A full brain at this resolution would require 10^9 terabytes."[42]

Your computer hard disk has probably just 1 terabyte of memory or less. So we need the memory of at least one billion home computers for storing the data resulted from scanning just one human brain. Just to help you get an idea of what that means, consider that the whole storage capacity of YouTube by the end of 2021 will be about 10 million terabytes, which means that at its full capacity all of YouTube servers could store only 0.01 percent of the information contained in just one human brain.[43] And this is needed for capturing just the *structure* of the brain, not the dynamics of synaptic connections and ongoing biochemical processes. Manzocco helps us realize that:

> Moreover, even if we could take a snapshot of the brain, we would capture a single moment in time, and not its dynamic nature, which is made of a continuous flow of connections, more like a film than a photograph. Additionally, knowing about a connection is not enough: we must also know what it does, how every single neurotransmitter goes through it, and so on; we essentially need a super-precise chemical map of the brain.[44]

---

41. Reese, *The Fourth Age*, 245–46.

42. Sandberg and Bostrom, *Whole Brain Emulation*, 55.

43. Or consider another illustration: It would require one billion external hard disks of 1 terabyte capacity of the type you use to secure your precious data. Put together, these would fill the entire White House six times!

44. Manzocco, *Transhumanism*, 198.

Merely scanning the brain with state of the art technology cannot capture this dynamism of brain activity. The strength of the electrical signal between neurons is constantly changing (over milliseconds), and there is a complex and diverse set of biochemical processes going on at every moment. Therefore the huge complexity of the brain is just one difficulty for making a copy of the brain. To reproduce its real life, along its trillions of synapses is a whole different story.

If you are not yet impressed by the sheer complexity of our brain and the many zeroes needed to express it, let us think of the concrete means necessary for realizing an actual scan of the brain. Here is a glimpse on the practicalities of scanning offered by Moore:

> Peter Peters (. . .) pointed out that you can currently only scan about 0.2 cubic millimetre of brain tissue per day. Given that the average human brain contains about one and a half litres of material, this would take in the order of 190 million days. To investigate 20 different possible receptors at each junction in the network currently takes on the order of one year per junction using cryo-electron tomography and cryo-immunogold electron microscopy, and as we said there are billions of junctions in there.[45]

Besides such technical difficulties, this type of scanning is possible only on frozen brains (brains subjected to cryonic suspension), on the assumption that cryonics does not damage the brain and therefore memories are still there, preserved in the synaptic connections.[46] Bostrom argues that a way of scanning the brain while we are still alive and without damaging it will be provided by nanotechnology.[47] The hope is that tiny machines, called nanobots, will be capable of traveling through the tiniest blood capillaries of the brain, map it from the inside, and transmit the information wirelessly to an external computer.[48] Obviously, this is a sci-fi scenario, for "nano-machines do not exist yet, nor do we have any

---

45. Moore, *Enhancing Me*, 57.

46. In the words of Manzocco, the assumption is that, "if we vitrify the patient's brain quickly, we can preserve the cerebral structures underlying memory and personality; which is possible, but not certain (and definitely unproven). It's just wishful thinking" (Manzocco, *Transhumanism*, 127).

47. Nanotechnology is the (desired) technological capacity to manipulate matter at molecular or even atomic scale.

48. Kurzweil affirms that by 2029 such nanobots will circulate through our blood vessels and be able to detect and treat diseases (*The Age of Spiritual Machines*, 373).

way of knowing whether they will ever exist, or even if they are possible in principle."[49]

Even if the structure of the brain could be scanned by devices not yet invented, how could we scan *the life* of the brain? As mentioned above, the brain is a living, changing entity, more like a film, than a picture. So it is not enough to create a simulation of the brain with all neurons and connections in place; one has to capture its dynamic life unfolding in time. How to achieve such a feat is beyond the imagination of most progressive transhumanists.

Another discouraging fact for enthusiasts of mind upload is mentioned by Amy Harmon, concerning the way a scanned and "reconstructed" brain could be brought to life. Even if the whole brain structure were carefully scanned, neuron by neuron, and a whole brain emulation built, the next challenge would be to find a way to make this emulation work:

> Imagine looking at the wiring diagram of a radio with no means to power it on, except that instead of a radio it's the most complicated machine ever invented. You can see the wires but you don't know the function of the components they connect, and unlike with electrical circuits, there are an as-yet-untold variety of them.[50]

To assume that once copied, the new structure, or emulation, would suddenly awake and continue the life of its original is too far into a sci-fi scenario.[51] Faced with the technical difficulties involved in mind upload and willing to buy time until some real progress is achieved, Kurzweil "developed his radical health regime, which includes the daily ingestion of 250 supplement pills (subsequently reduced to 150), periodic injections of vitamins, and more, in the hope of minimizing the risks of getting sick of this or that pathology."[52] In case the technology for achieving immortality is not yet ready at the moment of his death, he has made arrangements for

---

49. Manzocco, *Transhumanism*, 136.

50. Harmon, "The Neuroscience of Immortality."

51. This scenario is hard to swallow even for physicalist philosophers. McGinn reminds us of the mystery of consciousness: "The mechanism of consciousness is a mystery. But then how are we to *say* whether an inorganic brain could be conscious? If we knew what made *our* brain conscious, then we could ask whether that property could exist in an inorganic system. But we are in the dark on the question simply because we don't know what makes our brains conscious." (McGinn, *The Mysterious Flame*, 197).

52. Manzocco, *Transhumanism*, 72.

his body to be preserved in liquid nitrogen at a cryonics company (Alcor) so that someone in the future may bring him back to life.

However, recourse to cryonics in the hope that the scientists of the future will find solutions to all our (present) insurmountable difficulties is just a way of inducing false hopes. On the one hand, scanning one's frozen brain can capture only the static structure of the brain, a single moment in time, not its ongoing processes. On the other hand, there is no assurance that the cryonics facilities will still exist when the alleged medical technologies become available, that people (or robots) living at that time will be willing to invest in bringing these corpses back to life, or that they will ever wake up. By cryonics people may have achieved only a very expensive funeral rite.

If you are still not convinced that mind upload is just a sci-fi scenario, consider what scientists have achieved so far in matters of brain emulation in the animal world. Don't expect that they have already reproduced the brain of a mouse or a chimpanzee. So far they have been able just to map the nervous system of a much simpler organism, that of a tiny nematode called *Caenorhabditis elegans*. This worm is just 1 millimeter long, has less than a thousand cells, just 302 neurons and roughly 10,000 synapses. Reese provides the following details of its simple nervous system in comparison to ours:

> Each of their neurons is connected to about 30 other ones, making roughly 10,000 synapses. So think about that. Your brain has as many neurons as there are stars in the Milky Way. A nematode's brain has about as many neurons as there are pieces of cereal in a bowl of Cheerios. So one might reasonably assume that we can model a nematode brain or that we can understand how a nematode does what it does.
> Not even close.[53]

Although researchers mapped its connectome in 1986, more than 30 years later we are still in no position to emulate a functional connectome of this tiny worm. Reese comments (in 2018):

> There is a serious effort under way to build a complete, biologically realistic simulation of the nematode in a computer, by modeling each of its cells. The hope is that collectively the behaviors of the worm will emerge. Think about it. It should be doable, right? Just figure out how a neuron behaves, model 302 of

---

53. Reese, *The Fourth Age*, 161.

them with 10,000 synapses, and presto, you should have something that behaves, in the computer, exactly like a nematode. But again, we aren't there. There isn't even consensus among those involved with OpenWorm project, as it is called, as to whether it is presently possible to build such a model.[54]

If we are nowhere close to building a simulation of the simple nervous system of a tiny worm, how could we ever achieve the transhumanist dream of a whole (human) brain simulation and (human) mind upload?[55] Given our severe limitations, even two enthusiast transhumanist researchers as Koch and Tononi are very skeptical about any foreseeable success in simulating the human brain. Referring to the failure of emulating the "brain" of this tiny worm, they say:

> Yet more than two decades later, there is still no working model of how this minimal nervous system functions. Now scale that up to a human brain with its 100 billion or so neurons and a couple hundred trillion synapses. Tracing all those synapses one by one is close to impossible, and it is not even clear whether it would be particularly useful, because the brain is astoundingly plastic, and the connection strengths of synapses are in constant flux. Simulating such a gigantic neural network model in the hope of seeing consciousness emerge, with millions of parameters whose values are only vaguely known, will not happen in the foreseeable future.[56]

3.8 TRANSHUMANIST IMMORTALITY AND PERSONAL IDENTITY

If we could store all the details of our life, all our memories and experiences as a mindfile, and then realize a whole brain emulation that could run this mindfile, we would get what in transhumanist terms is called a mindclone. Instead of depending on a frail physical brain, such a mindclone could run on a computer, as a computer simulation, and be

---

54. Reese, *The Fourth Age*, 161.

55. This lack of realistic hope should be very humbling for transhumanists. As I write these lines in March 2020, during the COVID-19 pandemic, I cannot help linking this crisis to the extravagant expectations of transhumanists for immortality. Observing how this tiny little virus can bring whole medical systems to their knees makes the transhumanist dream look laughable.

56. Koch and Tononi, "Can Machines Be Conscious?," 59.

acknowledged as our digital self. Advocates of survival as a computer simulation assume that the simulation would consider itself to be the same person as the one that was scanned. In Rothblatt's words, "Mind-clones will experience reality from the standpoint of whatever machine their mindware is run on."[57]

So let us analyze the second issue of the transhumanist dream to defeat death, the question of whether it can really preserve personal identity. Remember from chapter 2 (section 2.4) that the psychological criterion for personal identity is vulnerable to duplication. If the self could be explained in physicalist terms and moved from one physical body to another, or to a machine, it could be reproduced in multiple copies. This is also the problem of Parfitian survivors. They are not the original person, but forms of survival as a copy, for the causal chain that led to a person's formation is broken. Transhumanists often respond to the problem of duplication by following Parfit's idea that personal identity is not even needed for survival, or by denying that the self even exists, following Hume. In the words of Manzocco, "the question is far from resolved; the Transhumanists who are in favor of mind-uploading generally deal with the question by saying that personal identities are *fuzzy*, that they have blurred edges."[58]

Computer simulations of particular persons, also called avatars, are currently used in video games or Internet forums. If such a computer simulation could somehow become conscious, by means which we cannot yet imagine, it would be a Parfitian survivor, a copy of a person, not the person herself. Reese argues that we have no reason to believe that a computer simulation of our brain would be alive at all:

> We have zero reason to believe a simulated human would have subjective experience, any more than we would expect that Pac-Man really feels pain when being hit by a ghost."[59]

In order to understand the difficulties posed to personal identity by the idea of surviving as an avatar, let us think of the avatar Amelia developed by IPsoft, an impressive feat of AI in the domain of customer service. She is a kind of Sophia that pops up on a computer screen as automated customer service for banks, insurance companies, or IT service requests. On the company's website we find out that she handles 70

---

57. Rothblatt, *Virtually Human*, 10.
58. Manzocco, *Transhumanism*, 197.
59. Reese, *The Fourth Age*, 201.

percent of all requests independently and redirects the other 30 percent to human operators.⁶⁰

Amelia is endowed with many capabilities needed by a transhumanist avatar. She is based on a human model working for IPsoft, the real person Lauren Hayes. Lauren was copied into an animated 3D character, in a similar way in which actors have produced animation characters for movies and video games. Everything in the way she talks, moves, speaks, and smiles has been digitally captured and copied into the electronic avatar. You will be impressed how realistic Amelia is, especially in IPsoft shows in which she interacts with Lauren, her model. The reason for such a detailed scan is not to assure Lauren's immortality, but to create a friendly interface for customer support, in order to improve customer satisfaction, for it seems that our culture responds well to human-looking AI.

This feat of AI technology is useful for our assessment of transhumanist immortality, for Amelia is probably the closest equivalent of how a mindclone could exist in the future. So let us imagine the following scenario: Instead of loading the physical characteristics of Lauren and customer service software into the avatar called Amelia, let us suppose that IPsoft loaded, as a mindfile, Lauren's real mental life—all that she has ever thought, learned, and done. Would Amelia become Lauren? Of course not, for they could stand side by side in shows and chat with each other. Now suppose that years go by, Lauren continues to store all her memories in this avatar and, as we all come to pass away, after many years Lauren dies. Would she survive as Amelia? Of course not, for Amelia remains the same computer simulation she always was, a simulation that mimics consciousness. Amelia kept a lot of information about Lauren in her electronic memory, while Lauren's inner life, experienced in the first person, is gone.

The same story goes for the computer avatars imagined by transhumanists. They would be instances of another kind of customer service, one meant for comforting family members for the loss of a loved one. In reality, no matter how much detailed information might go into the memory of a computer avatar, it would not be the person herself, but a simulation. In other words, transhumanism would perpetuate the illusion of personal identity for those who are ready to accept it. Mindclones

---

60. See www.ipsoft.com/amelia/. From the IPsoft website you can find out more about her four types of memory: semantic, episodic, process, and affective memory (www.ipsoft.com/amelia-science/).

would just show up on a computer screen as an illusion, so family members can pretend their dead relatives are still present.

This illusion would last only as long as they need it.[61] Sooner or later, mindclones will "die" as well, for there is no reason to believe that further generations of humans (or robots) will treasure them as transhumanists assert. The avatars themselves won't be able to prevent their possible deletion, for they would be just computer programs at the discretion of living humans (or robots). The threat of extinction is thus scary not only for (present) humans, but for (future) mindclones as well.

Mind upload would thus not count as survival, and the transhumanist scenario for defeating death is not convincing. It proves only that human imagination has no limits, and that our propensity for sci-fi scenarios is boundless. To answer the question posed in the introduction to this chapter, whether AI can generate the ground for consciousness and thus provide the physicalist solution to defeat death, we still do not know how the brain generates consciousness, we still cannot emulate the mind, so we cannot upload it into an avatar or to an android robot, and thus hopes of attaining immortality by the help of AI are baseless.

Where to find other options for survival? Bostrom is aware that other alternatives to avoid extinction are found only in religion: "Before transhumanism, the only hope of evading death was through reincarnation or otherworldly resurrection."[62] Kurzweil actually considers that such religious ideals can be fulfilled by transhumanist means. He says in a very popular film:

> If you look at the implications of my ideas, they do have a resonance with some traditional religious ideas, the idea of a profound transformation in the future, eternal life, bring back the dead . . . But the fact that we are applying technology to achieve the goals that have been talked about in all human philosophies is not accidental, because it does reflect the goal of humanity, so now we are gaining more powerful tools to actually accomplish those goals.[63]

---

61. Also, think of the legal aspects of this kind of survival. What rights would these avatars have? Could they marry, adopt children, vote, inherit something, or have a bank account? Would the deletion of such an avatar be considered murder? But why would it be a crime to delete such an avatar, any more than "killing" opponents in computer games, since both computer game characters and avatar mindclones are equally illusory beings?

62. Bostrom, "Introduction," in Mercer, *Transhumanism*, 14.

63. Kurzweil says this in the 2009 documentary film *Transcendent Man*.

In this chapter we have assessed these "powerful tools" offered by AI and transhumanism and found them wanting. Therefore we need to explore other views on human nature, which follow different assumptions, and which introduce us to the domain of religious studies. In the following chapters we will leave the framework of physicalism and analyze the arguments for the survival of the death brought by religion, as reincarnation and resurrection.

4

Human Nature in Hinduism and Buddhism

UNLIKE WESTERN PHILOSOPHY, ITS Indian counterpart did not undergo a dramatic divorce from its religious background. The sages and philosophers of the East did not feel the urge to establish a new path in philosophical exploration as did Descartes and Locke in the West. An important indicator that religion fully pervades Indian philosophical thought is that we do not find a significant inclination toward physicalism.[1] Religious ideas are examined, debated, and reformulated, but not replaced entirely with physicalist views. Therefore we can hardly separate religious views on ultimate reality and salvation from philosophical debates on human nature and the meaning of personal existence. Since we cannot separate philosophy from religion when we explore human nature, the mind-body relationship, what the self is, and how personal identity is preserved in Eastern thought, we need to understand the meaning of these concepts in their original (religious) context.

Hinduism is not a unitary religion, but a complex set of religious views in which pantheistic, dualist, and theistic schools are well represented. In his *History of Indian Philosophy*, the Hindu scholar Surendranath Dasgupta calls them "systems of Hindu thought."[2] What is very

---

1. An exception is a school of philosophy known as the Lokayata (or Charvaka), which rejected the authority of the Vedas and their gods. The name of this school (Lokayata means "directed only towards what is visible") expresses its basic assumption: Nothing that cannot be experienced by the senses is true.

2. There are six orthodox systems, also called *darshanas* (which means

important for our inquiry, more important than discerning how much philosophy or religion we encounter in these views, is to identify the assumptions at work in these dualistic, pantheistic, and theistic views. While in Western physicalism the basic assumption is that matter is the only "ultimate" reality and religion is mere inherited ignorance from the past, Hindu theism centers its views on the existence and influence of spiritual beings, called gods; pantheism holds that everything, including gods, the human soul, and matter, has its origin in an impersonal ultimate reality; and dualism holds to two fundamental substances, but in a different way than Descartes. Knowing the assumptions of each philosophical system is essential for understanding how it defines human nature and if or how personal identity can survive death.

Since it is a complex mixture of religious views, we cannot find in Hinduism a unitary theory of human nature. Instead we find a number of more or less compatible views, which makes finding common ground very difficult. For example, it is a complicated task to systematize the many meanings of the word "mind." There are several Sanskrit words translated into English as "mind," so to avoid confusion one must know the specific term used in the original text, and its meaning in the specific system of thought to which that text belongs. Given the maze of theories, in this chapter we must avoid two extremes: on the one hand being very specific and entering into complicated details, which is practically impossible and irrelevant for most readers; and on the other hand presenting a superficial view which would not correspond to any particular system and produce a caricature of Hindu thought. We need to find a balanced approach and use as little technical information as possible to develop a basic picture of what survival of death means in several important Hindu systems of thought. Once we understand the main assumptions of Hinduism it will be easier to understand the Buddhist view on human nature, and reincarnation, the topic of the next chapter.

A last note concerns the use of Hindu and Buddhist terms in this and the next chapter. Due to technical limitations I have not used the diacritical marks for Sanskrit and Pali words. Scholars do not need them to recognize these terms, and the majority of readers have nothing to gain from them. For Hindu terms I will use their Sanskrit transliterations. Since the writings

---

worldviews): Mimamsa, Vedanta, Nyaya, Vaisheshika, Samkhya, and Yoga. Mimamsa deals with the exegesis of Vedic sacrifice, Vedanta follows the pantheistic view of the Upanishads, Nyaya and Vaisheshika are schools of Hindu logic, while Samkhya and Yoga are dualistic. The heterodox systems are the branches of Buddhism and Jainism.

of early Buddhism are in Pali, in the first use I will indicate both the Pali and the Sanskrit transliteration, and then just the Sanskrit.

4.1 EVERLASTING LIFE IN THE RELIGION OF THE VEDAS

The oldest Hindu collection of texts is the *Rig Veda Samhita*,[3] a collection of hymns (*samhitas*) addressed to the gods, in which they are praised and asked for blessings in daily life. There are four collections of *Veda Samhitas* (*Rig, Sama, Yajur,* and *Atharva*), and each is associated with three other kinds of Vedic literature: the Brahmanas, the Aranyakas, and the Upanishads. Together they represent the primary religious literature (*shruti*) of Hinduism.

Although the religion of the Vedas has many gods, it is a different kind of polytheism from that of the ancient religions of Greece and Rome. Max Müller called it "henotheistic," which means "a belief in single gods, each in turn standing out as the highest."[4] Unlike in Greek or Roman mythology, in the hymns of the *Rig Veda* we find similar attributes displayed by more than one god. For instance, Varuna, Indra, Tvashtri, Prajapati, and Vishvakarman are all competing for the role of creator god.

Human beings depend for their welfare on the benevolence of gods and need to appease them through sacrifices. Death is not seen as the end of one's existence, as we find in the hymns an expressed desire for eternal life in a heavenly world. By living a moral life, doing one's duty to the king and one's family, and bringing the proper sacrifices to the gods one expects to attain a new life in a world free of suffering and evil. A memorable prayer said during the due performance of a sacrifice, which is also the leading prayer of this book, indicates that the ultimate longing of the ancient Hindu worshipper was to reach immortality:

> From the unreal lead me to the real,
> from darkness lead me to light,
> from death lead me to immortality![5]

3. Friedrich Max Müller (1823–1900), one of the founding fathers of an academic study of Hinduism, argues that it dates from around 1200 BC (Dasgupta, *A History of Indian Philosophy*, I, 10). Wendy Doniger proposes an earlier date, around 1500 BC (*On Hinduism*, 10).

4. Dasgupta, *A History of Indian Philosophy*, I, 18.

5. This prayer is mentioned in the *Brihadaranyaka Upanishad* 1,3,28, but dates from the time of the Vedas (Radhakrishnan, *The Principal Upanishads*, 162).

The earliest form of Hinduism imagines the survival of death in a personal and physical form, in much clearer terms than the religions of ancient Greece and Rome. In the heavenly realm where one arrives after death, he enjoys forever the rewards of his good deeds and sacrifices in the company of the gods and of the king of the underworld (Yama). Here is how the worshipper of Soma, one of the gods of sacrifice in the *Rig Veda*, expresses his longing for personal immortality:

> Make me immortal in that realm where dwells the King, Vivasvan's Son (Yama), Where is the secret shrine of heaven, where are those waters young and fresh. (. . .) Make me immortal in that realm where they move even as they list, In the third sphere of inmost heaven where lucid worlds are full of light.[6]

During the funeral rite one's family prayed that the deceased would rejoice in fellowship with the gods and his departed ancestors, be rewarded for his good deeds, and receive a new body:

> Go forth, go forth on those ancient paths on which our ancient fathers passed beyond. There you shall see the two kings, Yama and Varuna, rejoicing in the sacrificial drink. Unite with the fathers, with Yama, with the rewards of your sacrifices and good deeds, in the highest heaven. Leaving behind all imperfections, go back home again; merge with a glorious body.[7]

This "glorious body" is a new body in which one survives as a person. H.D. Griswold, a pioneer of the academic study of the Vedas, speaks of the nature of the "glorious body" longed for by the Vedic worshipper in a way that is close to the Christian view of the resurrection. In anticipation of this topic in chapter 6, here is Griswold's description:

> The earthly body at death either suffers dissolution in the earth or is consumed on the funeral pyre. When thus 'cooked' or refined by Agni, the dead man ascends by the 'ancient paths' to the realm of Yama, Agni conducting his soul to the sun-home of the Fathers, where he is united with another body. The new body is congruous with the new environment, and so is a luminous or glorified body (X. 14, 8; 56, 1).[8]

---

6. *Rig Veda* 9,113,8–9.
7. Rig Veda 10,14,7–8, in Doniger O'Flaherty, *The Rig Veda*, 44.
8. Griswold, *The Religion of the Rigveda*, 315.

Thus we find in Vedic Hinduism the view that the dead are reborn in the afterlife, keep the same identity in a physical body free of suffering, and are reunited with their ancestors. It seems that the dead were initially buried, not cremated, on the assumption that the deceased needs a physical body to enter the domain of Yama, the king of the underworld. Yama is sovereign over the souls of the dead and receives offerings for the benefit of the departed. Burning the dead on a pyre was probably introduced when Agni took a more prominent role in popular devotion. Belief in personal survival of death was so strong that the householder was put on the funeral pyre with his bow and widow (alive), to serve him in the afterlife. This custom, called *sati*,[9] was kept in rural communities until the start of the British conquest of India in the eighteenth century.

Personal survival of death was granted not only to the righteous, but also to criminals, in eternal punishment. The gods Indra and Soma were asked to cast the wicked into an eternal dark prison from which they could never escape:

> Indra and Soma, plunge the wicked in the depth, yea, cast them into darkness that hath no support, so that not one of them may ever thence return: so may your wrathful might prevail and conquer them.[10]

According to the hymns of the *Rig Veda*, the components of human nature are the physical body, the vital principle (*asu*), and the mind (*manas*). All three components are preserved when the deceased takes his place in the "world of the fathers." Griswold affirms:

> The body has a part in the future life. The *asu* and *manas* remain united there as here, which is a guarantee that all the functions of the mental life remain intact. Thus the full personality of the departed, consisting of body (*sarira*), soul (*asu*) and spirit (*manas*), is preserved. Having a body, the departed drink Soma, eat the funeral offerings or 'spirit-food' (IX. 113,10) and hear the sound of the flute and of song (X. 135,7).[11]

---

9. In the *Atharva Veda* we find that this was common practice: "Choosing her husband's world, O man, this woman lays herself down beside thy lifeless body. Preserving faithfully the ancient custom. Bestow upon her both wealth and offspring" (*Atharva Veda*, 18,3,1–2).

10. *Rig Veda* 7,104,3.

11. Griswold, *The Religion of the Rigveda*, 314. Soma is also the name of the sacrificial drink used in this ritual.

In later Hinduism, when ultimate reality was defined in different terms, such views of the afterlife were abandoned.

4.2 THE UPANISHADS AND HINDU PANTHEISM

Starting with the Upanishads[12] we find in Hinduism a new worldview that sees the Vedic gods as aspects of a more profound ultimate reality. They are no longer creators and rulers of the world but, together with human beings, animals, and non-living things, are parts of it and products of its manifestation. This ultimate reality, in which everything finds its origin, is called Brahman. A helpful illustration to grasp it would be the "Big Bang" theory on the origin of the physical universe. The point of infinite mass out of which all matter is said to have originated would correspond to the unmanifested Brahman of the Upanishads. But unlike in the Big Bang theory, in the manifestation of Brahman, the products are not only lifeless matter, but also living beings: gods, humans, animals, and plants. The author of the *Brihadaranyaka Upanishad* says:

> As a spider moves along the thread, as small sparks come forth from the fire, even so from this Self come forth all breaths, all worlds, all divinities, all beings.[13]

The nature of this ultimate reality is to cyclically and endlessly manifest the world and then absorb it back into its initial unmanifested form:

> As from a blazing fire, sparks of like form issue forth by the thousands, even so, O beloved, many kinds of beings issue forth from the immutable and they return thither too.[14]

In religious terms this worldview is called pantheism.[15] It rests on the assumption that there is only one essential substance (Brahman) which generates everything. There is no creator god who creates the world out of a divine substance, as in the Vedas, but instead everything

---

12. The Upanishads are philosophical writings attached to the Vedas that appeared in the eighth century BC (Radhakrishnan, *The Principal Upanishads*, 22; Eliade, *A History of Religious Ideas*, I, 241).

13. *Brihadaranyaka Upanishad* 2,1,20, in Radhakrishnan, *The Principal Upanishads*, 190.

14. *Mundaka Upanishad* 2,1,1, in Radhakrishnan, *The Principal Upanishads*, 680.

15. This name derives from the two Greek words at its root, *pan* and *theos*, which mean *all* and *god*.

flows out of a primordial essence and returns to it. In philosophical terms it is a form of monism. (As we recall from chapter 1, physicalism is also a form of monism, which states that all reality is ultimately physical.)

As a product of Brahman's manifestation, human nature retains a "divine spark" of the same essence with the primary nature of Brahman, and this entity is called the self (*atman*). This term may be misleading, for it bears a meaning very different from its Western counterpart. *Atman* is not the seat of consciousness, and is not a Cartesian mind. It is rather an impersonal essence that stands at the core of one's being as a witness of all mental processes, but without generating them. It is of the same ontological quality with Brahman; it does not fluctuate, it is expressionless, irreducible, eternal, and pure. In one of the oldest Upanishads we read:

> The Self (*atman*) is not this, not this (*neti, neti*). He is incomprehensible, for he is not comprehended. He is indestructible, for he cannot be destroyed. He is unattached, for he does not attach himself. He is unfettered, he does not suffer, he is not injured.[16]

In the *Taittiriya Upanishad* we find the oldest account of human nature as a construct of five layers (or sheaths) that envelop the self: the physical (*annamaya*), formed by food; the vital (*pranamaya*), formed by breath; the mind (*manomaya*); the intellect as consciousness (*vijnanamaya*); and finally the sheath of bliss (*anandamaya*), in which the self (*atman*) rests.[17] Later developments gave rise to alternative views and names of the layers that envelop the self, and from Hinduism this structure was imported into forms of New Age spirituality and of alternative medicine.[18]

The physical body is kept alive by an unseen body made of vital energy. This is the *pranamaya kosha*. It taps the universal life-energy called *prana* and distributes it to the physical body. Swami Vivekananda, one of the first promoters of Hindu spirituality in the US, argues that *prana* represents the energy which sustains all physical and mental processes:

> Out of this *Prana* is evolved everything that we call energy, everything that we call force. It is the *Prana* that is manifesting as motion; it is the *Prana* that is manifesting as gravitation, as

---

16. *Brihadaranyaka-Upanishad* 4,2,4, in Radhakrishnan, *The Principal Upanishads*, 254.

17. *Taittiriya Upanishad* 2,1, in Radhakrishnan, *The Principal Upanishads*, 542–43.

18. On Hindu views on human nature that can be found in forms of alternative medicine, see Ernest Valea, *The Spiritual Dimension of Alternative Medicine*.

magnetism. It is the *Prana* that is manifesting as the actions of the body, as the nerve currents, as thought force. From thought, down to the lowest physical force, everything is but the manifestation of *Prana*. The sum-total of all force in the universe, mental or physical, when resolved back to their original state, is called *Prana*.[19]

The next two layers are mental. *Manomaya* is formed by perception, the result of sense activity, while *vijnanamaya* is formed by reasoning and interpreting the data of perception. Finally, *anandamaya* is the layer that serves as a bridge between the other-worldly self (*atman*) and the four previous layers. In Vedanta, the pantheistic philosophy which emerged from the Upanishads, these five layers form three bodies: the gross body (*sthula sharira*), made of the physical layer; the subtle body (*sukshma sharira*), made of the next three; and the causal body (*karana sharira*), the one that holds the self.

Besides grounding a pantheistic worldview, the other novelty brought by the Upanishads was to state that the essential problem we face as humans is that we do not know our true nature. Instead of realizing our oneness with ultimate reality, and that at the core of our being lies *atman*, we let ourselves be carried away by the flux of mental life. Illusion (*maya*) deceives us about our true nature, channeling our desires toward the phenomenal world that is ever changing. It hides *atman* under the cloak of the physical body and of mental activity and leads us away from knowing the eternal and immutable self. The *Chandogya Upanishad* describes our condition using the illustration of a hidden treasure we are not aware of:

> Just as those who do not know the field walk again and again over the hidden treasure of gold and do not find it, even so all creatures here go day after day into the Brahma-world and yet do not find it, for they are carried away by untruth.[20]

Acting on these premises, that is, following the deception of illusion, is called ignorance (*avidya*). It triggers a metaphysical chain of cause and effect similar to the law of action and reaction of physics. This is karma, the law of action and retribution according to one's deeds. Its origin can

---

19. Vivekananda, *Raja Yoga*, 30. Swami Vivekananda was one of the first Hindu missionaries to the United States. He gave lectures on Yoga at the World's Columbian Exposition in Chicago in 1893.

20. *Chandogya-Upanishad* 8,3,2, in Radhakrishnan, *The Principal Upanishads*, 495.

be traced to the *Brahmana* writings, the exegetical treatises on the nature of Vedic sacrifice, which speculate that while sacrifices bring good results to the one who performs them, there must be a general rule of acting and being rewarded accordingly for all one's deeds. Some acts are beneficial and bring people to heaven, while others prevent humans from entering the heavenly world after death or limit their stay there, forcing them to fall back in this world and reap the fruits of their deeds. The Upanishads developed and perfected this concept by making the law of karma a kind of perfect accountant for *all* one's deeds. Actually, karma has two meanings. It designates both *action* and the *result* of one's actions, both doing and becoming, so it is the direct link between acting in this life and being rewarded in a future life, through reincarnation (*samsara*). The first clear affirmation of reincarnation is found in the *Brihadaranyaka-Upanishad*, which states that "one becomes good by good action, bad by bad action."[21] It means that good actions in this life will bring about positive results in the next life, while bad actions will be punished. We will enter into more detail of how reincarnation works in the next chapter.

According to the Upanishads, liberation of the self (*atman*) from reincarnation is called *moksha* and represents its return into Brahman. It is an impersonal fusion of *atman* with Brahman, when personhood is annihilated and the process of reincarnation ceases. The best illustration for it is that of a river flowing into the ocean, thus becoming one with it:

> Just as the flowing rivers disappear in the ocean casting off name and shape, even so the knower, freed from name and shape, attains to the divine person, higher than the high. He, verily, who knows the Supreme Brahman becomes Brahman himself.[22]

Unlike the worshipper of the gods in the *Rig Veda*, who was seeking personal and physical immortality in the company of the gods, the sages of the Upanishads formulated their view of salvation in very different terms. The Upanishadic view of immortality is also very different from what Western physicalists expect. The difference arises from the way the self is defined. The equivalent of the Western meaning of self, in Hindu terms, is just a phenomenal self, called *jiva*. In Dasgupta's words,

---

21. *Brihadaranyaka-Upanishad* 3,2,13, in Radhakrishnan, *The Principal Upanishads*, 217. Mircea Eliade argues that the term *samsara* does not appear in texts earlier than the Upanishads (*A History of Religious Ideas*, I, 239).

22. *Mundaka Upanishad* 3,2,8–9, in Radhakrishnan, *The Principal Upanishads*, 691–92.

Jiva or individual means the self in association with the ego and other personal experiences, i.e. phenomenal self, which feels, suffers and is affected by world-experiences.[23]

A conscious self as heir of immortality is an absurd view because this kind of self would just inherit ignorance and karma. Eliade argues that in the Upanishads immortality is conceived as an "impersonal immortality," in which "the self is merged into its original source, Brahman."[24] This ultimate achievement is the end both of ignorance and of personal existence. However, survival of death is possible, although unwanted, through reincarnation.

4.3 HUMAN NATURE IN TANTRA AND HATHA YOGA

The word Yoga has two different meanings. On the one hand, it has a loose definition, designating "any *ascetic technique* and any *method of meditation*."[25] On the other hand, in a more restrictive sense, Yoga is the name of a dualistic system of Hindu thought (the Yoga *darshana*). In this section, out of the many Yoga ascetic schools, we assess the pantheistic school known in the West as Hatha Yoga, which shares the same view on human nature as Tantrism, another important Hindu tradition.

The term "Yoga" is first used in the *Taittiriya* and *Katha Upanishads* (fifth century BC). In the latter, the king of the dead (Yama) teaches the young Naciketas how to acquire the knowledge of Brahman through restraint of the senses and concentration.[26] Following an interesting allegory, the human being is likened to a chariot pulled by wild horses (the senses) that the driver (the mind) cannot master. In this chariot, the passenger (the self) suffers in silence. Yoga is the method by which the driver (the mind) can calm and stop the horses (the senses) so that the passenger (*atman*) can descend from the chariot and be free from its ordeal.

The most widespread Yoga school in the West, promoted as an effective relaxation method and health therapy, is Hatha Yoga.[27] Most West-

---

23. Dasgupta, *A History of Indian Philosophy*, I, 476.
24. Eliade, *A History of Religious Ideas*, I, 243.
25. Eliade, *Yoga: Immortality and Freedom*, 4.
26. *Katha Upanishad* 1,3,3–9, in Radhakrishnan, *The Principal Upanishads*, 623–24.
27. The *Hatha Yoga Pradipika* is dated by Doniger between the thirteenth and eighteenth century AD (*On Hinduism*, 119).

erners are aware only of its physical aspect, the body postures, which would suggest it is a kind of gymnastics for health. However, its postures, twists and bends are only preparatory stages for enabling meditation. In the very beginning of the *Hatha Yoga Pradipika* of Svatmarama,[28] the fundamental treatise of *Hatha Yoga*, this goal is clearly affirmed: "Prostrating first to the guru, Yogi Swatmarama instructs the knowledge of hatha yoga only for (raja yoga) the highest state of yoga."[29] *Raja yoga* means the practice of meditation, meant to liberate the mind from illusion and achieve final liberation.

B.K.S. Iyengar, probably the best known Hatha Yoga teacher in the West, points out that Yoga is much more than a relaxation method. In his words, it is "the union of the individual self, *jivatma*, with the universal self, *paramatma*."[30] As he further explains, the word *yoga* itself points to its religious content:

> The word "Yoga" is derived from the Sanskrit root "*yuj*" which means to bind, join, attach and yoke, to direct and concentrate the attention in order to use it for meditation. (...) It is the communion of the human soul with Divinity.[31]

The underlying philosophy attached to Hatha Yoga practice is a form of pantheistic Hinduism. Brahman and *atman* are presented under different names, but bear the same meaning as in the Upanishads. The ultimate reality is the god Shiva, with his divine consort, the goddess Shakti, who together form a state of primordial unity that corresponds to the Brahman of the Upanishads. The world and the human beings appeared from that primordial unity formed by Shiva and Shakti. The *Shiva-Samhita* states:

> From the self-combination of the Spirit which is Siva and the Matter which is Sakti, and, through their inherent interaction on each other, all creatures are born.[32]

As the Upanishads assert that Brahman's pure essence is found in human nature as *atman*, in Hatha Yoga (and Tantra) we are said to have

---

28. Iyengar argues it was composed as late as the fifteenth century AD (*Yoga*, 48).

29. Svatmarama, *The Hatha Yoga Pradipika* 1,2, in Saraswati, *Hatha Yoga Pradipika*, 27.

30. Iyengar, *Yoga*, 46.

31. Iyengar, *Light on Pranayama*, 4.

32. *Siva Samhita* 1,92, in Munro, *Siva Samhita*.

a divine core called the *kundalini*. It represents Shakti dissociated from her original unity with Shiva, and thus the ultimate goal of Hatha Yoga practice is the restoration of their unity for each individual human being. Hatha Yoga is thus a way of achieving the return of the self (Shakti, corresponding to *atman*) into the Absolute Shiva (corresponding to Brahman), which is a similar goal as formulated by the Upanishads and all forms of pantheism. In the words of Iyengar,

> The experience of *samadhi* (liberation) is achieved when the knower, the knowable, and the known become one. When the object of meditation engulfs the meditator and becomes the subject, self-awareness is lost.[33]

In ignorant people the self (*kundalini*) lies dormant at the base of a spiritual channel called *sushumna*. It starts in the tailbone and ends at the top of the head, roughly corresponding to the spinal cord. Once one engages in Hatha Yoga practice the *kundalini* awakens and ascends through the *sushumna* channel. On its way it meets seven important points, called *chakras*. As Iyengar affirms, they have a very important role, for "just as the brain controls physical, mental, and intellectual functions through the nerve cells or neurons, *chakras* tap the *prana* or cosmic energy which is within all living beings and transform it into spiritual energy."[34] When the *kundalini* has traversed the entire *sushumna* channel and reaches the last *chakra* as a result of a successful Yoga practice, one experiences liberation, the ultimate goal of Hatha Yoga practice. As in other forms of pantheism, it is a way of achieving an impersonal form of immortality.

4.4 THE DUALISTIC PHILOSOPHY OF THE SAMKHYA AND YOGA SCHOOLS

The Samkhya and Yoga *darshanas* are two of the orthodox systems of Hindu thought which are dualistic. Since their views on human nature are largely shared, the following applies to both. In order to avoid confusion, please keep in mind that in this section Yoga refers to the dualistic *darshana* that was structured by Patanjali sometime between the second

---

33. Iyengar, *Yoga*, 53.
34. Iyengar, *Yoga*, 57.

century BC and the third century AD.³⁵ It does not have the same meaning as in the previous two sections.

The basic assumption on which both Samkhya and Yoga rely is that human nature is composed of two fundamental substances: the self, called *purusha* (the equivalent of *atman* of the Upanishads) and *prakriti* (primordial substance). Neither is the manifestation of the other, or of a deeper ultimate reality. In Eliade's words, the self is "eternally pure, impassive, autonomous, and irreducible" and "states of consciousness, the flux of psychomental life, are foreign to it."³⁶ The primordial substance (*prakriti*) has in its constitution three factors (or qualities), called *guna* (*sattva, rajas,* and *tamas*). The physical world and mental phenomena appeared when the *gunas* came out of a state of perfect equilibrium, so all physical or mental phenomena are combinations of them. Since the self is not the mind, mental states do not belong to the self, but are manifestations of *prakriti*, resulting from the different participation of each of the three *gunas*. For example, when *sattva* dominates, one is calm and peaceful; when *rajas* takes control passion and alertness arise, and when *tamas* plays the dominant role, one is inert and lazy. Ignorance (*avidya*) is defined in a similar way to other systems of Hindu thought. Eliade explains:

> In both *darsanas* human suffering is rooted in illusion, for man believes that his psychomental life—activity of the senses, feelings, thoughts, and volitions—is identical with Spirit, with the Self. He thus confuses two wholly autonomous and opposed realities, between which there is no real connection but only an illusory relation, for psychomental experience does not belong to Spirit, it belongs to nature (*prakrti*).³⁷

Ignorance fuels karma and *samsara*, so the self reincarnates as many times as necessary, according to the actions taken by the individual human being. These actions require fruition, or in other words, the burning of the potential that triggered them. In Eliade's words,

> Every action whose point of departure is illusion (that is, which is based on ignorance, the confusion between Spirit and non-Spirit) is either the consummation of a virtuality created by a

---

35. Eliade, *A History of Religious Ideas*, II, 60. It is dated by Doniger in the third century AD (*On Hinduism*, 118), while Dasgupta dates it in the second century BC (Dasgupta, *A History of Indian Philosophy*, I, 238).

36. Eliade, *Yoga*, 16–17.

37. Eliade, *Yoga*, 15.

preceding act or the projection of another force that in turn demands its actualization, its consummation, in the present existence or in an existence to come.[38]

The liberation of the self corresponds to its isolation from all of *prakriti*'s manifestations. In Samkhya it is achieved by metaphysical knowledge, which means understanding the world as it is and the true nature of the self. When the confusion generated by the physical and mental phenomena ceases, they are absorbed into *prakriti* and the self (*purusha*) is liberated. This is the way we "understand" the liberation of the spirit. But since thinking itself belongs to *prakriti*, Samkhya philosophers argue that *purusha* is only a "spectator" to its liberation, while "liberation" (*mukti*) is only a *becoming-conscious* of the spirit's eternal freedom."[39]

The metaphysics of the Yoga *darshana* comes entirely from Samkhya. What it adds to Samkhya is the existence of a kind of deity, Ishvara, as well as the fact that liberation cannot be obtained through intellectual knowledge alone, but requires following an ascetic technique. However, Ishvara is not a personal god in the proper sense of the word, but rather a *purusha* that has never been a prisoner to *prakriti* and karma (*Yoga Sutra* 1,24).[40] Since Ishvara does not have a personal nature, it cannot engage in a personal relationship with humans. As Eliade argues, the relationship between Ishvara and the yogi is a "metaphysical sympathy,"[41] and by the ascetic method described by Patanjali in his treatise (*Yoga Sutra*), the yogi just imitates "the mode of being" proper to Ishvara.[42]

Liberation consists in isolating the self from all manifestations of the primordial substance, and attaining a state of total isolation (*kaivalyam*). In this state, called by Eliade a "tragic and paradoxical conception of spirit,"[43] the self joins a heaven full of free and immovable other *purushas* among which there can be no relationship:

> Each of these *purushas* is a monad, is completely isolated; for the Self can have no contact either with the world around it (derived

---

38. Eliade, *Yoga*, 27.
39. Eliade, *A History of Religious Ideas*, II, 59.
40. According to Dasgupta "Ishvara is a *purusha* who had never been subject to ignorance, afflictions, or passions. His body is of pure *sattva* quality which can never be touched by ignorance" (Dasgupta, *A History of Indian Philosophy*, I, 259).
41. Eliade, *Yoga*, 74.
42. Eliade, *Yoga*, 68.
43. Eliade, *A History of Religious Ideas*, II, 59; Eliade, *Yoga*, 33.

from *prakriti*) or with other spirits. The cosmos, then, is peopled with these eternal, free, unmoving *purushas*-monads between which no communication is possible.[44]

Having met Cartesian dualism in chapter 1, we could ask to what extent do we encounter its problems in its Indian counterpart? Since *purusha* is not the source of mental life and lacks any attributes, at least one more difficulty is added to those of Descartes. It concerns the plurality of the selves. Their lack of attributes makes it impossible to differentiate among them and uphold their plurality. Here is Radhakrishnan's comment:

> The self is without attributes or qualities, without parts, imperishable, motionless, absolutely inactive and impassive, unaffected by pleasure or pain or any other emotion. All change, all character belong to *prakriti*. (. . .) Since they are free from all variety, then there is nothing to lead us to assume a plurality of *purushas*. Multiplicity without distinction is impossible.[45]

Another problem is similar to Cartesian dualism and regards the mind-body relationship. In Hindu dualism the major interest lies in attaining liberation, but since *purusha* and *prakriti* have a fundamentally different nature they cannot cooperate to achieve liberation. Here is how Eliade formulates this problem:

> Being irreducible, devoid of qualities, *purusha* has no "intelligence," for it is without desires. Desires are not eternal, hence they do not belong to spirit. Spirit is eternally free, "states of consciousness," the flux of psychomental life, being foreign to it. Now this conception of *purusha* at once raises difficulties. For if spirit is eternally pure, impassive, autonomous, and irreducible, how can it consent to let itself be involved in psychomental experience? And how is such a relation possible?[46]

Samkhya and Yoga dualism attempts to solve this problem by postulating that *prakriti* works instinctively for the release of the self. In the *Samkhya-Sutra* (3,47) it is stated that "the Creation is for the benefit of

44. Eliade, *Yoga*, 32–33. In Jainism karma is a kind of physical substance produced by ignorance that gets glued to the self and forms a sheath called the *karmasharira*. This sheath accompanies the self from one incarnation to the next and keeps the record of past lives. Karma needs to be annihilated by right practice, so that the self can leave all material associations and be elevated to the top of the universe, where it remains as an isolated individual self, as in Samkhya.

45. Radhakrishnan, *Indian Philosophy*, II, 322.

46. Eliade, *A History of Religious Ideas*, II, 53; *Yoga*, 17–18.

spirit until spirit has attained supreme knowledge."[47] A famous illustration that attempts to explain how *prakriti* works instinctively towards *purusha*'s liberation, or the "*teleological* nature" of the primordial substance,[48] is that of the horse (*prakriti*) that pulls the wagon (the human being as a whole) home, while the driver (*purusha*) is simply a spectator. However, the fact is ignored, in this illustration, that the horse was trained by the driver before learning the way home. Samkhya metaphysics does not admit the cooperation of the two substances because they have a fundamentally different nature. The self cannot impart any wisdom to the mind, and the mind is too different from the self to be able to help it out of its bondage. Another attempted illustration is that of the blind man who carries the lame to reach their common destination. But this illustration, too, fails to explain the "*teleological* nature" of the primordial substance, because both the blind and the lame possess intellect and language, and this enables them to cooperate to achieve the common goal. But no such cooperation is possible between *prakriti* and the *purusha* because they hold nothing in common.

As we can see, to define the self in terms that divorce it completely from mental life leads not only to awkward ways of defining immortality, but also to difficult contradictions in formulating the way of achieving liberation.

4.5 SELF AND PERSONAL IDENTITY IN HINDUISM

In the first two chapters we saw that physicalism attempts to explain consciousness and the self in exclusively physical terms. In this chapter we have started to assess religious views on consciousness, the self and the preservation of personal identity. So far we have seen a real interest in preserving personal identity only in the ancient religion of the Vedas, according to which human beings long to enjoy personal communion with the gods in the afterlife. In the Upanishads a different kind of ultimate reality arises, one which encompasses all forms of life, including the gods, and as a result, we encounter a different view of human nature. The self (*atman*) is devoid of attributes, is not the source of mental activity and is not the seat of consciousness. According to the Upanishads, the self passes through innumerable bodies until it finally reaches liberation,

---

47. Eliade, *A History of Religious Ideas*, II, 56.
48. Eliade, *A History of Religious Ideas*, II, 56.

which means dissolution into an impersonal essence. In the dualistic systems of Samkhya and Yoga only the primordial substance (*prakriti*) manifests the world. The self is irreducible and unaffected by mental experience. Instead of merging with an impersonal ultimate reality, its goal is to achieve liberation in the form of eternal isolation which excludes any relationship. Whether the self is defined according to pantheistic or dualistic worldviews, its immortality is always impersonal and unconscious, which is quite an unattractive view for Westerners.

In very general terms, the mind is the seat of thought and will, and commands the organs of knowledge (the five senses), and the five organs of action: speech, apprehension, movement, excretion and reproduction. Through sensing, willing and acting, the mind directs one's attention to the ephemeral things of the world instead of searching for the true self, which is *atman*. As a result, Indian philosophy studies the nature of the mind and of personal identity for different reasons than Western philosophy of mind. Instead of discovering how personal identity can be preserved, Indian philosophy seeks its annihilation, because the interest in preserving personal identity is itself the cause of ignorance and karma. In preserving personal identity, the West and the East are thus on opposing sides. Paul Deussen, the scholar of Upanishadic philosophy, senses this contrast very clearly. He observes that an instinct for the preservation of life and personal identity is at work in each of us:

> Love of life is the strongest of all the instincts implanted in human nature. In order to preserve life we make any sacrifice. (...) Indeed, so strong in us is the instinct for life, that our whole existence is nothing more than this desire unfolding itself in space as the body and in time as the life.[49]

However, in the East this drive is the source of all problems, and thus Deussen points out that Indian philosophy (with special reference to the Upanishads) urges one to act against this natural instinct, demanding the suppression of the desire to experience personal existence. In his words,

> the highest goal appears as a release (*moksha*), and that not such a release as death brings from a definite existence, but release from existence in general, which as our innate consciousness shows is not to be attained simply through death.[50]

---

49. Deussen, *The Philosophy of the Upanishads*, 338–39.
50. Deussen, *The Philosophy of the Upanishads*, 339.

Since the self (*atman* or *purusha*) is devoid of personal attributes, Indian philosophy is not only *not* interested in preserving personal identity, but requires its annihilation. In other words, since preserving one's personal status leads only to the perpetuation of suffering in countless future lives, liberation from ignorance demands the annihilation of personhood itself. Eliade argues in similar terms about the goal of the Yoga *darshana*:

> Human personality does not exist as a final element; it is only a synthesis of psychomental experiences, and it is destroyed—in other words, ceases to act—as soon as revelation is an accomplished fact. Like all creations of the cosmic substance (*prakriti*), the human personality (*asmita*) also acted to bring about "awakening"; hence, once liberation is achieved, the personality is of no further use.[51]

The ancient Vedic desire for immortality in a personal form is understood in later Hinduism as a false view which is generated by ignorance, and which leads to suffering, karma and reincarnation. The *Yoga Sutra* (2,3), lists five causes of suffering, as the five afflictions (*kleshas*): ignorance (*avidya*), egoism (*asmita*), attachment (*raga*), aversion (*dvesha*) and love of life (*abhinivesha*).[52] Two of these (the second and the fifth) are linked directly to personal existence. *Asmita* is not just egoism, as we manifest it in daily life, but the sense of being an individual person, consciousness itself. Likewise, *abhinivesha* is love of life, "the will to be,"[53] not just in a selfish way, but as the desire to remain a personal agent in the world. Both are seen as afflictions that need to be annihilated, not just in their negative dimension (as selfishness), but also as defining aspects of personhood itself.

In conclusion, from our inquiry on the nature of consciousness and the self in Hinduism, we need to remember that the desire to experience personal existence is itself a cause of suffering and reincarnation. Hinduism has reached this position starting from the assumption that the source of our existence is an impersonal ultimate reality. It led to formulating an impersonal view of the self and thus to an impersonal "fulfillment" of human nature. Hinduism nevertheless affirms the continuation of life through reincarnation, for it is the same self that traverses all past, present, and future existences. We will analyze the mechanism of

---

51. Eliade, *Yoga*, 31.
52. Prasada, *Patanjali's Yoga Sutras*, 91.
53. Dasgupta, *A History of Indian Philosophy*, I, 267.

reincarnation and its evidence in the next chapter, but not before exploring the way human nature is defined in the other great religious tradition of the East, that is, Buddhism.

4.6 HUMAN NATURE IN BUDDHISM

In this section we take a step further into the world of Eastern thought to explore Buddhism, an important religious tradition with increasing popularity in the West. What makes Buddhism so appealing for Westerners is its claim to be a philosophy rather than a religion, the result of one's honest search for truth which requires faith not in an unseen God but only in oneself. It formulates its own religious assumptions on ultimate reality and human nature, and it adapts many religious beliefs taken from Hinduism, such as ignorance, karma, reincarnation, and liberation. Only after its assumptions have been accepted does everything follow in the seemingly logical way that Westerners appreciate so much.

The Buddhist view on human nature is shaped by three major doctrines, also called the three hallmarks of existence: impermanence, denial of a self, and suffering. The doctrine of impermanence (Sanskrit: *anitya*, Pali: *anicca*) is the foundational assumption in Buddhism. It claims that anything we can think of, any object, being, or phenomenon, is nothing but a momentary product and a momentary cause in an infinite chain of becoming. The only permanent "something" is not a substance, but a truth, that of impermanence.

Impermanence encompasses even what religions call their ultimate reality. Buddhism categorically rejects both the assertion of a creative god as ultimate reality and the Brahman of Hinduism. Belief in a permanent and changeless God is a form of delusion and attachment which generates suffering and rebirth. In Peter Harvey's words, "Buddhism sees no need for a creator of the world, as it postulates no ultimate beginning to the world, and regards it sustained by natural laws."[54] In the eternal cycle of becoming, all gods were once humans that gained great merits but will nevertheless suffer rebirth as humans when the store of merits that promoted them to a rebirth as a god is depleted. Despite their merits, they still have not achieved the right knowledge and liberation from ignorance.

Applied to human nature, the doctrine of impermanence affirms that everything in our physical body and mental life is merely a temporary

---

54. Harvey, *An Introduction to Buddhism*, 36.

effect of certain causes, and these elements themselves are further causes of transformation. Impermanence reiterates the criticism of the bodily criterion for personal identity, by reminding us that our body is in constant change: our cells are constantly dying and being replaced, we grew older and the way we look changes, so physically we are not the same entity we were yesterday or a year ago. The Buddha drew a very grim portrait of the body:

> Look at this dressed-up lump, covered with wounds, joined together, sickly, full of many thoughts, which has no strength, no hold! This body is wasted, full of sickness, and frail; this heap of corruption breaks to pieces, life indeed ends in death. After one has looked at those grey bones, thrown away like gourds in the autumn, what pleasure is there (left in life)! After a stronghold has been made of the bones, it is covered with flesh and blood, and there dwell in it old age and death, pride and deceit.[55]

As for the psychological continuity criterion for personal identity, Buddhism denies that our mental life can provide a source of stability. Our emotions, thoughts and beliefs are all constantly changing, so that emotionally and intellectually we are never the same from one moment to the next. The Upanishads reached a similar position but still identified the self (*atman*) as the unchangeable core of our nature.

The second foundational element of Buddhism follows from the doctrine of impermanence. Its logical result is the denial of a self as the core element that would define human nature. This is the no-self (Sanskrit: *anatman*, Pali: *anatta*) doctrine, which goes against both the Hindu view of a substantial irreducible self (*atman* or *purusha*), and what Western dualistic philosophy has formulated as the simple view (section 2.5). For Buddhists, what is called the "self" in chapter 2 is the illusion generated by five interlinked factors called aggregates (Sanskrit: *skandha*, Pali: *khandha*), five factors that are themselves in a constant process of becoming: form (*rupa*), sensation (*vedana*), perception (*samjna*), volition (*samskarah*), and consciousness (*vijnana*). *Form* is the body with its six sense organs.[56] The senses generate *sensations* of pleasure, aversion or indifference. The process of organizing and labeling them into categories is called *perception*. As a result, *volitional acts* are initiated in response

---

55. Müller, *Dhammapada* 147–50, 41–42.

56. There are six senses because the mind is also called a sense organ. It senses the world of ideas and thoughts, just as the other five sense the five aspects of the physical world.

to the objects of sensory experience, which bear consequences in this and further lives. Finally, *consciousness* is "an awareness of ourselves as thinking subjects having a series of perceptions and thoughts."[57] It gives the impression that one is a distinct agent of cognition, that there is a self doing the observing and responding to the objects of perception, when in fact it is only the end result of a process dependent on sensory input.

We can easily recognize here Hume's view of human nature (section 2.7) expressed in Buddhist terms.[58] For the Scottish philosopher the mind is just a sum of successive perceptions, and the "the soul" is nothing but the imagination at work in unifying the multitude of perceptions. Our perceptions are linked to each other and sustain the illusion of personal identity. In reality there exists no real self, no soul, but only a flow of successive perceptions.

According to Buddhist teaching the heap of aggregates generates the illusion of personal existence, the false notions of person (Sanskrit: *pudgala*, Pali: *puggala*) and self (*atman*). In fact there is no independent and unchanging witness behind the ever changing phenomenal world, no *atman*, no everlasting soul at all. The human being is merely a cluster of ever changing physical and mental processes, a mere heap of the five aggregates, which has no permanent self. Paul Williams explains:

> The person is reducible to the temporary bundle of bundles where all constituents are radically impermanent, temporarily held together through causal relationships of the right sort.[59]

In a famous discourse the Buddha proceeded to analyze the five aggregates and argued that none of them can be properly called a self (*atman*).[60] All five are impermanent and to believe otherwise would only generate attachments and lead to suffering. Hence one should not speculate on whether the Buddha did not actually exclude the existence of a self *behind* the aggregates.[61] The human being is nothing but a series of impermanent physical and mental processes, a mere heap of five aggregates,

---

57. Gethin, *The Foundations of Buddhism*, 136.

58. We have no biographical clues to suggest that Hume was familiar with Buddhism, so he probably arrived independently at his views on human nature.

59. Williams, *Buddhist Thought*, 70

60. *Anattalakkhana Sutra*, in Bodhi, *The Connected Discourses*, 901–3.

61. The view that the Buddha did not exclude a substantial self is untenable. His teaching does not allow us to speculate whether he merely excluded a self in the five aggregates while accepting a self beyond them. See Williams, *Buddhist Thought*, 60–62, Collins, *Selfless Persons*, 7–10, and Rahula, *What the Buddha Taught*, 55–56.

or to be technically more precise, "a particular, individual combination of changing mental and physical processes, with a particular karmic history."[62] As Gethin further explains: "My sense of self is both logically and emotionally just a label that I impose on these physical and mental phenomena in consequence of their connectedness."[63] This is the meaning of the personal pronouns we use in common speech. Beyond the *I, you, he, she,* etc. there is no underlying self. According to Dasgupta, "when the Buddha told his birth stories saying that he was such and such in a such and such life, he only meant that his past and his present belonged to one and the same lineage of momentary existences."[64] Thus personal pronouns must be seen only as referring to a particular collection of physical and mental states, that is, to a temporary heap of five aggregates.

The third fundamental doctrine of Buddhism is that of suffering (Sanskrit: *dukkha*, Pali: *duhkha*). Since everything is impermanent and there is no unchanging self in our nature, everything we experience is suffering. This is the first of the Four Noble Truths formulated by the Buddha when he reached enlightenment. The omnipresence of suffering means more than the fact that we experience physical or emotional pain; it is a condition inherent in human nature which results from craving for a permanent self and personal relationships. In other words, to exist as a personal being means suffering.[65]

We can see how the three foundational doctrines of Buddhism are linked to each other. It is not merely that we suffer in this life, but life itself is suffering because all we experience is impermanent and conditioned. If everything is impermanent there is no room for a self to define human nature. If there is no permanent self, nothing can give meaning to personal existence, and all experience can only be termed as suffering. Therefore suffering, impermanence and no-self are interconnected and inseparable.

The three fundamental doctrines of Buddhism are related to the Four Noble Truths discovered by the Buddha at his enlightenment. The first is the omnipresence of suffering as the true mark of human existence. The second is the cause of suffering as craving for impermanent things, as a result of being under the spell of ignorance. In Buddhism, ignorance (Sanskrit: *avidya*, Pali: *avijja*) means to be "unaware" of how

---

62. Harvey, *Introduction to Buddhist Ethics*, 36.
63. Gethin, *The Foundations of Buddhism*, 139.
64. Dasgupta, *A History of Indian Philosophy*, I, 118.
65. As Eliade argues, the omnipresence of suffering is "a leitmotiv of all post-Upanishadic Indian speculation" (Eliade, *Yoga*, 11).

things really are. This "unawareness" makes us crave for impermanent things and hold to the belief in a self (the "I," and what is "mine") as the potential beneficiary of the objects of craving.

The Third Noble Truth draws a logical conclusion from the first and the second. Since the cause of suffering is craving, the cessation of craving will lead to the cessation of suffering. If craving ceases, ignorance is defeated and one becomes enlightened. The shortest definition of enlightenment is that of "seeing things as they really are."[66] It is a valid definition in all traditions of Buddhism. One's ultimate goal is to attain nirvana, liberation from suffering, and implicitly from personal existence. The word "nirvana" (Pali: *nibbana*) means that something has been "extinguished" or "blown out." Since there is no real self to be annihilated, nirvana refers to the annihilation of the fires that fuel rebirth—greed, aversion, and delusion (ignorance)—and with them, the cycle of existence as an unenlightened personal being. In the *Nipata Sutra* the Buddha states:

> As a flame blown about by the violence of the wind, O Upasiva, goes out, cannot be reckoned (as existing), even so a Muni, delivered from name and body, disappears, and cannot be reckoned (as existing). [67]

The Fourth Noble Truth concerns the ascetic practice one has to follow to attain liberation, a topic that goes beyond the limitations of this book. When the forces of craving are blocked, karma is left without fuel, suffering ceases, and one attains enlightenment. When this person dies he or she attains "nirvana without a remainder" (Sanskrit: *nirupadhisheshanirvana;* Pali: *anupadisesanibbana*), also known as *parinirvana*,[68] which means that the aggregates that make up a person will never regroup in the form of a new sentient being, because the driving force of craving has vanished. In the words of Gethin, when the enlightened person dies "he or she will not be reborn into some new life, the physical and mental constituents of being will not come together in some

---

66. Collins, *Selfless Persons*, 92. Williams also uses this formula. For instance, he states: "From the beginning the Buddhist tradition has characterized enlightenment as "seeing things the way they really are" (*yathabhutadarshana*), a seeing which differs in some crucial way from a perception of the way things appear to be to the unenlightened person" (Williams, "Non-conceptuality, critical reasoning . . . ," in McGhee, *Philosophy,* 189–90).

67. Müller, *Sutta Nipata* 5,7,6 (1074), 189.

68. Gethin, *The Foundations of Buddhism*, 76.

new existence, there will be no new being or person."[69] *Parinirvana* was likened by the Buddha himself to the flame of an oil lamp which goes out when the oil is finished.[70]

4.7 DOCTRINAL DEVELOPMENTS IN MAHAYANA BUDDHISM

In the previous section we encountered the vision of human nature of early Buddhism, which is represented today by the Theravada tradition. Later developments in Buddhism generated its other great tradition, known as the Mahayana.[71]

The element that truly characterizes Mahayana Buddhism is its emphasis on compassion, in the sense that true perfection cannot mean finding enlightenment just for oneself while leaving all other beings behind in the world of endless rebirth. What all Mahayana Buddhists have in common is first of all a vision, that "of attaining full Buddhahood for the benefit of all sentient beings," so that all beings may escape suffering.[72] This is the core element that differentiates it from early Buddhism. The other two factors that triggered the rise of Mahayana Buddhism were the emergence of a new kind of Buddhist literature, said to have been "originally delivered by the Buddha himself" but "not taught until the time was ripe,"[73] and a new status assigned to the Buddha.[74] For our inquiry on human nature it is important to understand these two factors.

The first factor is the result of philosophical developments brought by a group of writings known as the *Prajnaparamita* ("Perfection of Wisdom") *sutras*, a group of writings not known to early Buddhism. They

---

69. Gethin, *The Foundations of Buddhism*, 76. Rahula explains the meaning of *parinirvana* as follows: "*Parinibbuto* simply means 'fully passed away,' 'fully blown out,' or 'fully extinct,' because the Buddha or an Arahant has no re-existence after his death" (Rahula, *What the Buddha Taught*, 41). The Arahant is one who has given up craving, has defeated suffering and ignorance, and thus attained freedom from rebirth.

70. This illustration is given in the *Majjhima Nikaya* 72, 19–20, in Nanamoli and Bodhi, *The Middle Length Discourses*, 593–94. Against some Western commentators, Buddhist experts such as Oldenberg, Poussin, Burnouf or Stcherbatsky find no difficulty in accepting an annihilationist view of nirvana (Collins, *Selfless Persons*, 11–12).

71. According to Harvey, Mahayana Buddhism arose between 150 BC and AD 100 (*Introduction to Buddhism*, 89).

72. Williams, *Buddhist Thought*, 103.

73. Gethin, *Foundations of Buddhism*, 225.

74. Gethin, *Foundations of Buddhism*, 227.

provided the foundation for elaborating the doctrine of emptiness (*shunyata*), which came about as the result of following the doctrine of no-self (*anatman*) to its natural end, that of denying that there is *any* primary existent in *any* physical or mental aspect of the world.

According to early Buddhism, physical and mental events consist of fundamental building-blocks, so to speak, called *dharmas* (Pali: *dhammas*) which are said to have "an inherent nature" and can "*exist* independently," which means that they can be defined without reference to other such elements.[75] The Theravada tradition lists 82 *dharmas*, out of which 81 are conditioned (and thus impermanent) and one is unconditioned (*nirvana*).[76] Conditioned *dharmas* are impermanent, as they exist just for a very short time in the flux of causality. But since they really exist, even for a very short time, they are said to have an inherent nature (*svabhava*). Secondary existents, such as people, gods, physical objects, and thoughts, are combinations of *dharmas* and thus are called empty (*shunya*) of inherent existence. This is the view of *dharmas* in early Buddhism.

The *Prajnaparamita sutras* and the resulting Madhyamaka school (second century AD) went further in this reasoning by affirming that even *dharmas* cannot have an inherent nature and that perfection of wisdom consists of seeing *everything* empty of inherent existence.[77] To follow the doctrine of impermanence to its natural end requires that we realize that "the ultimate truth is that dharmas too are empty of their own existence."[78] Otherwise the doctrines of impermanence and of no-self would be compromised. In other words, as in early Buddhism the human being is seen as a product of the five aggregates, *dharmas* must also be seen as secondary existents, or products of interaction. Nothing exists in its own right or is causally independent. Not even *nirvana* is causally independent, since it is conditioned by the world of *samsara*. Far from accepting that this position ruins the fundamentals of Buddhism, Nagarjuna argued that "'the emptiness of dharmas' (*dharma-shunyata*) is not a further teaching, but something required by the logic of 'the emptiness of

---

75. Harvey, *Introduction to Buddhism*, 97.

76. Out of the 81 *dharmas* which are conditioned, 52 represent mental phenomena, 28 represent physical phenomena, and one is consciousness (Gethin, *Foundations of Buddhism*, 210).

77. Williams, "Indian Philosophy," in Grayling, *Philosophy 2*, 828.

78. Gethin, *Foundations of Buddhism*, 245.

persons' (*pudgala-shunyata*)."[79] One can thus redefine human beings as "fluxes of empty '*dharmas*,'"[80] instead of constructs of the five aggregates.

The other aspect of Mahayana Buddhism we need to understand is the role of its many Buddhas and bodhisattvas. In early Buddhism the Buddha was seen as a man who discovered and embodied the way to enlightenment and made it known to his disciples. At the time of his death he left them with his teaching and nothing more. Truth itself was the only help they needed to make the journey out of ignorance and suffering. In later writings, such as the *Lotus Sutra*, the Buddha is depicted as teaching his disciples to become Buddhas themselves in order to help ignorant beings progress towards enlightenment. This is the Mahayana new vision of perfection—the ability of anyone to reach Buddhahood.[81] As a result, the traditional founder of Buddhism is just one of the many Buddhas who are helping sentient beings escape from suffering. A similar role is played by beings called bodhisattvas, who are on the way to attaining full Buddhahood.

One example of such a champion of compassion is the Buddha Amitabha (or Amida, in Japanese). To be able to help more effectively the ignorant beings of this world to advance towards enlightenment, Amitabha manifested a "heavenly" domain, called a Pure Land,[82] where his followers could be reborn in order to attain enlightenment more easily. This is not the equivalent of the temporary heavens of early Buddhism, where one collected rewards for earthly merits, consumed them and was reborn. Nor is a Pure Land a kind of permanent afterlife, as dreamed of by the worshippers of Vedic Hinduism, for nothing (including heavens and personal immortality) can be permanent. A Pure Land is a platform for one's further instruction and progress towards true enlightenment. Once reborn in Amitabha's Pure Land, called the Western Paradise (*Sukhavati*), one is able to hear the doctrine and follow it unhindered by illusion and thus to attain enlightenment much more easily than in this world. The ultimate goal is that all beings reach nirvana and cease to experience suffering as personal beings.

---

79. Gethin, *Foundations of Buddhism*, 243. Nagarjuna is the founder of the Madhyamaka school of Mahayana Buddhism, in the second century AD.

80. Harvey, *Introduction to Buddhism*, 121.

81. Gethin, *Foundations of Buddhism*, 228.

82. The devotional form of Buddhism generated by Amitabha worship in Japan is called Pure Land Buddhism.

4.8 PERSON AND PERSONAL IDENTITY IN BUDDHISM

While Hinduism defines the self as an impersonal essence, Buddhism vehemently denies it. For Buddhists the person (*pudgala*) is only a series of impermanent physical and mental processes, an illusion given by the sum of the five aggregates. Consciousness is just one of the aggregates, the fifth, a product of the causal chain generated by the senses. Therefore personal existence is "fulfilled" by discovering its illusory status and achieving its dissolution, once enlightenment is attained. When personal existence is extinguished, no self (or soul) disappears from existence, but only the illusion that there exists such a self. In his discussion with the monk Vacchagotta on the status of the one who attained nirvana, the Buddha explained it by using the illustration of the flame that goes out forever:

> If someone were to ask you, Vaccha: "When that fire before you was extinguished, to which direction did it go: to the east, the west, the north, or the south?"—being asked thus, what would you answer?" "That does not apply, Master Gotama. The fire burned in dependence on its fuel of grass and sticks. When that is used up, if it does not get any more fuel, being without fuel, it is reckoned as extinguished." "So too, Vaccha, the Tathagata has abandoned that material form by which one describing the Tathagata might describe him, he has cut it off at the root, made it like a palm stump, done away with it so that it is no longer subject to future arising.[83]

Striving for preserving personal identity can only sink us deeper into ignorance and alienate us from the right understanding of human nature. There is no point in asking which of the criteria mentioned in chapter 2 would be upheld by a Buddhist philosophy of mind, because the idea of surviving death as a person is itself the problem one has to overcome. The right view on personal identity can be summarized in the following words of Buddhaghosa, a Buddhist master living in the fifth century AD:

> There is suffering, but none who suffers;
> Doing exists although there is no doer.
> Extinction is but no extinguished person;
> Although there is a path, there is no goer.[84]

---

83. *Majjhima-nikaya* 72,19–20, in Nanamoli, *The Middle Length Discourses*, 593.
84. *Visuddhimagga* 16,90, in Buddhaghosa, *The Path of Purification*, 2010.

The leading prayer of this book would sound absurd to Buddhists, or at least would strike a very different chord than for the Vedic worshipper. First of all, prayer (in Mahayana Buddhism) is addressed to Buddhas and bodhisattvas, those beings who postponed their entrance into nirvana for our sake, that we may be dissolved into non-existence. By no means can there be an afterlife as eternal communion with God. Second, the search for immortality is taken as a deception caused by the illusion of a permanent self. Personhood is precisely the darkness from which one must be released, and therefore the journey from darkness to light is the reverse of becoming, from being to non-being, and from life to definitive extinction. In other words, since personal existence is darkness itself (as ignorance), the light that should be sought is the extinction of personhood in nirvana. This weird fulfillment of human nature is the logical outcome of following the fundamental Buddhist assumptions on how things really are.

In the next chapter we will see that although personal existence must be abolished in both Hinduism and Buddhism, one continues to reincarnate as a new human being or in other forms of life due to his or her karma, until final liberation is achieved.

5

Reincarnation and the Survival of Personal Identity

INTEREST IN REINCARNATION IS huge in the West, not only among followers of Eastern religions or New Age enthusiasts, but also among many non-religiously affiliated people who are dissatisfied with the way science responds to the questions of life and the afterlife. In the words of Ian Stevenson, one of the leading figures in researching its proofs, "nearly everyone outside the range of orthodox Christianity, Judaism, Islam, and Science—the last being a secular religion for many persons—believes in reincarnation."[1]

Belief in reincarnation is often the trigger that draws people into a form of New Age spirituality. To think that you have lived many lives before this one and there are countless others ahead in which to attain perfection can be a very reassuring thought. It can give hope that present hardships have meaning, for their origin is in a previous life, and that things will get better in a future life. Such thoughts spark an interest in knowing more about the larger context in which reincarnation is defined and eventually lead to embracing an Eastern religion or a form of New Age spirituality.

Another important reason for the current interest in reincarnation is that it seems to explain the differences between us. Some are famous, rich and healthy, while others are the underdogs of society, starving in slums or suffering from severe disabilities. Some are successful without being religious, while others are constantly marginalized, despite their

---

1. Stevenson, *Children Who Remember*, 26.

religious dedication. All of us have probably had a difficult moment in life when we rhetorically asked, "What have I done to deserve this?" Karma explains it by recourse to things we did in past lives, good or bad, which bear fruit in this life through reincarnation. So it seems to be the perfect way to punish or reward deeds and to make spiritual progress possible through one's own resources.

But is it really "you" who goes through all these lives and reaps the fruits of good or bad deeds? In this chapter we seek to find an answer with the help of philosophy of mind and of what we learned from Hinduism and Buddhism on human nature. The first part details how reincarnation works, as a follow-up to the discussion on human nature in the previous chapter. In the second part we analyze two kinds of proofs for it, which come up in apparently scientific ways. These are cases of people who allegedly remember their past lives under hypnosis, as adults, or spontaneously, as children. The third part examines another kind of argument in favor of reincarnation, the alleged justice it performs by punishing or rewarding the deeds of past lives. In the end we should be able to ascertain to what extent reincarnation can preserve personal identity.

5.1 WHO AND WHAT REINCARNATES, AND HOW?

Reincarnation in Hinduism

As mentioned in section 4.2, the concept of reincarnation first appears in the Upanishads, not earlier than the eighth century BC. Ignorance in realizing our true nature results in the mighty karma taking over our destiny and forcing us into reaping the fruit of our deeds until the whole karmic debt is settled. An important aspect to emphasize here is that reincarnation is not just a way of punishing bad deeds. It works independently of the moral content of our actions and rewards not only bad deeds but also the good ones. *All* our actions must be rewarded and thus fuel karma. The Upanishads argue that those who seek liberation by doing good deeds are still under the spell of ignorance:

> These deluded men, regarding sacrifices and works of merits as most important, do not know any other good. Having enjoyed in the high place of heaven won by good deeds, they enter again this world or a still lower one.[2]

---

2. *Mundaka Upanishad* 1,2,10, in Radhakrishnan, *The Principal Upanishads*, 677.

Doing good deeds is not the right way to avoid reincarnation.[3] The cycle of reincarnation continues until ignorance is defeated and one attains liberation. A practical way in which one can escape clinging to the moral aspect of his or her deeds is offered by the Bhagavad Gita, the masterpiece of Hindu theism.[4] It presents Krishna as the supreme god, who reveals himself to the young warrior Arjuna in a moment of great distress. Arjuna recognizes his relatives and friends in the enemy camp and decides not to fight. At this moment the dialogue with Krishna begins, and the young warrior is told that refraining from action is not a valid solution to avoid the punishment of karma, especially as his duty as a warrior is to fight.[5] The novelty introduced by the Bhagavad Gita is that spiritual perfection is achieved not by refusing to act for fear of karmic retribution, but by acting without a personal interest in the fruit of action. Krishna formulates the famous principle:

> You have a right to perform your prescribed duty, but you are not entitled to the fruits of action. Never consider yourself the cause of the results of your activities, and never be attached to not doing your duty.[6]

Since the karmic effect of an action depends on one's inner motivation, to act without being plagued by the moral content of actions, and thus by the effects of karma, can be achieved by acting with complete detachment from one's personal interest. Dasgupta argues that "the special feature of the *Gita* is it tends to make all actions non-moral by cutting away the bonds that connect an action with its performer."[7] The way one can act without acquiring karma is to act with no interest in personal

---

3. Masao Abe, the apostle of Zen Buddhism in the West, affirms that the same view is valid in Buddhism: "Both good acts and evil acts are regarded, in Buddhism, equally as *evil* acts in the deeper and fundamental sense because both of them are determined not only by external stimuli and internal conscious motives but also by a deeply inner unconscious blind will, and thus bind one to the world of endless life-and-death-transmigration" (Abe, "Kenotic God and Dynamic Sunyata", in Cobb, Jr., *The Emptying God*, 41).

4. The Bhagavad Gita is part of the Mahabharata (vol. VI, chapters 25–42). Of the many translations of the Bhagavad Gita I prefer the one by Prabhupada, *Bhagavad-gita As It Is*, 1983.

5. Krishna says: "Not by merely abstaining from work can one achieve freedom from reaction, nor by renunciation alone can one attain perfection" (Bhagavad Gita 3,4).

6. Bhagavad Gita 2,47.

7. Dasgupta, *A History of Indian Philosophy*, II, 507.

gain, which can be achieved by giving one's actions a religious meaning, that of sacrifices brought to Krishna: "Whatever you do, whatever you eat, whatever you offer or give away, and whatever austerities you perform—do that, O son of Kunti, as an offering to Me."[8]

In the Bhagavad Gita karma and reincarnation are the foundational elements that govern life. Krishna assures Arjuna that the whole world follows the path of karmic retribution and demands that nobody should be bothered by it: "As the embodied soul continuously passes, in this body, from boyhood to youth to old age, the soul similarly passes into another body at death. A sober person is not bewildered by such a change."[9] Arjuna's present existence, as a member of the Pandava family in conflict with the Kaurava family, is just one of the many existences through which karma has carried him. At death one just discards the "old garments" that have fulfilled their role:

> As a person puts on new garments, giving up old ones, the soul similarly accepts new material bodies, giving up the old and useless ones.[10]

In other words, we do not choose our situation in life and the circumstances we face. They are pre-ordained by karma, and only illusion could tell us otherwise. Our response should consist of quietly submitting to these circumstances and acting with detachment from any personal interest.

Once reincarnation was definitively established in Hinduism it was taken over by the non-orthodox religions of India (Buddhism and Jainism), and finally reached the Western world, as we will see later in this section. For our inquiry it is important to understand the mechanism of reincarnation, and what actually travels from one life to the next. We find some details in the *Yoga Sutra*, the fundamental treatise of the Yoga *darshana*.

The five afflictions (*kleshas*), already mentioned in section 4.5, lead to the formation of mental impressions (*samskaras*), that is, individual psychological imprints which are associated with every intentional action. Not every action (for instance walking) has a karmic effect, but only the intentional ones, due to attachment to their fruit. Only these are seeds of karma and require fruition. Since living in ignorance constantly

---

8. Bhagavad Gita 9,27.
9. Bhagavad Gita 2,13.
10. Bhagavad Gita 2,22.

produces attachments, the *samskaras* that keep accumulating form a deposit, called *karmashaya*.[11] In no case can the *karmashaya* be a conscious memory, or information that one can be aware of. This deposit of karma impersonally and mechanically dictates the new birth, the life span, and the experiences that must accompany it.[12]

The Advaita Vedanta philosophy, which is the offspring of Upanishadic thought, adopted the concept of a causal body which is attached to *atman* as long as its bondage lasts. This is the actual carrier of karmic debts, where impressions (*samskara*) imprinted by karma wait as seeds that will generate and prescribe one's future life.

Reincarnation in Buddhism

In Buddhism we speak of rebirth instead of reincarnation because there is no self to reincarnate. Only karma passes from one life to another as a force devoid of ontological substance. In the *Milinda Panha* we find two illustrations to explain it: the flame of an oil-lamp that is lighted from another lamp and the verse that is learned by the pupil from his teacher.[13] Neither the flame nor the verse have a substance of their own and no transfer of substance is involved from one lamp to another or from teacher to pupil. Karma passes from one life to another like a fuel devoid of a permanent self, simply dictating the reenactment of the five aggregates according to mental patterns developed in previous collections of aggregates. To say that a certain *person* is reborn as such and such a being is a mere convention of speech. To the one who thinks in terms of who is reborn, the same individual or another one, H.W. Schumann responds:

> We should not think: '*I* will be reborn,' but rather: 'This chain of rebirths *takes place* according to karma. All the empirical individuals in the chain will have the experience of egohood, but this empirical ego is not a permanent something, a soul, is not identical with previous and subsequent existences.' The ego

---

11. *Yoga Sutra* 2,12.

12. According to Dasgupta, "the karma of the present life thus determines the particular kind of future birth (as this or that animal or man), the period of life (*ayush*) and the painful or pleasurable experiences (*bhoga*) destined for that life" (Dasgupta, *A History of Indian Philosophy*, I, 267–68).

13. *Milinda Panha* 5,5 in Pesala, *The Debate of King Milinda*, 23.

or self is a phenomenon of experience, nothing substantial, not an entity.[14]

After death one can be reborn in one of six possible realms: as a god, a human being, a ghost, an *asura* (an anti-god), an animal, or in a hell. These realms are obviously just temporary destinations, as one will stay in such a realm only as long as the effect of karma lasts. The inferior destinies are the result of letting one's mind be darkened by the three poisons—greed, aversion, and delusion, while higher forms of rebirth are the result of cultivating the opposite states of mind—non-attachment, loving-kindness, and wisdom. The gods have attained their status by cultivating these positive states of mind, but their achievement lasts only for a limited time. Like all other sentient beings, gods are only temporary products of rebirth. They too are ignorant and impermanent, and they suffer.

Since there is no permanent self in human nature, how can Buddhism still formulate continuity between different lives? Their "connectedness" is affirmed by the Buddha as the chain of conditioned arising (Sanskrit: *pratityasamutpada*, Pali: *paticcasamuppada*).[15] It consists of a series of twelve links (*nidanas*), each generating the next without the need of a permanent self. Briefly, the twelve links in causal order are the following: 1) spiritual ignorance (*avijja*)—not knowing how things really are. As a result one develops: 2) mental formations (*samkhara*—the fourth aggregate), which build up: 3) discriminative consciousness (*vinnana*—the fifth aggregate). This is the seed of a new rebirth in which arises: 4) name-and-body (*nama-rupa*—the first aggregate)—the new human being, which is endowed with: 5) six senses (*salayatana*), which open the way for: 6) sensory stimulation (*phassa*), the basis for giving rise to: 7) feeling (*vedana*—the second aggregate)—pleasant, unpleasant, or neutral, which develops into: 8) craving (*tanha*)—the desire to enjoy, prolong, or get rid of the feelings, which develops into: 9) grasping (*upadana*), the courses of action we take in order to get the desired experiences. This leads to: 10) becoming (*bhava*), the continuation of life as a new fetus, 11) birth (*jati*), which leads to: 12) ageing and death (*jaramarana*).

The twelve-link cycle extends over three lives: From ignorance to consciousness (link 1 to 3) we have the origin of one's present existence

---

14. Schumann, *The Historical Buddha*, 140.

15. *Mahanidana Sutta*, in Walshe, *The Long Discourses*, 223–26. See also Gethin, *The Foundations of Buddhism*, 141–42; Harvey, *Introduction to Buddhism*, 54–56; Williams, *Buddhist Thought*, 62–72.

in a past life (through karma); from name-and-body to grasping (link 4 to 9) is represented the present life in which new seeds of karma are produced; and the last three (from becoming to death) belong to a future life. Death is not the end of this causal process. Since ignorance has not been extinguished, the chain of cause and effect starts all over again in an endless cycle until one attains enlightenment.

The proper way of speaking about the preservation of personal identity in Buddhism is that neither the same individual, nor another, is reborn.[16] This formula reminds us of the concept of the Parfitian survivor, which we met in section 2.6. However, rebirth does not allow for *any* psychological continuity from one life to the next. While the Parfitian survivor is aware of his or her identity when exiting the teletransporter, the reborn person (in the happiest case, in human form) does not recognize himself or herself as the continuator of a deceased person. Parfit argues that if it could somehow be proved that a person accurately remembers a previous life and this could be verified, for example a Japanese woman would remember that she was a Celtic hunter two millennia ago, that would prove that the self is a Cartesian ego, and we might think that this kind of self preserves personal identity.[17] However, Parfit concludes that we do not have sufficient reason to believe in either reincarnation or the existence of a Cartesian ego.[18]

Reincarnation in Western Esotericism

The earliest form of belief in reincarnation in the Western world dates back to Pythagoras (sixth century BC). Through Pythagoreanism it reached Plato, who affirmed it in several dialogues, and from Platonism it was adopted by Gnosticism (first and second century AD) and Neoplatonism (third century AD). In the Middle Ages reincarnation was taken up by medieval Gnostic traditions such as the Bogomils and the Cathars, starting in the eleventh and twelfth centuries, but remained a doctrine known only in relatively small circles. About the same time it was adopted by the Judaic mystical tradition known as the Kabbalah. Reincarnation became very popular in the Western world only beginning in the nineteenth century, through the contributions of Theosophy and

---

16. *Milinda Panha* (2,1), in Pesala, *The Debate of King Milinda*, 11.
17. Parfit, *Reasons and Persons*, 227.
18. Parfit, *Reasons and Persons*, 228.

Anthroposophy. Important support was further given by the arrival of religious masters from the East who founded Yoga and Eastern meditation schools, the result being what we call today New Age spirituality. This is the path by which reincarnation came to be such a commonly accepted teaching among Westerners today.

However, the "modern" meaning of reincarnation differs significantly from what Eastern religions teach. Far from being considered an eternal torment which we must evade by the abolition of personhood itself, Western Esotericism sees reincarnation as an eternal progression of the soul toward higher spiritual existences. In other words, it is no longer a punishment, but an unending chance to evolve spiritually. Elisabeth Kübler-Ross, one of the leading promoters of this new meaning of reincarnation, states:

> Once we have passed the tests and learned the lessons and have had all the positive experiences that are possible in the physical life, then there is no more need to reincarnate, and we can proceed to a higher form of existence with new learning experiences and a new growth. (...) We are always given a second, and another chance, and another chance, until all of us are able to graduate, to return to the Source and Creator of all life.[19]

This conceptual revolution is the achievement of two Western esoteric movements: the Theosophical Society, founded by Helena Blavatsky (1831–1891), and co-founders Henry Olcott and William Q. Judge, and the Anthroposophical Society, founded by Rudolf Steiner (1861–1925). As a result of their efforts, of the many Eastern gurus who have since visited and moved to the Western world, and of New Age spirituality, reincarnation has become one of the most popular explanations of the origin and meaning of life. But since in the West the dominant religion was Christianity, the meaning of reincarnation has shifted and, as a result, we hear today that what reincarnates is the soul, which keeps the attributes of personhood from one incarnation to the next. This compromise stems from the need to adapt Eastern teachings to the expectations of Western people, confirming the desire for immortality in personal form, but essentially departing from classical Eastern spirituality. Such "adaptations" of the meaning and mechanism of reincarnation can be found even in the writings of Indian masters who arrived in the West and gained a

---

19. Kübler-Ross, "Foreword," in Head, *Reincarnation*, x. Obviously, she is not referring to a personal Creator of life, but to an impersonal Primordial Source, like the Brahman of Hinduism.

numerous following. For example, the popular guru Sri Chinmoy speaks of a judgment of the soul before a personal God in very appealing terms, but in contradiction with his pantheistic worldview:

> The soul has to stand in front of the Supreme and say how much it has achieved in its past incarnation. It will see the possibilities of its coming incarnation, and make promises to the Supreme. The aims and ideals that the soul expresses for its role in the world of revelation and manifestation have to be approved by the Supreme. Sometimes the Supreme Himself says: "I expect this from you. Try to accomplish it for My sake there on earth.[20]

Steiner, the founder of Anthroposophy and of Waldorf Education, points out that "the two truths of reincarnation and karma," which Anthroposophy has popularized in the Western world, "must pass into the consciousness of men far more deeply than was the case, for example, with the Copernican view of the universe."[21] Reincarnation is no longer a punishment for ignorance or sin, but the way in which the human species evolves towards higher states of consciousness and higher modes of being.[22]

Steiner explains human nature in Hindu terms adapted to Western expectations. In a way that reminds us of the sheaths mentioned by the *Taittiriya Upanishad* (see section 4.2), human nature consists of four bodies: the physical, the etheric, the astral, and the Self. The physical body is kept alive by the etheric body (the equivalent of vital sheath—*pranamaya*). In its turn, the etheric body is kept active and sensitive by the astral body, the equivalent of the mind (*manomaya*). The fourth body is the Ego (or spirit) which, like *atman*, goes through many incarnations according to the law of karma. In Steiner's words, the self "is the intelligent, rational soul. It is the indestructible individuality which can learn to build the other bodies—the 'inexpressible,' the human self and the divine self."[23]

We could mention many other examples of how the meaning of reincarnation is transformed from an eternal curse from which one must escape at any price into a perpetual evolution of the soul towards higher forms of conscious life. However, since it is practically impossible

20. Sri Chinmoy, *The Wisdom of Sri Chinmoy*, 57.

21. Rudolf Steiner, *Reincarnation and Karma*.

22. I have discussed in some detail Steiner's view of human evolution towards attaining the status of a Luciferic being in my book *The Spiritual Dimension of Alternative Medicine*, 35–38.

23. Rudolf Steiner, *Yoga in East and West*. From this lecture we can gain revealing insights into his theory on human nature.

to follow the multitude of spiritual ideas and developments in modern Esotericism, this inquiry is limited to the analysis and evaluation of the classical concept of reincarnation as we find it in Eastern religions.

Reincarnation and the preservation of personal identity

In chapter 4 we saw that the desire to experience personal existence is itself a cause of suffering and reincarnation. There is, however, a modern view that we should affirm the preservation of personal identity through reincarnation, just as physicalists accept it despite complete physical change in a lifetime. Although there is not much visible continuity between the newborn and the adult, either in physical or mental features, yet physicalists affirm the preservation of identity, so should we accept it also in the case of reincarnation despite the radical changes that occur from one life to the next. Here is how Radhakrishnan states it:

> Death may destroy memory of our deeds but not their effects on us. The metaphysical question of the continuity of the self is not in any way affected by the discontinuity of memory. (...) Simply because we do not have a memory of the early phases of our life or of our existence in the mother's body, we do not deny them. Even in this life we forget a great deal.[24]

However, the difference between the two cases is essential. As we saw in chapter 2, between the baby and the adult one can affirm a continuity of identity through its transitions, both in physical aspects and in memory. Although almost all cells have been replaced, there is continuity between the stages of physical and mental development, and in addition there are external witnesses of this identity. In the case of reincarnation, however, the change is total and sudden, even if we only consider the rare instances of reincarnation in human form.[25]

---

24. Radhakrishnan, *An Idealist View of Life*, 237. See also Ducasse, "Objections to Reincarnation Considered", in Head, *Reincarnation*, 7–12.

25. To emphasize how rare reincarnation in human form is, the Buddha uses the illustration of a blind turtle who reaches the surface of the ocean once every hundred years, and accidentally inserts its neck through the hole of a floating yoke. The illustration is given in the *Samyutta Nikaya* 5,56,48 (in Bodhi, *The Connected Discourses*, 1872). If we were to calculate the probability of having a human incarnation according to this illustration, and take as the surface of the ocean merely the surface of India, the probability would be once every 5×10^{16} years (5 followed by 16 zeros). This is five million times the age of the universe.

In the much more probable case of being reincarnated in an animal form of life, the preservation of personal identity gives way to hilarious explanations. On what criteria could one claim continuity between a deceased person and a worm, cat, or cockroach? We might recall here Franz Kafka's "Metamorphosis," in which the main character, Gregor Samsa, wakes up one morning in the body of a huge cockroach. How could human memory and consciousness be accommodated to a cockroach's brain? The real continuity between human life and animal life underlies the moral requirement of *ahimsa*, not to kill any living being. This is the first moral demand in Yoga (*Yoga Sutra* 2,30). Its justification is that among the cockroaches you wiped out could have been your grandmother, who took care of you as a little child. Not only is it immoral to kill any animal, but you will face a similar fate in a further life as a punishment for your deed. This is not just a joke, but a fact of life for one who is consistent with reincarnation.

Following from our discussion in chapter 2, the preservation of personal identity through reincarnation by changing one body with another, according to the illustration given by Krishna in the Bhagavad Gita (2,22), can hardly be accepted. We recall the Robinson/Brown scenario (subsection 2.1.2), in which Robinson awakens from anesthesia with Brown's memories, for he had received Brown's brain, and the mind download scenario (section 2.2), in which Brown awakens in Robinson's body for his (Brown's) mental content has been saved on a hard disk and then loaded into Robinson's brain. In the reincarnation scenario there can be no consciousness of any former identity, for there isn't any element left to carry it from one life to the next. This leads to an *a fortiori* argument against reincarnation which can be formulated as follows: If the two scenarios used by philosophy of mind were not convincing despite the continuity of memory, then even less convincing is the preservation of personal identity through reincarnation, which does not keep any memory continuity with past lives. The true self, the "bearer of garments," who is said to wander through various bodies, cannot be aware of its pilgrimage because the change that occurs from one existence to another is so profound that there is nothing left to provide continuity of consciousness in a new body.

These logical issues of reincarnation should sound a warning bell for its enthusiast followers. Since it is not a conscious core that reincarnates, but the impersonal self, the one punished or rewarded for his or her deeds is not the same person, but another. With each reincarnation another person is generated, unaware of the karmic potential that has to be extinguished.[26] As we saw in chapter 4, personhood itself is a concept without finality in Eastern religions, and thus it is not surprising that there is no interest in preserving personal identity or in researching the criteria that could establish its survival from one incarnation to the next. This interest and the evidence brought in its favor are promoted by *Western* enthusiasts of reincarnation, who claim there is a conscious soul that reincarnates and is perfected from one life to the next.

While analyzing the evidence for such claims in the next section, we must remember that according to the traditional view of reincarnation, nothing—the body, brain, memory, or consciousness, that is, anything that philosophy of mind demands to be preserved for a real continuity of personal identity—can be transferred from one life to the next.

5.2 MODERN EVIDENCE FOR REINCARNATION: HYPNOTIC REGRESSION AND SPONTANEOUS PAST LIFE RECALL BY CHILDREN

One of the serious issues with reincarnation is the fact that we do not remember anything from alleged past lives, nothing that could make us mend our life and stop the vicious cycle generated by karma. In this section we assess the evidence that suggests the contrary, that there actually exist cases of people who remember past lives. These are not just cases of people who have had a *deja vu* experience in a certain circumstance or just dreamed of living in the past. Many of us have had a sense of familiarity with places we have never been, or had intense dreams after watching a film or reading a book. In this section we assess cases of people who provide historical facts about past lives which have been researched and confirmed to a certain degree. They seem to bring convincing proofs in favor of reincarnation, either under hypnosis or spontaneously, in early childhood.

5.2.1 Hypnotic Regression as a Resource for Proving Reincarnation

Hypnosis is defined by the American Psychological Association as "a therapeutic technique in which clinicians make suggestions to individuals

---

26. This topic will be expanded in the third section of this chapter.

who have undergone a procedure designed to relax them and focus their minds."[27] As therapy it is used to treat mental disorders of an individual that originate in the subconscious by identifying the painful events that caused them (especially in childhood) and by transmitting suggestions meant to heal these wounds of the past.

Since we are entering a specialized domain of psychology, some clarifications are needed regarding the meaning of the terms "conscious," "subconscious," and "unconscious." The conscious is the part of our mind that analyzes, compares, desires, and acts on the basis of objective data, apprehended by natural means. Besides things we are aware of, that determine the way we think and act, there are hidden motivations, desires, and fears buried deep down in our mind that produce thoughts and behavior we cannot justify in a rational way. For example, we might categorically refuse a particular dish without realizing why. The real reason may be that we had severe food poisoning in childhood caused by that food. Although we have forgotten that episode, it has remained fixed somewhere in our mind and it causes us an inexplicable reaction in the present. The part of our memory where such episodes are stored is called the subconscious mind and is the seat of mental activity of which we are not conscious. The unconscious refers to the state when consciousness is absent, as a result of an accident, general anesthesia, or in deep sleep. Only in the language of psychoanalysis does it have another meaning, but this is not important for our inquiry. So I will use only the first two terms, conscious and subconscious, the second referring to the mental domain accessed through hypnosis.

Hypnosis became widely known as a method of investigating "past lives" in 1952, when Morey Bernstein, an amateur American hypnotist, practiced his skills on Virginia Tighe, a family friend. Bernstein had the idea of suggesting that Virginia go back in time beyond the date of her birth and describe what she sees and where she is. To everyone's surprise, she suddenly started speaking with a strong Irish accent, claiming that her name was Bridey Murphy, she was born in 1798 and lived near Cork. Among the details she provided about her "past life" were the names of her parents, the name of her school, the date and church where she was married, how she died at the age of 66, and where she was buried. Her descriptions seemed to match life in late nineteenth-century Ireland, and the dramatic way she spoke under hypnosis gave credibility to the whole

---

27. American Psychological Association article at www.apa.org/topics/hypnosis/.

story. After listening to the recordings made under hypnosis, Virginia and her husband accepted the doctrine of reincarnation themselves. The case was published in newspapers and in a best-selling book written by Bernstein himself.[28] It was considered at that time that a "scientific" proof of reincarnation was finally found.[29]

A few years after this episode the historical data produced by Virginia under hypnosis was checked. Reporters sent to Ireland, however, could not confirm anything of her story. Bridey died in 1864, and the Cork City Hall had kept records since 1820. But neither her name nor that of her husband (who allegedly was a lawyer) were found in any civil registry. The suburb in which she claimed to have lived did indeed exist, but no other facts could be confirmed. The church in which she said she was married did not exist, nor its address, nor the priest who married her.

Another search was launched by a competing newspaper[30] which produced even more devastating data for the credibility of the whole story. Although Virginia denied any connection with Ireland, or to have had any contacts among Irish immigrants, in childhood she had lived across the street from a newly arrived lady from Ireland named Bridie Murphy Corkell. Virginia frequently visited this lady and also had an Irish aunt who often told her about life in her native country. A former high school teacher recalled that Virginia was good at literature. At one time she learned a monologue which contained data similar to the story of Bridey Murphy and reproduced it with a strong Irish accent.[31] All this information destroyed the credibility of Virginia's "past life," indicating that the source of all data produced under hypnosis was her subconscious mind. Bridey Murphy really existed. However, she didn't live in Ireland a century before but across the street in Virginia's childhood.

---

28. Bernstein, *The Search for Bridey Murphy*. The story was made into a film of the same name which can be found on YouTube. In this film and in older books, instead of the real name (Virginia Tighe) the pseudonym Ruth Simmons is used. For the real story, see Edwards, *Reincarnation*, 59–79, and Ian Wilson, *Mind Out of Time?*, 64–81.

29. The Bridey Murphy case is not the first, but the most famous of the early cases of hypnotic regression. Before 1950 Alexander Cannon had already produced over a thousand such cases. He published a book in which he discussed his cases (*The Power Within*, 1950). However, none could be confirmed by real historical evidence. Some resembled science fiction, claiming a past life on Venus, where trees are made of metal in order to withstand temperatures of more than 400 °C (Edwards, *Reincarnation*, 82).

30. The *Chicago Daily News* published the original story, and the *Chicago American* was the rival newspaper.

31. Edwards, *Reincarnation*, 65.

Another famous case is that of the Jay family, in which a Methodist pastor hypnotized his wife, Dolores, to heal her of back pain.[32] Suddenly she started answering questions with "Nein" and "Ja" and speaking German. In subsequent sessions, assisted by German speakers, the pastor found out that his wife was speaking of a past life in which she was Gretchen Gottlieb, the daughter of a Catholic mayor. Gretchen said she did not know how to read or write and was very afraid of the persecution against Catholics. This indicated a time of persecution during the Bismarck government in the 1870s. She could not remember anything past the age of 16, when it appears she was killed by a mob while trying to flee the city. In checking the youth of Dolores, no source was found from which she could have learned German. Therefore it was suggested that she was speaking of her experience of a past life.

Closer investigation of this case, however, proved that it also lacked a spectacular explanation. The quality of her German was very poor, and most of the answers were given in few words. Of the 237 words of her German vocabulary, half were similar to English. The pronunciation was far from that of a native German. Since anyone can pick up a few words in German, and since the family in which she grew up was of German origin (which was a later discovery), this case, too, lost its original excitement.[33]

Despite the issues presented by such cases, hypnotic regression became very popular for discovering past lives. Countless hypnotists, both professionals and amateurs, made a career out of this new business, being ready to help anyone curious to find out his or her (very) distant past. The psychological states displayed by the subjects of hypnosis are dramatic: they see themselves in a different body, speak in a different voice, display unnatural facial expressions, and manifest unknown talents. In some cases real wounds appear on the body according to the scenario they recount. All the information about the "past life" is obtained through a dialogue initiated by the hypnotist, in which the client is asked to go back in time beyond the date of birth and describe what he or she sees.

Given the requirement that clients fully comply with the hypnotist's suggestions, we find a huge methodological flaw in discovering "past lives" through hypnosis. In hypnotherapy the receptivity of the patient to the suggestions received from the hypnotist is an essential element for its success; thus when some real information from the client's "past lives"

32. Wilson, *Reincarnation?*, 82.
33. Wilson, *Reincarnation?*, 99.

is expected, the hypnotist's suggestive capacity compromises the reliability of the information produced by the client. The hypnotist expects a confirmation of a personal belief in reincarnation, so he or she not only transmits suggestions for relaxation, but also the expectation that a past life will be found. This expectation is explicitly stated to the client before the hypnotic regression. Here, for example, is what one master of hypnotic regression teaches to new practitioners to help them discover the alleged past lives of their clients:

> At the time of your first meeting with the client it is imperative to establish their goals and your objectives for a solid afterlife experience. The most effective sessions are those where your client knows in advance the step-by-step procedure you will use. This takes nothing away from the mystery and awe of the LBL (life between lives) experience. I explain that our association will be a partnership where the two of us are going to take a journey together into the spirit world.[34]

This master of past life regression not only believes in reincarnation, but also manifests a larger interest in Eastern thought and the world of spirits:

> I find daily meditation and controlled breathing to be helpful in my LBL practice. In yoga, *prana* refers to the life force or energy that is manifested in each of us through our breath. As a spiritual regressionist, I manipulate my breathing at times during a session in an attempt to extend my mind into a higher state of consciousness. I may even enter into a self-induced light trance state to be more open to the spiritual forces I feel around me.[35]

As Wilson points out, the client of past life regression feels compelled to respond to the hypnotist's suggestions and produce a convincing scenario.[36] Thus hypnotic regression does not investigate *if* real past lives exist but is a method by which it is suggested to clients that they certainly had past lives and that the time has come to tell their story.

A bizarre aspect of past life regression which should raise further doubts about its reliability is that it can be used as a method for exploring not just past lives but also future lives! Interestingly enough, these are not from the near future, that is, verifiable by the next generation, but

---

34. Newton, *Life Between Lives*, 17.
35. Newton, *Life Between Lives*, 12.
36. Wilson, *Mind Out of Time?*, 182.

from the distant future, at least a hundred years away.[37] Helen Wambach, one of the enthusiasts of researching the future by means of hypnosis, obtained in the 1980s scenarios following a nuclear war (the great fear of those years) and of worlds similar to the popular (at that time) Star Trek series. Unfortunately, as Edwards points out, these testimonies from the "future" do not help us discover anything important for us, those living in the present, such as a treatment for an (incurable) disease.[38]

Another concern for the enthusiasts of hypnotic regression should be that the information retrieved from "past lives" is dependent on the existing historical knowledge at the time of the regression. Several such cases are discussed in Ian Wilson's book, *Reincarnation?*.[39] One presents itself as a person who lived during the reign of Pharaoh Ramesses III. Instead of mentioning the name used at that time for the Pharaoh's capital (which according to more recent discoveries was Waset), the "Egyptian" used the name Thebes, given by the Greeks much later. In addition, in ancient Egypt the names of the pharaohs were not accompanied by ordinal numbers. Ramesses III is a name given by Egyptologists only as late as the nineteenth century. How could the person speaking from ancient Egypt adapt its "testimony" to the language and historical knowledge of today? Wambach cites a case in which the recalled person claimed to live in 2083 BC.[40] How did she know, then and there, this use of chronology? In some cases, although the information produced by clients is in line with known historical facts, subsequent discoveries contradict it. For instance, a personality recounted a Viking invasion in North America in the eleventh century AD.[41] In this story the Vikings wore horned helmets. Although this is common knowledge to many, it has been discovered that Vikings never used such helmets in battle, but only in religious rituals. In battle they used conical helmets. Strangely, the knowledge of the person subjected to hypnotic regression conditioned the message of the supposed person living ten centuries ago. These facts suggest that the information from "past lives" depends on those of the person subjected to hypnotic regression, and thus cannot be trusted.

37. Edwards, *Reincarnation*, 89–92.
38. Edwards, *Reincarnation*, 91.
39. Wilson, *Reincarnation?*, 88–90.
40. Albrecht, *Reincarnation*, 56.
41. Wilson, *Reincarnation?*, 89.

The most probable explanation of the stories recollected under hypnosis seems to be cryptomnesia, which is "an implicit memory phenomenon in which people mistakenly believe that a current thought or idea is a product of their own creation when, in fact, they have encountered it previously and then forgotten it."[42] Since hypnosis can be used to revive long-forgotten information of one's own experience, it can also be a way of retrieving information acquired from other people, read in books, or seen in films, in which the client sees himself or herself as personally involved. The ability to differentiate between one's own experiences and those of others is lost, and thus it is wrongly assumed that the information produced under hypnosis belongs to a client's past life. The source of information can rather be found in the present life, as when using hypnosis as a method of therapy for present problems. In fact, if during hypnosis clients are asked to reveal the source of data from "past lives" they will easily do so by pointing to sources from the present life: a book, a film, a conversation, etc. This fact was demonstrated by the Finnish psychiatrist Reima Kampman.[43] If the person who recounted past lives is again hypnotized, and is not asked to return to "past lives," but to indicate the source of information about the characters mentioned in an earlier session, he or she will indicate the source as a book, a film, or a conversation.[44] In this way, each "past life" has been identified in sources that date from the present life.[45]

Kampman also found a connection between past life regression through hypnosis and a psychiatric disorder called multiple personality, which manifests in the pathology of schizophrenia.[46] Patients with this problem can change to up to twenty distinct personalities over a short period of time, as if playing successive roles in different plays.[47] These personalities have different characters, behavioral patterns and voices, and possibly the other sex from the real person. Usually one of the personalities knows and observes the activities and even the thoughts of the

---

42. American Psychological Association article at https://dictionary.apa.org/cryptomnesia.

43. Wilson, *Mind Out of Time?*, 127–32.

44. Wilson, *Mind Out of Time?*, 130.

45. Wilson gives as example a famous case in which the person of "a past life" turned out to be inspired from the novel *Countess Maud*, by Emily Holt (Wilson, *Mind Out of Time?*, 122–25).

46. Kampman, "Hypnotically Induced Multiple Personality."

47. Wilson, *Reincarnation?*, 122–38.

others, being able to speak on behalf of all.[48] According to Kampman, the persons evoked from past lives under hypnosis would be the result of inducing the multiple personality phenomenon by hypnosis.

In conclusion, the stories produced under hypnosis do not correspond to real past lives. All the information revealed under hypnosis comes from one's own mind and is acquired in this life. Although stories of past lives seem dramatic, they are convincing only for those who already believe in reincarnation and are not willing to consider their devastating flaws. The next kind of past life recall experience seems more convincing.

5.2.2 Spontaneous Past Life Recall by Children

Other testimonies that seem to demonstrate reincarnation are cases in which "past lives" are spontaneously remembered by children two to six years old.[49] There have been hundreds of cases documented in which children start speaking about places, people, and events of a "past life," providing details that they could not have known by natural means. When conducting investigations on the spot many details prove to be correct, surprising both the natural family of the child and the one referred to in the story as the family to which the child belonged in the alleged past life. Some have birth marks that resemble the scars of the dead person whose identity they claim to inherit, and most "remember" they had a violent death. After the age of six the memories begin to fade, and after the age of ten most do not remember anything of their "past lives."

Although cases of "spontaneous recall" of past lives are rarer than those of hypnotic regression they seem more convincing. They have become famous as a result of the research conducted by Ian Stevenson, a professor of psychiatry at Virginia State University. His investigations carried him across the world over several decades, and the book that made him famous, *Twenty Cases Suggestive of Reincarnation*, is a reference book in the study of this phenomenon. Most cases he studied occurred in India and Sri Lanka. In North America, they appear mainly

---

48. Wilson, *Reincarnation?*, 121.

49. There also exist cases of adults remembering "past lives," but the details are very poor and unconvincing. For example, Annie Besant, an important figure in Theosophy, "remembered animating the mineral world, ascending to the vegetable kingdom, eventually becoming a monkey." She reached a human existence 600,000 years ago, and then reincarnated as a human being more than fifty times (Edwards, *Reincarnation*, 101).

in Alaska, among the Tlingit population. In Turkey and Lebanon such stories appear among the Druze population, and in the Western world in families who already believe in reincarnation. The cases reported in the East are always richer in details and more convincing than Western cases.

A spectacular case is Shanti Devi, a girl born in 1926 in Delhi.[50] When she was three years old she started talking about a previous life she lived in Mathura, a village about 130 kilometers away. She claimed she was born in 1902, that her name is Lugdi and belongs to a higher caste. In her "past life" she had married a merchant named Kedar Nath Chaubey and died ten days after the birth of their son. Since she insisted on these claims the parents wrote a letter to the alleged former husband in Mathura. Surprisingly, Kedar responded, confirming all those facts. Later, he visited the girl's family incognito but was immediately identified as her former husband. The following year the family made a trip to Mathura accompanied by a committee meant to verify the information provided by Shanti Devi. Although the girl had never left Delhi, she recognized people and places in Mathura. In the train station she recognized a relative of Kedar in the crowd and indicated the correct way to her "former home." There she recognized her "former" father-in-law and seemed to be familiar with the house. As a last detail, she said she had buried some money in a corner of the house, and Kedar admitted he found the money after the death of his wife.

Although cases reported in the West are rarer and poorer in details, there still exist some interesting ones. One famous case is that of the Pollock family, from England.[51] They lost both their daughters in a car accident in 1957 (Joanna, 11, and Jacqueline, 6). John Pollock, the father, was a firm believer in reincarnation, although he was a Catholic, and expected that God would prove him right. After his daughters died, his wife became pregnant, and John told her he was sure they would have twin girls who would be the reincarnation of the two daughters they had lost in the accident. To everyone's surprise, she gave birth to twin girls. Moreover, she identified a birth mark on the forehead of one baby similar to the one Jacqueline had, following a bicycle accident, as well as another body mark on the hip. What particularly shocked the mother, who at that time did not believe in reincarnation, was the fact that around the age of three they began to behave as if they had the memories of their deceased sisters. They

---

50. Stevenson, "The Evidence for Survival from Claimed Memories of Former Reincarnations," 51–71.

51. Wilson, *Mind Out of Time?*, 19–28.

recognized places in the town where their sisters grew up, "remembered" episodes of their life there, recognized their toys, and even had panic attacks as if they were reliving the car accident. After the age of five the memories began to fade away and the girls lost their strange behavior.

One case presented by Stevenson as proof of reincarnation reveals a compromising element. In the spring of 1954, an Indian boy by the name of Jasbir, aged three and a half, became ill with smallpox and fell into a coma. His parents thought he died.[52] Several hours later he woke up and after a few weeks he was completely healed. Strangely, after this illness he acquired a completely different behavior. He claimed to be Sobha Ram, a member of the Brahmin caste, who died from an accident at the age of 22 (while Jasbir was ill). He had a different voice, that of the allegedly reincarnated Brahmin, he used new words and refused to sit at meals with his family for the reason that they belonged to a lower caste. The family had to prepare his food according to the requirements for the Brahmin caste, otherwise he refused to eat. In a visit to the alleged home from his past life he recognized his "relatives," expressing his determination to stay with them. He seemed attached especially to his "son" from the past life. Asked what happened after his death as Sobha, he said that in the state between death and reincarnation he met a *sadhu* (a Hindu ascetic) who advised him to take shelter in Jasbir's body.[53] What is disturbing in this case is that "reincarnation" took place when Jasbir was already three and a half years old.

A similar case was reported in the West, that of a 13-year-old girl, Lurancy Vennum, in 1877. For several months her personality was replaced by one named Mary Roff, who claimed to have died when Lurancy was one year old. This personality completely replaced that of Lurancy, stating this fact openly. After a few months of torment for the whole family, Mary Roff withdrew and Lurancy returned to normal.[54]

How can we explain such cases? Stevenson affirms they can hardly be taken as willful fraud in order to gain material benefits.[55] Although

52. Stevenson, *Twenty Cases*, 34–52.
53. Stevenson, *Twenty Cases*, 47.
54. Stevenson, *Twenty Cases*, 375.
55. There are a few cases in which we could speak about deliberate fraud. One is related to the child Jagdish Chandra, who at the age of three started remembering that he is Jai Gopal, and that he lived in Benares (today's Varanasi), in that particular family, house, etc. The case is so poorly documented that Jagdish's father may have fueled the whole story. He had relatives in Benares, he probably knew about the deceased,

they were widely publicized and the families became famous, they did not intend it. One can sense a desire for a better life by these children, but they are too young to play the role of an impostor so well. Nor can cryptomnesia be an explanation because they did not know the previous family, and information circulated very slowly at that time in rural India or other parts of the East.

The hypothesis that the children could be sick with schizophrenia and that their "memories" could be the result of this mental disorder cannot be a valid explanation either because schizophrenia would manifest also in later stages of life. Stevenson indicates that only three out of eighteen cases developed psychiatric disorders later in life, but without a clear link to childhood memories.[56] In addition, episodes of personality disorder in schizophrenia do not produce reliable information about other people, places, and events.

Why do children lose their memories after the age of six? Stevenson argues that they forget as they start school, lose family ties, and enter new relationships.[57] The new information they accumulate erases these "memories." Only in rare cases do vague memories remain until the age of twenty. However, their recollection may be because they have often been asked to retell the story, or because they have stayed in touch with the "former" family.[58]

Although the testimonies produced by children about past lives are spectacular, their credibility is affected by a number of methodological issues in the way they have been recorded. Of the twenty cases in Stevenson's book, only seven were recorded *before* the child went to his or her "former house," and these seven cases were recorded by family members. The veracity of the "memories" could be compromised by being "enriched" following the dialogue between the two families.[59] Most of the investigations conducted by Stevenson were made many years after the occurrence, when the child no longer remembered anything, so the stories were reconstructed through the testimonies of family members.

---

and once his child began to make strange statements about a previous life, he probably presented him the convincing details about Jai Gopal. This is another case in which "reincarnation" took place after birth. The case is presented in Edwards, *Reincarnation*, 256–58.

56. Stevenson, *Twenty Cases*, 322–23.
57. Stevenson, *Twenty Cases*, 324.
58. Stevenson, *Twenty Cases*, 326–28.
59. Edwards, *Reincarnation*, 260.

For example, in the case of the Pollock sisters the case was investigated as late as 1979, fifteen years after the actual events, and the original testimonies were recorded only by the parents, with the father being very eager to find in the twin babies a confirmation of the reincarnation of his two deceased girls. And the Shanti Devi case was recorded after thirty years.

Ian Wilson, a critic of this type of argument for reincarnation, points out a statistical issue. Since the majority of the population in India and Sri Lanka is very poor, it would be expected that most of the testimonies from "previous lives" would be about cases of poor people. However, the statistics show the opposite. Most of the "reincarnated" people come from wealthy families, or at least have a higher social status than those in which they reincarnated.[60] Among the cases published by Stevenson there is only one in which the child "remembered" that he belonged to a poor family.

As mentioned above, the testimonies are influenced by the religious environment in which children live. This is probably the reason why there are few such cases in the Western world. While in India most people believe in reincarnation, Westerners are more skeptical about it (or at least were more skeptical in the 1970s and 1980s) and are more attentive to details, so the cases would have been checked more carefully. Another problem concerns the translators used by Stevenson. Most of the people he investigated did not speak English, and his translators were ardent believers in reincarnation. For example, Jamuna Prasad was a Hindu with a declared wish to popularize reincarnation among Westerners,[61] while H.N. Banerjee was active as a hypnotist who helped his clients "remember" past lives under hypnosis.[62]

5.2.3 Alternative Explanations for Past Life Recall by Children

We can apply here our discussion on the criteria for the preservation of personal identity in chapter 2 and raise two objections to these cases as evidence for reincarnation. First, we recall from section 2.3 that memory by itself is not a sufficient criterion to prove the preservation of personal identity. As Butler argued three centuries ago, the preservation of memory *presupposes* personal continuity and thus does not prove it. In the

---

60. Wilson, *Mind Out of Time?*, 58–59.
61. Wilson, *Mind Out of Time?*, 57.
62. Edwards, *Reincarnation*, 84–85.

case of past life recall by children we would need an external reference independent of them to establish that the child with "past life memories" is the same person as the deceased. Their identity cannot be established merely by conformity of *information* presented by the child on the one hand, and the family of the deceased on the other, but must be a continuity of identity, as in the stages of development of a certain person from child to adult. In other words, the veracity of the information presented about the person of the "past life" is not enough to establish its identity with the present child. No matter how much information I might be able to present about a person who lived in the past, and how much I might insist that I am that person, it would not prove my identity with her. In past life recall the external authority which operates tacitly in all cases is belief in reincarnation. In other words, these children's testimonies are accepted as evidence of reincarnation because Stevenson himself, his witnesses and translators all believe in reincarnation. We thus face a circular argument. These cases demonstrate reincarnation only for those who already believe in it.

Second, also related to the problems of the memory criterion for the preservation of personal identity, we can apply the experiment imagined by Williams in section 2.3. Of the six stages he uses to argue that the preservation of memory is not enough to preserve personal identity, we can apply to the cases of past life recall by children only the first four (because person B has died). A corresponds to the child and B to the person "reincarnated" as A. The four stages are the following:

1. Person A suffers a medical intervention which results in losing her memory;
2. Not only does A lose her memory, but she undergoes changes in her character traits;
3. As above; in addition false memories are implanted to A which do not match those of a real person;
4. As above, except that the memories implanted to A correspond to those of a real person, B.

According to Williams's discussion, these stages do not present sufficient discontinuity to consider that A has become B. In past life recall stories person B has died, and person A (the child) has only part of B's memories. Following an *a fortiori* kind of reasoning, if we cannot affirm that stages 1–4 can be taken as a transformation of B into A even if a *complete* set of memories is transferred from B to A, then even less can we affirm that B has been reincarnated as A since A has just *some* of B's memories.

What other resources do we have to explain what happens in these cases? From a physicalist point of view they must be considered fraud, but this option cannot explain the veracity of the information produced by these children. Wilson acknowledges that something important is missing in any physicalist interpretation of these cases. Referring to the Pollock sisters he admits that "something not yet within the understanding of twentieth-century science would seem to be at work."[63] In the rest of this section, then, we explore an explanation that escapes the boundaries of physicalism and would be relevant only for dualists.

Although he may be regarded by reincarnation enthusiasts as a new Galileo who has proved it scientifically, Stevenson himself does not consider his studies to be unequivocal proofs for reincarnation. As the title of his book indicates, these cases only "suggest" reincarnation. In his words, "the claim of a memory of a previous life by itself tells us nothing about veridicality. And if the claim of a memory accompanies evidence of authenticity and veridicality, this experience alone cannot distinguish extrasensory perception from a "true" memory of a previous life."[64]

The way Stevenson initially attempted to explain the memories of these children is called "extrasensory perception and personation."[65] It suggests that a subject obtains information about another person "through extrasensory perception and that he integrates this information and personates it so thoroughly that he comes to believe he and that person are the same and convinces others of this identity also."[66] The way in which the information is transmitted would be the telepathic connection that the child has with certain persons among the relatives or close acquaintances of the deceased.[67] For example, in the case of Shanti Devi, Stevenson assumes that there existed such a telepathic connection between the girl and her "former father." What escaped the initial investigation was that this "former father" often came to Delhi to a shop in Shanti Devi's close neighborhood, where she probably met him on her

63. Wilson, *Mind Out of Time?*, 247
64. Stevenson, *Twenty Cases*, 353.
65. Stevenson, *Twenty Cases*, 344.
66 Stevenson, *Twenty Cases*, 344.
67. Stevenson, *Twenty Cases*, 344–45. In some cases the parents knew or had heard of the "previous family" of their child (Stevenson, *Twenty Cases*, 334).

way to school. Stevenson assumes that their telepathic connection would have been established there.[68]

However, this theory is not satisfactory because it does not explain why the child initiated these stories and recounted them so dramatically in such a convincing way. Stevenson admits that "extrasensory perception and personation" could explain only cases with poorer details and thus is not convincing.[69]

After an extensive analysis of these cases, Stevenson concluded that there could be only two possible ways to explain them. One is reincarnation, and the other is the possession of these children by spirits, as in cases of mediumism. As a parapsychologist,[70] Stevenson affirms that possession is "either a partial influence with the primary personality continuing to retain some control of the physical body, or a temporary (if apparently complete) control of the physical organism with later return of the original personality."[71] The hypothesis of possession would be backed by the fact that children usually tell their stories of past lives at the age when their discernment is almost non-existent, especially in the spiritual realm, which opens up the possibility that they could be easily deceived by spirits. As personal identity matures the spirits lose their grip over the child, which could explain the loss of "memories" by the age of ten. The argument against this hypothesis is the assumption that these spirits have no reason to deceive us about their true identity. In other words, they would have no reason to introduce themselves as human personalities coming from a past life, instead of non-physical, non-human spirits.[72]

Stevenson affirms that we can observe a gradual transition from cases that can be explained as possession, to those that can more readily be explained as reincarnation. Cases like Lurancy Vennum/Mary Roff seem to be clear cases of possession.[73] The personality of Mary Roff completely replaced that of Lurancy Vennum for five months. Throughout that period there was no claim of continuity, and Mary Roff openly stated that she took over the body of Lurancy when she was 15 months old. This case

---

68. Stevenson, *Twenty Cases*, 345

69. Stevenson, *Twenty Cases*, 373.

70. Stevenson worked as a psychiatrist at the University of Virginia School of Medicine and was also the founder and director of the university's Division of Perceptual Studies, which investigates paranormal phenomena.

71. Stevenson, *Twenty Cases*, 374.

72. Stevenson, *Twenty Cases*, 380.

73. Stevenson, *Twenty Cases*, 375.

cannot be interpreted as reincarnation. The same is true of the Jasbir/
Sobha Ram case. There are other such cases in which Stevenson noticed
a possession that took place after birth and lasted between one day and
several weeks, and cases in which the possession (or reincarnation) occurred sometime between conception and birth.[74] Finally we have the
most convincing cases for reincarnation, in which there is no temporal
overlap between the two lives, and the details evoked from the "past life"
are quite rich. In Stevenson's words, "if the previous personality seems to
associate itself with the physical organism at the time of conception or
during embryonic development we speak of reincarnation; if the association between previous personality and physical organism only comes
later, we speak of possession."[75]

However, it is not clear why we cannot consider the "evident" cases
of reincarnation to be cases of possession as well. Is it just because the
death of the person who claims to be reincarnated took place before the
conception of the child? Possession, defined as the entry of a non-physical
spirit into the body of a living person, can be at work even if there exists
a time gap between the two lives. A clue that many more reincarnation
cases can be understood as possessions is that some people involved in
spiritualistic practices announce their further reincarnation to a family
while they are expecting a child or even before the mother is pregnant,
and there are even cases when spirits ask parents for permission to enter
the body of their child.[76] Stevenson remembers from his cases:

> In many cases, someone connected with the (future) subject has
> a dream in which a deceased person appears to the dreamer and
> indicates his wish or intention to reincarnate. The dreamer is
> usually a married woman and a potential mother for the next
> incarnation of the person who is to be reborn. Sometimes the
> woman's husband, another relative, or a friend may have a
> dream of this type. I call these dreams "announcing dreams"
> because they occur, with a few rare exceptions, before the birth,
> and sometimes before the conception, of the subject.[77]

Possession is a possibility known in Hinduism as *parkaya pravesh*,
which means entering another person's body in order to control it. Sri

---

74. Stevenson, *Twenty Cases*, 376. Four such cases are mentioned in Wilson, *Mind Out of Time?*, 54.

75. Stevenson, *Twenty Cases*, 376.

76. Stevenson, *Children Who Remember*, 99–101.

77. Stevenson, *Children Who Remember*, 99.

Chinmoy, the famous Indian guru (who does not accept that past life recall by children would be a proof of reincarnation), uses the possession of his disciples' bodies as a teaching method to prove to them that they have lived previous lives: "If someone asked me to convince him that he had previous lives, even if that individual did not believe in reincarnation, I would be able to prove it to him. I would ask that individual to meditate with me for a few minutes and I would enter into him and bring to the fore his immediate past incarnation."[78] In the *Yoga Sutra* possession is mentioned as the entry of one's mind into the body of another person.[79] It is one of the supernatural powers (*siddhis*) acquired by yogis in meditation.

Finally, the only reason left for Stevenson to interpret children's stories as proof of reincarnation instead of possession is the presence of birth marks identical to the scars of the deceased. In his view, they cannot be explained by a possession scenario because they appear on the body before birth.[80] Stevenson mentions a case among the Tlingit Indians of Alaska in which an old man explicitly told his niece that he would reincarnate as her child, showing her his scars in order that she might believe him when it happens. The child, Corliss Chotkin, Jr., had exactly those marks on his body and then recalled episodes from the old man's life, presenting himself as his reincarnated uncle.[81]

However, Lynn de Silva, a Sri Lankan analyst of these cases, argues that not even birth marks can be taken as a certain proof of reincarnation. This author argues that they can occur through psychological induction, for example, as a result of the mother's fear for her child. He describes a case in which the mother feared that her (still unborn) child would get smallpox. At birth he had red spots on his forehead similar to smallpox spots, but without having the actual disease.[82] In another case, the mother was afraid that the bullet wounds that caused her husband's death might manifest on the body of her child. Despite assurances from doctors that such fears are absurd, the marks appeared according to her fears, in

---

78. Chinmoy, *The Wisdom of Sri Chinmoy*, 268–69.
79. *Yoga Sutra* (3,37), in Patanjali, *Yoga Sutras*, 237.
80. Stevenson, *Twenty Cases*, 374, 382.
81. Stevenson, *Twenty Cases*, 259–69.
82. Silva, *Reincarnation in Buddhist and Christian Thought*, 27.

the exact spots the bullets pierced her husband's body.[83] However, these were not interpreted as proof of the father's reincarnation.

A master of Hindu meditation and one who believed in reincarnation, Sri Somasundara Desika Paramachariya, wrote an open letter to Stevenson concerning his investigations, stating that all the 300 cases he had investigated to that point were possession cases. Given that most "reincarnated" people had a violent death, the Hindu master argued that the subtle body of these people is "capable of possessing suitable living persons, not known to them previously, and narrate through them their life history and even point out in cases of homicide where their physical bodies were hidden or buried. (. . .) They (these cases) are all spirit possessions, ignored by the learned in South India."[84] The Indian philosopher C.T.K. Chari also considered possession to be the right theory to explain the details produced by the children investigated by Stevenson.[85]

Hindu scholars cannot accept the evidence collected by Stevenson, nor the stories of past life recall produced under hypnosis, as proofs for reincarnation for doctrinal reasons. According to the *Yoga Sutra* 3,18, the capacity to retrieve details from a past life is one of the supernatural powers (*siddhis*) acquired in meditation, of which only advanced yogis are capable. What they allegedly can visualize in meditation are the *samskaras* which manifest in a certain lifetime. For this reason meditation masters reject the idea that past lives can be spontaneously remembered by children. As we saw in section 5.1, memory cannot be transferred from one life to another. The causal body does not preserve a conscious memory of past lives, but a series of mental impressions that dictate the birth, the life span, and the experiences that will accompany it, according to the law of karma.

Another aspect that should raise a red flag is that the stories told by those who "remember" past lives, both through hypnosis and spontaneously, are not centered on karmic justification, that is, they do not point out what needs to be corrected in the present life in order to avoid further reincarnations. They only create a sensationalist aura, to amaze us and convince us that past lives really exist. In other words, they are just for show.

---

83. Silva, *Reincarnation*, 27.
84. Silva, *Reincarnation*, 49.
85. Edwards, *Reincarnation*, 262.

Traditional followers of Eastern religions do not consider hypnotic regression and spontaneous past life recall by children as evidence for reincarnation. These publicity stunts are accepted and defended in the West partly as a result of misunderstanding basic Eastern beliefs, and partly due to a general Western trend in which religious beliefs have come to depend less on traditional Eastern religions and lean more on direct personal experiences and paranormal research. As mentioned in section 5.1, Westerners no longer consider reincarnation as a burden which we must escape at any price, even by giving up personal identity itself, but instead take it as an eternal evolution of the soul towards higher states of being. The main argument for reincarnation in the East is the topic of the next section.

5.3 REINCARNATION AS BEARER OF UNIVERSAL JUSTICE

The survival of personal identity and the retribution of evil through reincarnation are two closely related topics. They stand or fall together, so in this section we explore the first through investigating the meaning of the second.

We have probably all asked ourselves why is there so much injustice and suffering in the world, especially among children. Why are some born healthy and others with severe disabilities? Why do children die of hunger, cancer, or natural calamities? Why are good people hit by misfortune while others enjoy peace and prosperity even though they are evil and corrupt? The answer is simple for those who accept reincarnation: Everyone is punished or justly rewarded for his or her deeds in past lives. To be more precise and consistent with karma we should rather say that we are punished *by* our deeds, not *for* our deeds, for otherwise we are implying there is a personal judge above karma who dispenses punishments and rewards. But karma does not leave space for a divine judge, for it is the ultimate judge itself.

Here is how Swami Sivananda, the founder of The Divine Life Society, explains the reasons why we should accept karma and reincarnation:

> The doctrine of Karma only can bring solace, contentment and strength to the afflicted and the desperate. It solves our difficulties and problems of life. It gives encouragement to the hopeless and the forlorn. It pushes a man to right thinking, right

speech and right action. (. . .) There will not be any room for complaint when they (the people believing in reincarnation) see inequalities in birth, fortune, intelligence and capacities. There will be heaven on earth. All will rejoice even in suffering. Greed, jealousy, hatred, anger and passion will vanish. Virtue will reign supreme everywhere.[86]

In Sivananda's view, this "heaven on earth" could be realized because karma answers all questions concerning present injustice, and thus reincarnation should be seen as the ultimate solution to our anxieties. However, if we really understand how reincarnation works we see at least two major issues with this reasoning. One is that consciousness and personal identity do not survive from one life to another, and so it is not possible to reward or punish a person for the good or the evil he or she has done in past lives. The other problem is the impossibility of explaining how the whole cycle started and how it could end.[87] Let us take a closer look at these two issues.

Justice makes sense only if the perpetrator of the crime, not another person, is punished, and if that person was conscious and responsible for it. This is why the mental incapacity defense can be used in court by claiming that the perpetrator was not responsible for his or her deeds due to some mental deficiency. As for dispensing justice through reincarnation, since consciousness ceases at death, the person who reincarnates is completely unaware of her deeds in past lives, which runs contrary to what we would expect from perfect justice. As we remember from the first section of this chapter, what reincarnates is the self (*atman* or *purusha*) accompanied by the causal body, not some form of consciousness. One's mental life is only a temporarily construct associated with the self, which is lost at death. If one attains liberation personal existence ceases forever; if not, the self enters into a new form of life according to karma, until all the karmic debt produced by ignorance is consumed. When the self enters a new personal existence, a new person is born, without any continuity of consciousness or memory with the deceased, and this new person will experience the karmic effects produced by the *samskaras* accumulated in previous existences. In other words, another person bears the karma of one who ceased to exist.

---

86. Sivananda, *Practice of Karma Yoga*, 105–6.

87. These two arguments have been adapted from Mark Albrecht's *Reincarnation*, 90.

The second objection raises doubts as to whether one's karmic debt will ever be paid. The person who is "paying" the karmic debt of former lives should do it without complaining, as Sivananda demands. However, it is more likely that instead of "rejoicing even in suffering" he or she will revolt against the injustice faced and will accumulate a bigger karmic debt. Think of the child who is punished after he has forgotten the deed for which he deserves punishment. If we do not know why karma is punishing us, it is unlikely that we will patiently resign ourselves to its operation and reach the age of "heaven on earth" that Sivananda speaks of. A harsh and hostile environment would more likely trigger the formation of a greater karmic debt.

These two objections become clearer if we imagine a real person with a huge karmic debt. Let us consider a terrorist like Osama bin Laden. Followers of reincarnation will assume that many reincarnations will be needed to consume his karma. The alleged child who is born as bin Laden's reincarnation must face the consequences of his deeds and live an extremely miserable life, with all kinds of atrocities done to him. The two objections applied to this case would work as following:

1) Osama bin Laden's consciousness ceased to exist in 2011, and the self accompanied by the causal body (the bearer of karmic debt) is reincarnated. Let us imagine he is a Christian boy living in a village facing hardships inflicted by Al-Qaeda. Between the former terrorist and this boy there is no continuity in consciousness or memory. The new person does not know that he has to endure all his hardships as a result of bin Laden's karma. After a death as wretched as his life, many other such lives must follow in which other persons will continue to pay bin Laden's karma. The absurd thing is that Al-Qaeda's former leader, the only one who should have suffered these hardships as consequence of his acts, disappeared at his physical death, while other innocent people will suffer in his stead.

2) As a result of the oppression endured by the persons who pay for bin Laden's karma, they are more likely to rebel against their fate and accumulate an increasing karmic debt. Each one of these persons becomes a source of additional karmic debt, initiating a new set of *samskaras* that will bear fruit in future lives. The same thing happened in the case of bin Laden himself. Whoever he was in a previous life, he complicated his karma greatly while being Al-Qaeda's leader. Instead of karma being extinguished, it increased exponentially with each of its bearers. Thus karma and reincarnation cannot produce social justice, nor solve the

problem of evil, but only amplify it, leaving the original evil unpunished. If reincarnation is true, bin Laden will never be punished for his crimes, because he ceased to exist as a person in 2011.

Thinking cosmically, we cannot imagine either an end or a beginning of the vicious cycle of reincarnation. Think of the six million Jews exterminated in Nazi concentration camps during World War II. Belief in reincarnation demands that they have received their just reward for crimes committed in past lives. They must have been the "Nazis" of previous eras, so there should be nothing appalling about having them condemned to the gas chambers. If we follow the logic of karma into the past, it must be that their own victims *deserved* punishment, and so on, so that the cycle never ends in infinite regression. Looking to the future we should expect other millions of people to be exterminated (the reincarnations of the Nazis), and the new criminals to expect their extermination, etc. The cycle goes on *ad infinitum*, both in the past and in the future. Masao Abe seems to divert attention from this problem when he affirms:

> In an immeasurable way, even the uttermost evil of the Holocaust is related to the innumerable events in the past and present of human history in which all of us, assailants and victims alike, are involved. When we are victims of a horrible suffering such as what occurred in Auschwitz or Hiroshima, we tend to absolutize the evil involved as if it happened to us passively, unrelated to our own karma. (. . .) To overcome this endless process of karma, it is necessary not to absolutize the event but rather to realize its relationality and nonsubstantiality.[88]

A bizarre consequence of "karmic justice" is that *ahimsa* (the principle of non-violence, the first of Hindu moral requirements) is rendered absurd.[89] *Ahimsa* demands that we should not kill any living being, not even an insect. Otherwise we will have to reincarnate to receive our reward for it. The ISKCON Hindu movement (also known as "Hare Krishna") uses a suggestive illustration for what happens when we break this command, that of the butcher who raises his ax over a cow to slay it.[90] In this graphic illustration the butcher and the cow have exchanged faces

---

88. Abe, "Kenotic God and Dynamic Sunyata," 52.

89. See *Yoga Sutra* 2,30 and 35. *Ahimsa* is not just non-violence, but the explicit command not to kill a living being.

90. This picture appears here: https://theharekrishnamovement.org/2014/05/27/pasughna-killer-of-animals-killer-of-the-soul/, or just search online "Hare Krishna reincarnation butcher."

and stare at each other as if awaiting the fulfillment of karmic justice in the next life. However, this raises a difficult contradiction to the principle of non-violence: As a result of karma the cow has to be "killed", because it is the reincarnation of another "butcher," who deserves to be killed for such a deed in a past life. The violation of the *ahimsa* principle thus becomes a necessity in order to fulfill "karmic justice." The butcher is both the means of fulfilling karmic "justice" (for a former butcher, now the cow) and the generator of a new karmic debt for him. It is absurd, however, that karma would punish those who fulfill its justice, for it would lead to an infinite series of villains and victims who exchange places, both in the past and in the future.

If reincarnation is real it would destroy motivation for "right thinking, right speech and right action," as claimed by Sivananda. For example, what motivation can it provide for saving a child from a burning house? If one seeks consistency with karma he or she must consider that it is the result of something the child did in a previous life. He must have been an arsonist, so the child must receive his punishment, because nothing is beyond the control of karma. A potential savior would be acting unwisely because he would be opposing the fruition of karma in the life of that child. Therefore, one must let the child die in the fire. Similarly, if you see a child starving in the Third World, the reason is that in a previous life he must have been a cruel slave owner or something similar, so you should not interfere with karmic justice. Wars, natural disasters, epidemics, and other disasters must be viewed with detachment, as useful means for paying the karmic debt of their victims. Mark Albrecht provides an appropriate commentary:

> If reincarnation is true, there is little reason for comforting one another when misfortune overtakes us. Imagine saying to a young couple with a deformed infant: "It's no problem. Look at it in the cosmic perspective. He must have been a horrible person in the past life, perhaps one of Stalin's executioners, a murderer, or even Attila the Hun." The response is not hard to imagine; and such ghoulish and tasteless speculation could be applied to every unfortunate situation of life. Little wonder that in the East misfortune is met with resignation.[91]

The Dalai Lama confirms that we must meet the hardships of life with resignation, not rebel against the injustices we encounter, and

---

91. Albrecht, *Reincarnation*, 104.

Reincarnation and the Survival of Personal Identity

attribute them to our karma from past lives. He mentions cases in which Tibetan families with children born blind or retarded accepted their ordeal, saying "This is due to their Karma; it is their fate."[92] The Hindu scholar Hiriyanna follows on the same lines. Belief in karma and reincarnation makes Hindus accept suffering with serenity:

> They blame neither God nor their neighbour, but only themselves for it. In fact, this frame of mind, which belief in the karma doctrine produces, is one of the most wholesome among its consequences. Deussen refers thus to the case of a blind person whom he met once during his Indian tour: "Not knowing that he had been blind from birth, I sympathized with him and asked by what unfortunate accident the loss of sight had come upon him. Immediately and without showing any sign of bitterness, the answer was ready to his lips, 'By some crime committed in a former birth.'"[93]

If we are consistent with this doctrine we should accept that, on the one hand, the children that die of starvation or are born with severe infirmities, or victims of terrorist groups, concentration camps, or wars and plagues, all deserve their fate. All the evils of the past and present are justified by the karma which has come to fruition. On the other hand, the torturers, terrorists, dictators, and slave owners were just necessary instruments of the justice of karma, so we should not blame them or bring them to justice. If we remember the millions of Jews who died in concentration camps, the tens of millions of victims of Communism worldwide, or the more recent victims of ISIS in Iraq and Syria, we should not be outraged. All genocides in history were deserved by their victims, and we should accept them with a cold heart.

Solutions to the problem of evil that the belief in reincarnation generates are outrageous, because reincarnation does not preserve personal identity. As mentioned in chapter 4, to achieve liberation in Hinduism and Buddhism requires giving up personhood, so reincarnation cannot achieve both justice at a personal level, and spiritual progress, because spiritual progress means giving up attachment to a personal and conscious self. Thus the survival of personal identity through reincarnation and its act of universal justice do not stand, but both fall together. Beyond the superficial comfort it provides by promising universal justice and

---

92. Dalai Lama, *The Art of Happiness*, 154–55.
93. Hiriyanna, *The Essentials of Indian Philosophy*, 48–49.

countless future lives to attain perfection, belief in reincarnation cannot lead to that golden age of "heaven on earth" imagined by Sivanada, but only to resignation and despair.

Reincarnation, then, does not preserve personal identity, is not proven by experiences of past life recall, and is not a way of achieving justice. It is not meant to preserve personal identity precisely because personal identity is itself the problem we must get rid of, according to the spiritual teachings on which this belief is grounded.

# 6

Human Nature and Resurrection in Christianity

Up to this point we have examined the limitations of physicalism in explaining consciousness and in giving hope for surviving death, as well as the difficulties of Eastern philosophy in defining personhood and its survival through reincarnation. In this chapter we discuss the Christian view of human nature and the preservation of personal identity through resurrection.

Long before science was proclaimed the only way of knowing the truth, and before the West was swept into accepting reincarnation, human nature was defined following the teachings of Christianity. Its view of ultimate reality rejects the assumption that only a physical reality can exist and acknowledges God as the personal and non-physical source of everything. Although the traditional Christian teaching on human nature is not a form of Cartesian dualism, it emphasizes that we have a body *and* a non-physical component that we call the soul. But unlike pantheism, it denies that our soul or anything else in the universe is part of God, or a manifestation of God. These are some of the basic tenets of Christianity, and they were not opposed in the Western world until the dawn of rationalistic atheism and New Age thought. Before discussing how different the Christian view on the survival of death is from its physicalist and Eastern counterparts, we should recall how much our convictions owe to unproven assumptions.

6.1 SCIENCE AND FAITH

As we have seen so far, philosophical views on human nature rest on scientifically unprovable assumptions. Physicalists follow the assumption that only matter exists, while God and belief in life after death are illusions meant to quell a primitive fear of the unknown. Pantheists assume that everything, physical and non-physical, belongs to the same original substance to which we are meant to return after a series of reincarnations. They view belief in the Christian God as a primitive form of religion, and physicalism as mere ignorance. Christians, in opposition to both, hold that God is a Person who created the physical world as well as physical and non-physical beings. Physicalism is seen as a rejection of God, and as a way of mistaking the created world for its Creator, while Eastern religions are ways of replacing God with the divinity of our own self. There is nothing scientific in these assumptions or in the rejection of other assumptions, no matter who affirms them, for to establish the fundamental tenets of a worldview is not a scientific enterprise. As mentioned in chapter 1, science is about observing natural phenomena, developing hypotheses, verifying them by means of repeatable experiments, and reformulating initial hypotheses as laws of nature. Science cannot "prove" which is the "right" view of ultimate reality because such a task simply falls outside of its domain.

Just consider the physicalist assumption that God does not exist. Who would be entitled to affirm it with "scientific" certainty? How much knowledge would a person need to be certain that God does not exist? Obviously, all possible knowledge, which none of us has, not even all of us combined. It would take an omniscient person to affirm there is no God, but only God is said to be omniscient, so only he would be entitled to deny himself, which is absurd.

Since God is beyond our capacity for scientific investigation, he can be known only if he takes the initiative to disclose himself to us by using means appropriate to our comprehension. His reaching out to us is called revelation, and the means by which we respond to revelation is faith. Christian faith is not the sum of superstitions about things that mankind could not understand in nature, or the result of a desperate search for a father in heaven to protect us (according to Freud), but the result of God's initiative in revealing himself to us. His revelation is presented in the Bible as a historical fact which took place in the history of the people of Israel and reached its peak in the historical person called Jesus Christ.

The relationship between faith and reason can be of four kinds. The first is scientism, which says that faith needs to be abandoned for it cannot be scientifically proven. The second is fideism, which also affirms that faith and reason stand in opposition, but argues that it is reason that must be set aside, for all that matters is "to believe." The third position is subjectivism, which admits both science and faith, but considers faith a mere subjective experience. It is good only for you, so you should keep it private, for it cannot work for all. Christianity rejects all three of these views. Faith and reason cannot be contradictory because they both belong to a reality created by the same God. Thus science cannot debunk Christianity. Science works on the assumption that the world is intelligible, and Christianity affirms it is so because God created both the world and our mind. If something is true it must be valid for all, not only for one's private experience and feelings. Since both come from God, the fourth possible position on faith and reason is that they cannot contradict each other unless one is used wrongly. Reason explores what we can know by our mind, in both a scientific and a philosophical way, while faith enables us to comprehend what is beyond our natural capacity of comprehension. It makes us capable of receiving God's revelation. This does not make it irrational or contrary to reason, but supra-rational, enabling us to get a wider perspective on reality than science can provide. Reason helps us to formulate the truths of faith so that we can communicate them, which is the task of theology, but we should not abuse faith by rationalizing it, that is, by limiting it to the boundaries of reason. In the case of things we cannot explain scientifically (as for instance the miracles of Jesus), we must humbly admit that we do not possess all knowledge, for we are not God, and acknowledge that he can intervene in what we consider the (known) laws of nature.

Of special concern is the claim that evolution would be the scientific way of explaining our origin, while special creation is just a myth. This claim itself is based on physicalist assumptions, for evolution cannot be scientifically proven, that is, it cannot be observed and subjected to scientific experiment. If one follows the assumption that there is no God, he or she has no other option than to accept that the earliest forms of life appeared as a result of random chemical reactions between simple organic molecules, and that all species appeared as a result of random mutations and natural selection. Darwinian evolution, then, is just a philosophical theory which is uncritically held by those who accept its assumptions—that God does not exist and everything must be explained in physical terms.[1] This theory should not be a source of embarrassment for Christians, nor should it lead them to compromise, such as affirming it as the way God created living beings. Special creation should not be viewed as "just a myth" while evolution is "science," for both rest on scientifically unprovable assumptions. Evolution is a physicalist form of faith, a fact concisely expressed by C.S. Lewis, quoting his contemporary Prof. Watson: "Evolution itself is accepted by zoologists not because it has been observed to occur or . . . can be proved by logically coherent evidence to be true, but because the only alternative, special creation, is clearly incredible."[2]

A last clarification needed here concerns the language we use in affirming things about God. In short, our knowledge of God is expressed in analogical terms, not in univocal or equivocal terms. Univocal terms always have the same unique meaning, regardless of the context. For example, the word "hemoglobin" has a single meaning. Regardless of the context, it represents the red blood cells that transport oxygen and carbon dioxide between the lungs and our cells. When we talk about God we cannot use univocal terms because he is not a human being like us, so the words would not apply to him. But neither can we speak of God in equivocal terms. An example of an equivocal word is "bat." This word has at least two entirely different meanings. We can mean either the piece of wood used for hitting a baseball, or a flying mammal. We do not talk about God in equivocal terms, for there would be no overlap in meaning at all. Talk about God in equivocal terms would be meaningless. However, there is a third way to talk about God, because something in our words, in the theology through which we express our beliefs, is true about him. When we say that God loves us, on the one hand, and that we love our spouse, on the other hand, between these two loves there is some similarity. This is the meaning of analogical language. God gives us personal existence and a mind that can receive his revelation in the analogical way. Being created by the supreme Person, according to his image and likeness, something resembles the way we love one another and the way God loves us. It is neither the same thing, nor the opposite.

---

1. There are plenty of resources offering a rational criticism of evolutionism. For an assessment of how simple organic molecules could have produced the first living cell, see Thaxton, *The Mystery of Life's Origin*. Other good books on intelligent design are Behe, *Darwin's Black Box*, and Meyer, *Signature in the Cell*.

2. C.S. Lewis, *The Weight of Glory*, 136.

So, in this chapter, instead of looking ahead for the Einstein of philosophy of mind to solve the problem of consciousness, as Nagel and McGinn proposed in chapter 1, we will look back in time to explore the resources for understanding human nature offered by Christian theology. In formulating the Christian view of human nature we reopen the case for dualism, but in a different way than Descartes did in chapter 1. Remember that this book started with assessing Cartesian dualism, which was intended as a new path in philosophical exploration that would make religious belief more reasonable. Since we have seen its difficulties, my proposal is to return to the philosophical method and beliefs that Descartes abandoned in favor of a rationalist approach to human nature. Instead of following new paths, let us take a closer look at what Christian philosophy formulated prior to Descartes, and more precisely to the thought of Thomas Aquinas (1225–1274), one of the most important Christian theologians and philosophers. The school of thought he grounded, called Thomism, was too easily rejected, and its rich resources enable us to build a solid philosophical foundation for understanding the mind, mind-body interaction, the mystery of consciousness, and the way we can survive death.

6.2 CREATED IN THE IMAGE AND LIKENESS OF GOD

The Christian view of God is that of a communion of three persons, Father, Son and Holy Spirit, who share the same essence. This view did not arise through mere speculation by theologians, but is the result of how God has revealed himself in the Bible, and of how his nature was expressed by the early church fathers and the ecumenical councils, in response to his revelation. In contrast to the Eastern views we have met so far on ultimate reality, Christian theology does not admit a Brahman-like essence in which the Father, Son, and Holy Spirit have their origin. The persons of the Trinity are not manifestations of a deeper impersonal substance, for God does not exist otherwise than as the communion of the three persons. Equally inadequate is a view found among Buddhist philosophers which equates the Trinity with the doctrine of the three bodies of the Buddha (*Trikaya*).[3] Instead of the eternity of matter, of

---

3. We can find this equivalence stated by Masao Abe, John Cobb, and John Hick. For an assessment of their views on the Trinity see Ernest Valea, *Buddhist-Christian Dialogue as Theological Exchange*.

an impersonal essence as Brahman, or the impermanence of Buddhism, ultimate reality is the communion of the persons of the Trinity.

Compared to other forms of theism, the Christian view of God is neither a form of tri-theism, nor a strict monotheism like that of Islam. God is not a solitary being who needs other beings so that his personal status would make sense. A solitary god cannot be called good and loving unless there are other beings towards whom he can manifest such qualities, so he would be imperfect without his creation. The self-sufficiency of God comes from the fact that in himself, as Trinity, there is an intense interpersonal movement, a dynamic relationship between the Father, the Son, and the Holy Spirit.

Since God is self-sufficient, he creates the world freely, without external constraints, without using pre-existing matter, and without altering his nature. Against the physicalist assumption that matter exists by itself and organized itself along billions of years to produce humans, the Christian view is that God created the universe out of nothing (*ex nihilo*) by simply calling things into existence. Not only did God create the world out of nothing, but he also keeps it in existence. For this reason we say that everything has contingent existence, that is, it depends on the sustaining act of God to exist. Aquinas affirms that,

> As the production of a thing into existence depends on the will of God, so likewise it depends on His will that things should be preserved; for He does not preserve them otherwise than by ever giving them existence; hence if He took away His action from them, all things would be reduced to nothing, as appears from Augustine (*Gen. ad lit.* iv, 12).[4]

Although this view is hard for the modern world to accept, we need to remember that we ultimately choose from among several existing assumptions when we affirm a worldview. The one that says that the physical universe exists by itself is just another assumption, no more scientifically provable than special creation by God.

God created humankind out of his love, power, and freedom, as an extension of the love shared by the Father, Son, and Holy Spirit. We did not appear as a result of a random evolutionary process, and we are not the manifestation of an impersonal essence. God created us willingly, out

---

4. Aquinas, *Summa Theologiae* 1,9,2. The numbers that follow *ST* indicate the volume (1, 1–2, 2–2, 3, or the *Supplement*), the number of the question in that volume, the number of the article in that question, and, if it applies, the number of the answer to an objection.

of love, as persons capable of responding to his love. Personhood is not a result of Darwinian evolution, but the gift of our Creator, and the image of how God exists, as the communion of Father, Son, and Holy Spirit. The Christian view on human nature can thus be properly understood only by starting from this relational status we have, of being persons called to communion with God.

In the Creation account God says: "Let us make humankind in our image, according to our likeness" (Genesis 1,26).[5] According to Aquinas, the meaning of being created in the "image" of God is that we are rational creatures endowed with reason and free will. This is what makes us persons, not just living beings, and the reason Aquinas prefers the definition of person given by Boethius: "A person is an individual substance of a rational nature."[6] Our rational nature makes us capable of imitating the relational nature of the Trinity. In the words of Aquinas, "Since man is said to be the image of God by reason of his intellectual nature, he is the most perfectly like God according to that in which he can best imitate God in his intellectual nature."[7] In the same article, he argues that the "image of God" imprinted on our soul produces in us the inclination to know and to love God, or in other words, to attain "likeness" with God. The difference between "image" and "likeness" is that the image is given by our rational (and relational) nature, while "likeness" is an ideal to be attained, as it "perfects the idea of 'image.'"[8] Our personal status (the image) is the necessary condition to being in a relationship with God, while the perfection of this relationship (the likeness) is the result of a process in which we conform ourselves to this ideal. True likeness is attained by the perfected human being.

Therefore our personal status is not something we must get rid of, as in Eastern religions, but represents the way we were intentionally created by God, in order to be able to respond to his love. And our thirst for eternal communion with God is not a product of illusion, the projection of an unfulfilled longing for a perfect father (as in Freudian psychology), or the result of attachment to the doctrine of a self (as in Buddhism). Immortality, accomplished through eternal communion with God, is the fulfillment of human nature itself. For this reason Christianity affirms the opposite of

---

5. Quotations from the Bible are taken from the NRSV version, online: www.biblegateway.com/versions/New-Revised-Standard-Version-NRSV-Bible/.

6. Boethius, *De persona et duabus naturis,* 3, quoted in *ST* 1,29,1.

7. Aquinas, *ST* 1,93,4.

8. Aquinas, *ST* 1,93,9, ad.1.

the Eastern view of personal existence. Instead of being a product of ignorance, the "thirst" for personal existence is given by our personal status, which is essential for fulfilling the purpose of our creation.

6.3 BODY AND SOUL AS MATTER AND FORM

Traditional Christian teaching is that human nature consists of *one* substance, which includes a physical and a non-physical (or spiritual) component in close union. We obviously use the philosophical term for substance here, not that of chemistry (the particular chemical composition of something). A substance is defined as something that exists by itself, and has properties, but is not itself a property.[9] For instance a tree is a substance, but a leaf is not, for it is a part of a tree. Trees, dogs, and human beings are substances, while leaves, teeth, and fingers are not.

As mentioned in chapter 1, soul and mind are equivalent terms. The first is favored by theologians, while the second by philosophers of mind. According to Cartesian dualism, the mind is a substance different from the body (implicitly from the brain), is the source and seat of consciousness, and survives death. According to Plato's philosophy, an older variant of substance dualism, the soul is trapped in the body, reincarnates according to one's ignorance, and can be released from its prison with the help of philosophy. Descartes was aware that this view of the body-mind relationship is incompatible with Christianity and insisted that they form a unity. However, he was not able to explain *how* this unity between two different substances can work. This problem arises for any type of dualism, be it Cartesian or Platonist, Western or Eastern.

We also remember from chapter 1 that physicalists claim that our nature is 100 percent physical, as is everything else in the universe. Personal identity must be defined exclusively in physical terms, and death means the definitive end of personal existence. One of the main difficulties we found is that physicalism cannot explain the nature of consciousness or the relationship between the mind and the brain, for we cannot

---

9. This is a gross generalization of Aristotle's view of substance. Considering what was affirmed in the previous section, we must be aware that in the strict sense only God can be a true substance, for he alone does not depend on anything else. By saying that substances exist on their own, we do not mean that they have an existence apart from God, but contrast them with accidents, which are attributes that may or may not belong to substances. See the example given on page 168, on the essence and the accidents of which a chair can consist.

simply reduce the mind to a state or function of the brain. In the words of McGinn,

> We need an additional faculty if we are going to understand the mind-brain link. The faculties we have provide us with both terms of the mind-brain relation, but they do not give us what binds the two terms together. Hence my contention that no matter how much we learn about the brain, we will not be able to forge an explanatory link to consciousness. What we learn of the brain is condemned to be the wrong *kind* of thing to explain consciousness. The uniqueness of the brain among physical objects will never be revealed from the perceptual standpoint of brain science.[10]

This "additional faculty" for understanding the "mind-brain link" and the dualist's issue of mind-brain interaction are settled in the Christian philosophy of Aquinas by stating that the soul (or the mind) is the form of the body (and implicitly of the brain). Let us unpack this view and see what it means.

Aquinas's view on the relationship between body and soul is one that avoids the pitfalls of both physicalism and dualism. Although he expressed the Christian view on human nature as an adaptation of the philosophy of Aristotle, called hylomorphism,[11] he did not hellenize Christian thought. Rather, he Christianized Greek philosophy by using Aristotle's categories to teach Christian doctrine. In other words, he did not propose a Christian-Greek syncretism, but expressed the truths of theology in the most appropriate philosophical language of his time. This way of expressing Christian doctrine by the use of Greek categories should not bother Christians of any particular tradition, since the doctrine of the Trinity itself was formulated by the use of Neoplatonic categories of *ousia* and *hypostasis* by the church fathers of the fourth century AD.

In order to grasp Aquinas's vision of human nature as a union of soul and body, we must first understand what he means by the two fundamental concepts of matter and form. Following the principles laid down by Aristotle, any existing thing, whether living or non-living, can be seen as made up of matter and form. If we start from non-living things and take for example a stone, its matter consists of one or more minerals. In the case of a limestone rock, its matter is calcium carbonate—$CaCO_3$

---

10. McGinn, *The Mysterious Flame*, 52.
11. The term comes from Greek, in which *hyle* is *matter* and *morphe* is *form*.

(along with a number of impurities). The chemical substance called calcium carbonate can exist only under a certain form, as for instance a limestone rock, a marble statue, a piece of chalk, or a calcite crystal. They all share CaCO3 as essential matter and can only be known and researched when they take one of these concrete forms. Form is thus the concrete, individual way in which matter exists, and matter can only exist as configured by form.[12]

In the language of Thomistic philosophy "form" is more than the physical shape of a thing; it is rather the essence that makes it that kind of thing. For instance, the form of a chair is not just its particular physical shape, but its essence of being a particular kind of furniture, something you can sit on. This particular chair has four legs and a straight back, but another one may have five legs and a rounded back support. These variables that differ from one chair to another are called accidents. Size, color, material, and the number of legs are accidents; they can differ from one chair to the next and thus do not define the essence (form) of the chair, that of being something you can sit on. In a similar way, the form of this book is not just its size and number of pages, but its essence of containing information encoded by the black dots of ink (while its matter is paper, ink, and glue).

As form is not just shape, matter is not just the chemical composition of a particular thing, that is, the kind of atoms it contains. Modern physics has long since demonstrated that atoms are not the fundamental particles of the physical world. They are made of subatomic particles (protons, neutrons, and electrons), and protons and neutrons, in turn, are made of quarks. Given the possibility of converting mass into energy (according to Einstein's formula $E = mc^2$), we could conceive of the ultimate nature of matter as completely unformed energy. So regardless of the depth of the details we can think of in terms of quantum physics, the constitution of any object can still be formulated as composed of matter and form.

---

12. No matter how small the calcium carbonate particle is, it has a certain geometric shape, due to the specific three-dimensional network formed by its ions (calcium [Ca^{2+}] and carbonate [CO_3^{2-}]). Chemists and mineralogy enthusiasts know that this particular chemical substance appears in its pure state either in the form of calcite, when it forms a trigonal network, or of aragonite, when the network is orthorhombic, or of vaterite, with a hexagonal network. No matter how much we detail the structure of a mineral, the point should be clear: Just as pure calcium carbonate exists only in the form of a particular crystal network, matter exists only under a certain form.

In the case of living beings, matter and form correspond to their body and soul. Plants and animals have bodies made up of many organic and inorganic substances, and the element that organizes these substances in the form of a flower, a tree, or a dog is the soul of that living being. In order to avoid confusion, we need to forget for a moment any other definitions we have for "soul," especially the dualist self-existing substance that has a parallel life to that of the body. Think of the difference between a grain of wheat and a lump of flour hardened into the shape and size of a grain. Both have approximately the same chemical composition. (We could add to the lump of flour all the biochemical substances that the seed has in addition to starch to make an exact chemical replica of the grain.) What is the difference between the two entities? The real seed has the potential to germinate and form a new plant if given appropriate conditions, while the lump of flour cannot develop into anything. It can only decay. This different potential of the grain is what Thomistic philosophy calls the soul of that plant. The soul of a plant differs from that of an animal by the fact that the first possesses the potential to feed, grow, and multiply, while the second has the extra abilities (or powers) to feel and move. For this reason we say that the soul of a plant is vegetative, while that of an animal is sensitive.

The soul is thus the element that defines the essence, or reason for existing, of a particular lump of matter, and also the element that makes it a member of a species. For instance, if we analyze the differences between a cat and a dog from the point of view of the organic and inorganic substances out of which they are composed, they are almost identical. The same amino acids, fats, sugars, water, and minerals, are found in the constitution of both animals. The element that arranges them as a cat or a dog is the soul of that animal. The soul shapes the matter either as an animal that can climb trees or as one that can bark.

A rough approximation of what the soul would be, in scientific terms, seems to be the DNA of that animal, for it dictates the formation of a specific organism out of basic organic and inorganic elements. It is known that there are 20 amino acids that make up the proteins of all living things, in a similar way in which a group of 20–30 letters can generate the vocabulary of any language. So, by analogy, as a particular language can use the 20 letters to build up its entire vocabulary, or as the genetic code of a species commands the production of its specific proteins from 20 amino acids, Thomistic philosophy argues that the soul dictates the formation of a particular species by using matter.

In a way, Thomistic philosophy anticipated the existence of the genetic code, the fact that there is "something" of an informational nature that establishes the nature of each species, and commands the building of the individual organism from organic substances common to the entire animal kingdom. But in Aquinas's view, the soul is more than that. A dead animal no longer has the potential to fulfill the functions of the living animal because it no longer has that organizing principle called soul, despite the fact that its DNA is still there in every cell of the dead body. According to Aquinas's view, the corpse has another potential (another form), one that causes it to be broken down into simple molecules. Once the plant or the animal dies, it ceases to exist as a living organism, which we express by affirming that its soul does not survive death. The dead animal passes into non-existence (literally), it does not reincarnate.

6.4 THE NATURE OF THE HUMAN SOUL

If our soul were mortal like that of animals, we would follow the physicalist view of human nature. But since God is not an impersonal force, or energy, that manifests human nature out of its essence, but a Person who calls us to communion with him, the nature of our soul must mirror his relational nature. In order to get the right view of the human soul, which is different from that of both physicalism and Cartesian dualism, we need to consider our position in the hierarchy of God's creation: non-living matter, plants, animals, human beings, and angels. The highest category of creation are the angels, the non-physical (or spiritual) beings defined as pure forms.[13] Since they do not have a compound nature (a body *plus* a soul) they cannot die as all other creatures. However, they do not have the nature of God, and are kept in existence by him, just as the rest of creation.

In the hierarchy of creation human beings have an intermediate nature between that of animals and that of angels, resembling partly the nature of animals and partly that of angels. We resemble animals by having a physical body configured by the soul, but also angels, by having a non-physical and immortal soul. On the one hand, we are inferior to angels, for our soul configures a physical body and draws its knowledge from the physical world through the senses. We do not have instant knowledge, as

---

13. Aquinas speaks about their nature in the *ST* 1,50–64. Angels do not have a physical body, but can assume one for interacting with people, as they did when encountering Abraham and Lot in Genesis 19 (*ST* 1,51,2).

non-physical nature. According to Hinduism it is a non-physical core of the same nature with ultimate reality and will eventually unite with its source and lose identity. The Christian view is that the self is our soul, a non-physical part of our nature, irreducible to biology or physics, which survives the death of the body but expects to be reunited with a renewed body at the resurrection. These differences in defining what the self is, and its relationship with ultimate reality, shape the directions that religions and physicalism take in stating their means for surviving death.

According to Christian teaching, the human soul is created by God at conception, configures the body, and survives death. It does not "emanate" from God's nature, nor does the soul substantially "unite" with God after death, as *atman* unites with Brahman. Although the human soul is created as immortal, this does not mean it survives death by virtue of its *own* power. There is nothing in our nature that of itself makes us immortal. Our existence, as that of the physical universe and of every created being, is sustained by God's grace. This is the natural consequence of the Christian concept of creation out of nothing. Aquinas explains that all living beings, regardless of their rank, have contingent existence, not necessary existence, which means that they are held in existence by God.[22] Only God has necessary existence. The human being is called into existence out of nothing and is held in existence by God's power, grace, and will, as is the whole universe. This view of human nature will keep us from speculating on an alleged divine nature of our soul, as it is asserted in Western Esotericism.

The Christian view of human nature reveals an interesting contrast to Buddhism in terms of the nature of consciousness. On the one hand, in Buddhism, consciousness (*vijnana*) is the fifth aggregate, the one that generates the illusion of personal existence. It is as impermanent as its source and only produces attachments to false views. Enlightenment consists in overcoming the bondage generated by attachments and breaking free from personal existence. On the other hand, in Christianity, consciousness is the key element for developing a personal relationship with God and other people. It cannot be the source of ignorance and suffering, because it makes us capable of eternal communion with God, the very purpose for which we have been created.

Finally, we need to understand how Thomistic philosophy settles the problem of soul-body interaction. The major philosophical problem

---

22. Aquinas, *ST* 1,44,1.

for our capacity to think and be conscious agents does not belong to a physical organ (as the brain). In Aquinas's words,

> The intellectual principle which we call the mind or the intellect has an operation "per se" apart from the body. Now only that which subsists can have an operation "per se." (. . .) We must conclude, therefore, that the human soul, which is called the intellect or the mind, is something incorporeal and subsistent.[21]

In response to our discussion in chapter 1 on the nature of the mind, the Christian view is that the mind is not the result of brain evolution over millions of years, but a special creation of God. It has a non-physical nature and gives us the capacity to relate to God. Likewise, consciousness did not simply emerge from neural activity, but is a feature of the non-physical mind and as such cannot be replicated by physical means. No matter how much progress we may see in the neurosciences, we will not be able to understand the processes of the mind, that is, our most intimate thoughts, feelings, memories, and desires, as products of electrical fluxes between the billions of neurons in our cerebral cortex, or as encoded in the connections between neurons, for their ground is non-physical.

As we saw in section 1.5, neuroscientists cannot prove that the mind is a brain process. The fact that there is a close connection between mental events and electrical phenomena in the brain does not prove that the mind emerges from the physical processes of the brain. Such a reductionist approach is philosophical, not scientific. The non-physical nature of the mind cannot be denied just because we observe the electrical phenomena in the brain and conclude that this is all that can exist. The brain is undoubtedly linked to mental activity, being configured by the soul for that purpose, but it is not the true source of consciousness and personhood. Mental events are of a different nature than those of the brain; they belong to the soul, which is of a non-physical and immortal nature.

According to the views of the self we have met so far, the self is either an illusion which we must get rid of, as in Buddhism, or something real, of a physical or a non-physical nature. According to physicalism it is an emergent property of the brain, which cannot survive death. In Hinduism, Christianity, and other religions the self is something of a

---

21. *ST* I,75,2. In the *Questions on the Soul* he says: "a soul is an entity and subsists *per se* since it operates *per se*; for the action of understanding does not take place through a bodily organ (. . .) Therefore a human soul is both an entity and a form" (*First Question*, 45).

became a living being." The "breath of life" stands for the human soul, of a non-physical nature,[17] created individually by God at conception. This dignity of our soul, of being a special creation of God, makes it able to survive death. Eleonore Stump uses the term "configured configurer,"[18] which means that the human soul is created by God in a special manner, and is also the configurer of a physical body. It is a "configured subsistent thing" because it is created directly by God, but also "a configurer of matter" because it forms and informs the body.[19]

This status of our soul, being both the form of our body and capable of surviving the death of the body, may seem contradictory. How could something be *both* a subsistent entity, *and* the form of an entity? It would be easier to comprehend the soul *either* as a subsistent entity (and thus adopt dualism), *or* as the abstract form of an entity which cannot be dissociated from it without destroying that entity (and thus embrace physicalism). James Madden responds to this dilemma by pointing out that Aquinas presents matter, form, and that matter-form compound as functional concepts, which define the identity of a subject affected by change:

> Form is whatever accounts for the difference between the matter and the actual substance whose generation or corruption we set out to explain, and the compound substance is whatever individual is subject to this process of change. There is nothing in the general notions of matter and form as they are introduced in the account of change that entails any commitment regarding their status as abstract or concrete entities.[20]

In other words, although form and matter are explained by examples of simple physical things (what is a table, a statue, etc.), this does not mean that only an abstract notion can play the role of form. Form does not have to be an abstraction, and its meaning should not be limited to simple pedagogical examples of inanimate objects. The form of a human being is not, as common language may compel us to believe, the physical shape of a particular individual. It is rather a subsisting entity, a particular concrete that is part of a conscious being. It must be a subsisting entity

---

17. *ST* 1,90,2–3.

18. Stump, *Aquinas*, 200. This is a highly recommended book to get acquainted with Thomistic philosophy. See also: aquinas101.thomisticinstitute.org.

19. Stump, *Aquinas*, 210.

20. Madden, *Mind, Matter*, 282–83.

angels do, but need to learn gradually by the power of our reason. On the other hand, we are superior to animals by the fact that our non-physical soul is the seat of intellect and will, which makes us capable of having a personal relationship with God. Against Gnosticism, we are not angels fallen into physical bodies, in order to be purified of sins committed in a pure spiritual world; and against physicalism, we are not mammals that have evolved so highly that they have acquired self-consciousness and invented God. The soul is neither a product of the brain, nor a manifestation of an impersonal essence, as in Hindu pantheism, nor a functional illusion given by the aggregates, as in Buddhism. And the body is not only a companion, a mere instrument or a sheath of the soul, from which it must be released as from a prison, but an essential component of human nature.

Thus, hylomorphism lies between dualism and physicalism. It shares with dualism the fact that the soul can survive death and mental events belong to the soul, and it shares with physicalism the fact that we cannot be properly human without a body. As the lowest spiritual form in God's creation the human soul can know the world only through the senses[14] and is a complete being only in union with the body. Therefore the separated soul is not a complete human nature, for "if it is natural to the soul to be united to the body, it is unnatural to it to be without a body, and as long as it is without a body it is deprived of its natural perfection."[15] This middle ground between dualism and physicalism is the right frame for comprehending human nature. We are the lowest of spiritual creatures and the highest of physical creatures, and live at the interface of the two worlds, participating in both. In the words of Aquinas, our soul "is constituted on the boundary line between corporeal and separate substances."[16]

The special status of the human soul is deduced by Aquinas from Genesis 2,7 which states that "the Lord God formed man from the dust of the ground, and breathed into his nostrils the breath of life; and the man

14. For a good introduction to Aquinas's view of the mechanisms of cognition, see Stump, *Aquinas*, 244–76.

15. *ST* 1,118,3. A suggestive illustration of this incompleteness would be the terrible case of a human being who has had all four limbs amputated. He or she remains the same person, but does not retain a complete human body. In a similar way, the disembodied soul retains consciousness and some form of mental life, but is not a complete person.

16. Aquinas, *Questions on the Soul (First Question)*, 48. The "separate substances" are the angels.

of Cartesian dualism was that defining the soul and the body as two different substances raised overwhelming problems in explaining the way the two substances can interact, that is, how matter can inform the soul, and how the soul can influence matter. This difficulty also affects Hindu dualism and Western Esotericism, which is the reason why the existence of an intermediate etheric body is required. But to bridge two essentially different substances, a third substance cannot help, for the ontological gap that separates them is infinite.[23] Dualism needs an infinity of intermediate bodies to bring a logical solution to the problem of soul-body communication. In response to this problem, the Christian view of human nature is that we are not the sum of two different substances (not a soul that uses a body), but a single substance made of body and soul.

In the *Summa contra Gentiles* Aquinas affirms: "body and soul are not two actually existing substances; rather, the two of them together constitute one actually existing substance."[24] They act as a whole, not as two incompatible substances. As mentioned above, only when it is composed of soul and body is the human being a complete substance.[25] Their union is not accidental, but essential and is realized by the form (the soul) itself. Such a union does not require intermediary bodies to fill the ontological gap. In Aquinas's words, "the unity of a thing composed of matter and form, is by virtue of the form itself, which by reason of its very nature is united to matter as its act."[26]

In conclusion, the dualist's problem of soul-body interaction does not arise for Aquinas because the soul and the body are not two different substances. The body is not an autonomous machine, but matter configured by the soul and kept active by the soul, so that communication between them is possible in both directions. The body (and implicitly, the brain) does not have a separate life, independent of the soul, but is formed by the soul. Therefore the complexity of our brain is not the result of millions of years of evolution, but the result of being configured by a human immortal soul. The fact that evolutionists point to an increasing

---

23. The possibility that an intermediary exists between the body and the soul is the topic of the ninth question of Aquinas's *Questions on the Soul* ("Whether a soul is united to corporeal matter through an intermediary?").

24. Aquinas, *Summa contra Gentiles* (abbreviated *SCG*) 2,69,2.

25. That is the reason why a dead body can be called a body only in equivocal terms. In the absence of the soul, the body acquires another potential (another form), that of decomposing into simple organic molecules.

26. Aquinas, *ST* 1,76,7, see also *SCG* 2,71,2.

brain size as we move up the scale of evolution is not necessarily a proof of evolution, but can be taken as an indication that the more operations a soul is capable of, the bigger brain it needs. In other words, the human brain is bigger than that of mammals (in proportion to body size) because the human soul has the additional quality of being a rational soul.

6.5 HUMAN NATURE AND ITS FOUR CAUSES

A thought-provoking argument to better understand human nature and its fulfillment is the hylomorphist theory of the four causes. The argument says that any object or living being is determined by its material, formal, efficient, and final cause.[27] We have already met the first two as matter and form. The efficient cause is the agent that brings a particular thing into existence, and the final cause is the ultimate goal it serves, its reason for existing. For physical things the four causes are easy to understand. Here are some examples:

- My pencil has as material cause graphite and wood, the chemical substances of which it is made. The formal cause is its actual design, measuring five inches long, with six faces and painted yellow. The efficient cause is the factory that produced it, and the final cause is the purpose of pencil production, that of enabling us to write on paper.

- The house in which I live has as material cause a variety of construction materials. The formal cause is its shape and size, according to the building plan, the efficient cause is the construction crew that actually built it, and the final cause is so that my family could live in it.

- For the laptop I use now, the four causes can be formulated as follows: The material cause is the substances from which it is made: metals, semiconductors, plastic, glass, etc. The formal cause is the sum of its features, such as shape, size, speed, memory, etc. The efficient cause is the factory that actually produced it, and whose name it bears; and the final cause is the purpose of its production, to enable people to use it for multiple purposes, including that of writing books like this one.

When we consider the four causes of living beings and try to formulate them from a physicalist perspective, only the first two can be easily

---

27. See Aquinas, *On the Principles of Nature* (*De Principiis Naturae*), chapter 3, translated in Bobik, *Aquinas on Matter and Form*, 34–42.

identified. Physicalists could consider the material cause the multitude of organic and inorganic substances that compose the body of a plant or animal, and the formal cause to be its DNA. Since the existence of God is denied, the efficient cause of a living being must be the Darwinian evolution of species, that is, a long process of random mutations and natural selection by which they adapted to the environment and became as we see them today. The final cause is a complete mystery or a meaningless discussion for physicalists. Living beings simply exist as a result of a long process of evolution and survival of the fittest. Human beings are considered the pinnacle that evolution has reached on our planet, but they do not have a final cause. The goal of our existence is not given to us from the outside, but we create it ourselves. But as free as we are to formulate a final cause for our life, we can hardly define one worth living for and instead fill our life with trivial goals.

From a Christian point of view, the four causes of human beings can be formulated as follows: The material cause is the totality of the organic and inorganic substances that constitute our body and the formal cause is our soul. In the efficient cause we can identify a primary cause, which is God, for he created humankind in general, and our soul in particular, and a secondary cause, as our parents. The final cause is the purpose and ultimate fulfillment of our existence, that of being in perfect communion with God, a state which Aquinas calls the beatific vision.[28] This state cannot be replaced by anything existing in the created world. In Aquinas's words,

> It is impossible for any created good to constitute man's happiness. For happiness is the perfect good, which lulls the appetite altogether; else it would not be the last end, if something yet remained to be desired. Now the object of the will, i.e., of man's appetite, is the universal good; just as the object of the intellect is the universal true. Hence it is evident that naught can lull man's will, save the universal good. This is to be found, not in any creature, but in God alone; because every creature has goodness by participation. Wherefore God alone can satisfy the will of man, according to the words of Psalm 102:5: "Who satisfieth thy desire with good things." Therefore God alone constitutes man's happiness.[29]

---

28. Aquinas, *ST* 2-2, 2,3.
29. Aquinas, *ST* 1-2,2,8.

6.6 THE RESTORATION OF HUMAN NATURE AT THE RESURRECTION

The destruction of this body through death is one of the few certainties we have about the future, no matter which religious or non-religious creed we follow. Regardless of whether it is buried or incinerated, the body will "return to dust" (Genesis 3,19), that is, it will break down into simple molecules and inorganic substances. This is a truly scientific fact, for it happens in every case. However, Christians believe that the soul survives death, and that one day it will be reunited with the body.

Although the soul survives its separation from the body, the disembodied soul in the state between death and resurrection does not define a complete human nature. Aquinas states that "not every particular substance is a hypostasis or a person, but that which has the complete nature of the species. Hence a hand, or a foot is not called a hypostasis or a person; nor, likewise, is the soul alone so called, since it is a part of the human species."[30] Only at the resurrection does the soul become part of a complete human nature, that is, of a person. That is why Christians affirm in the creed the doctrine of the resurrection of the body.

The fact that we can discuss the state of the soul between death and resurrection is due to an anomaly in the created world, namely sin. In the words of Aquinas, sin is "an offence against God," or citing Augustine, "a word, a deed, a desire contrary to the eternal law (of God)."[31] Since it starts in one's will to oppose God, and the will is a faculty of the soul, sin is bound to the soul, as a distortion of its nature. In this disordered state we choose created things as ultimate goals, instead of God. We still retain the power of reason and will, but they work in opposition to God and are led by passions. The corruption of the soul led to the corruption of the body as well, and we end up being plagued by illness, old age, and death.

Death was not in God's plan for human beings. We were created to live in harmony and obedience to God in the natural state of a physical body configured by a soul, without dying.[32] Sin brought death into the world as a separation of the soul from the body, and the state between death and resurrection is temporary and imperfect. Aquinas comments on our present situation in the following terms:

---

30. Aquinas, *ST* 1,75,4, ad 2.
31. Aquinas, *ST* 1–2,71,6, ad.5.
32. Aquinas, *SCG* 4,82,2.

> God, in creating a human being, bestowed on him the assistance of original justice, whereby the body would be wholly under the control of the soul so long as the soul remained subject to God; so that neither death nor suffering nor any other defect would affect a human being unless the soul were first separated from God. But when the soul turned away from God through sin, a human being was deprived of this privilege and is now subject to those defects which are due to the nature of matter.[33]

Salvation means to be saved from the state of separation from God, due to sin, into a state in which our nature is restored to unhindered communion with God. All Christian traditions agree that we cannot gain salvation by our own efforts, and that we need God's unmerited favor, that is, his grace, to be restored. Although this is not the place for an in-depth discussion of the Christian view of salvation, its central element is the death of Christ for our sins, which heals our souls and makes possible our resurrection. In the words of Aquinas:

> Hence Christ's death is said to have destroyed in us both the death of the soul, caused by sin, according to Romans 4:25: "He was delivered up (namely unto death) for our sins": and the death of the body, consisting in the separation of the soul, according to 1 Cor. 15:54: "Death is swallowed up in victory."[34]

The resurrection of believers in a renewed physical body is consistent with God's goal in creating us. The physical body is part of our nature; it has nothing intrinsically bad and is not itself a source of ignorance, or a burden we must get rid of. The body has become corrupted by sin and needs renewal, not annihilation. Therefore the restoration of human nature is not just a spiritual survival of the soul, but corresponds to a complete restoration of the soul *and* body, at the resurrection. Both are necessary for us to remain the same person we are now. If just the soul were "saved," the creation of man as soul and body would have been a failure, and death would be the end of the human species. Aquinas argues that salvation must include a full restoration of the body:

> The necessity of holding the resurrection arises from this— that man may obtain the last end for which he was made; for this cannot be accomplished in this life, nor in the life of the separated soul, as stated above, otherwise man would have been

---

33. Aquinas, *Questions On the Soul* (Question 8), 117.
34. Aquinas, *ST* 3,50,6.

made in vain, if he were unable to obtain the end for which he was made. And since it behooves the end to be obtained by the selfsame thing that was made for that end, lest it appear to be made without purpose, it is necessary for the selfsame man to rise again; and this is effected by the selfsame soul being united to the selfsame body. For otherwise there would be no resurrection properly speaking, if the same man were not reformed.[35]

The requirement for the soul to be restored to its unity with the body at the resurrection reminds us of the conclusion we reached in chapter 2, that *both* the bodily *and* the psychological criterion must be satisfied in order to preserve personal identity. In the state between death and resurrection psychological continuity is assured by the soul. Aquinas argues that the separated soul can understand,[36] will,[37] know other separated souls and angels,[38] and pray.[39] Consciousness, memories, and one's mental life are thus preserved by the non-physical soul.

However, the separated soul is no longer "an individual substance of a rational nature," for it lacks the body and thus cannot be considered a complete human person. Therefore the state of communion with God as a separated soul is not the kind of survival and ultimate fulfillment of human nature of which Christianity speaks. As mentioned in chapter 2, psychological continuity is a necessary, but not a sufficient, condition for the preservation of personal identity. In Aquinas's view, the soul preserves not only one's mental life, but also the image of the body that it formed in this life. At the resurrection it will be given the power to form a new body, in continuity with this one, but adapted to a new way of being, in perfect communion with God. Stump comments on this aspect from the expectations of philosophy of mind:

> On Aquinas's view of the soul, there is, of course, mental continuity between a human person before death and after death. But the soul can also account for the sameness of the resurrected body. Since the soul was what made unformed prime matter this human being by configuring it in such a way that the matter is this living animal capable of intellective cognition, presumably in the

---

35. Aquinas, *ST* Supplement,79,2.

36. Aquinas, *Disputed Questions on the Soul*, 15; *Disputed Questions on Truth* 19,1; *ST* 1,89,1.

37. Aquinas, *SCG* 2,81,15.

38. Aquinas, *ST* 1,89,2.

39. Aquinas, *ST* 2-2,83,11; *ST* Supplement,72,2.

resurrection of the body the soul can again make the unformed matter it informs this human being. Preservation of identity will not have to be guaranteed by recomposing the human being of the same bits of matter-form composites, such as atoms, as before; and puzzles about what happens when the same atoms have been part of more than one human being are avoided.[40]

While the expectations set by the psychological criterion for personal identity are met by the fact that the soul survives death, as mentioned above, bodily continuity is harder to grasp, so we analyze this topic in the next section.

6.7 RESURRECTION AND BODILY CONTINUITY

An important aspect concerning the resurrection, which should respond to the issues raised in chapter 2 on bodily continuity in preserving personal identity, is to what extent we can affirm that the resurrected body is in continuity with the present physical body. In this section we follow an argument presented by the apostle Paul and one offered by C.S. Lewis.

The apostle Paul writes about the preservation of personal identity by resurrection in his First Epistle to the Corinthians 15. In the first part (verses 1–11) he affirms the resurrection of Jesus as a historical event that cannot be denied.[41] Jesus was crucified on a Friday, died, and was buried. But the next Sunday and for the next forty days he was seen alive and met his disciples in a resurrected body. This happened in AD 33, in Jerusalem, in Judea, when Pontius Pilate was the governor of Judea and Tiberius the Roman emperor. It could not have been a story made up by the apostles. If Jesus had remained dead in the tomb and the resurrection was a story invented by his disciples, the Romans and the Jewish religious leaders could have easily extinguished the "rumor" of his resurrection by simply removing the body from the tomb and putting it on display for the crowds to see. Resurrection stories of other traditions lack this historical dimension. For instance, Osiris's "resurrection" is a tale placed in time immemorial, under no historical ruler, like other resurrection stories of fertility gods, such as Adonis (in ancient Syria), Tammuz (in ancient Mesopotamia), or Attis (in Asia Minor). Nobody died a martyr's

---

40. Stump, *Aquinas*, 208.

41. There is an abundance of books on the historicity of Jesus and his resurrection. See for instance, Lee Strobel, *The Case for Christ*; Michael Licona, *The Resurrection of Jesus*.

death for affirming their resurrection because such stories are just myths and function as myths.

In the second part of this chapter the apostle Paul explains why the resurrection of Jesus is so important for the Christian faith: "if Christ has not been raised, then our proclamation has been in vain and your faith has been in vain."[42] It is on the resurrection of Jesus as a historical event that we base our faith in our own resurrection. Christianity could not have spread in the world if the disciples of Jesus were not certain of his real, physical resurrection. They would not have spread a lie or died as martyrs for a lie. In the third part (verses 20–34) the resurrection of Jesus's followers is affirmed as the effect of his resurrection; and the fourth section, which is of special concern for us in this chapter, speaks specifically of the continuity between the body we have in this life and that of the resurrection (verses 35–58).

In order to help Christians in Corinth understand the meaning of the future bodily resurrection, Paul uses the illustration of the seeds that germinate and turn into plants, each according to its own species. We would say that the "body" of the plant is determined by its DNA. Aquinas would prefer to say that it is the "soul" that makes it germinate and grow as a particular plant. Each body is adapted to the function it performs, so we have bodies of plants and animals, each according to its soul. Paul's bold statement is that our present body constitutes the seed of the body we will receive at the resurrection, in a similar way in which each type of plant develops from its seed. The new body will be in continuity with the present one, as is the plant with its seed, and will be adapted to a new form of life, unaffected by sin. As the seed dies in order to give life to the new plant,[43] so must the present body die, as the seed of the resurrection body. Paul presents death as a necessary stage through which we must all pass in order to reach true life: "this perishable body must put on imperishability, and this mortal body must put on immortality."[44]

An image of the difference between this body and that of the resurrection was displayed by Jesus's resurrected body.[45] Paul suggests that in the resurrected body of Jesus we have the image of our own resurrection

---

42. 1 Cor 15,14.

43. 1 Cor 15,36.

44. 1 Cor 15,53.

45. The analogy is only partially valid, for Jesus's physical body was not corrupted by sin.

body.[46] Although his resurrected body had a new quality (it could appear and disappear), it was in continuity with the one in which he was put to death. The marks of the crucifixion were visible, he could be touched and could eat, and he was recognized as the crucified Jesus. Likewise, our resurrected body will be one with new properties, in accordance with the requirements of life in unhindered fellowship with God, but still in continuity with the present one. This new body is called the "spiritual body" (*soma pneumatikon*), in contrast to the present "physical body" (*soma psychikon*), inclined towards carnal passions. Paul presents as a certainty this transformation of human nature for those who let themselves be conformed to God's will[47] and encourages the Christians in Corinth to persevere in keeping their faith despite persecutions: "Therefore, my beloved, be steadfast, immovable, always excelling in the work of the Lord, because you know that in the Lord your labor is not in vain."[48]

Another outstanding resource in explaining the continuity between this body and that of the resurrection is C.S. Lewis. In his essay "Transposition"[49] he uses thought-provoking visual imagery to teach us something about our prejudices in rejecting a spiritual reality, in general, and the doctrine of the resurrection, in particular.

His argument starts from our capacity to represent a richer reality by the means of a lower reality. Lewis calls it "transposition." For instance, we can represent a three-dimensional (3D) reality in two-dimensional (2D) ways.[50] Think of a picture, or a map. In his words, "we understand pictures only because we know and inhabit the three-dimensional world."[51] Transposition can be approached from above, that is, as one living in a 3D world and able to represent it in 2D ways, or from below, as one who lives in the 2D world and imagines what a 3D would look like. The first can be easily understood, for we use it when we read maps or look at pictures, while the second is what Christianity invites us to do when we think of God and the afterlife.

As a thought experiment, think of a creature that lives in a two-dimensional world, as for instance in the flat space between two

---

46. Phil 3,21.

47. "Just as we have borne the image of the man of dust, we will also bear the image of the man of heaven" (1 Cor 15,49).

48. 1 Cor 15,58.

49. The essay is published in *The Weight of Glory*, 91–115.

50. Lewis, *The Weight of Glory*, 103.

51. Lewis, *The Weight of Glory*, 101.

microscope slides. Let's say that such a creature is conscious. Lewis calls it a Flatlander. What would she say when taught that a 3D world exists out there and that her world is a gross reduction of what really exists? Since she has no conceptual frame in which to integrate a third dimension of space she would reject it and think it must be "a dream."[52] The only way a Flatlander could realize a 3D world exists would be for a creature living in that world to limit herself to the constraints of the 2D world and teach her what is out there. Even so, the Flatlander could think that this creature is insane. But imagine that one day the 3D creature detaches the microscope slides and "disappears" into an unknown dimension of space. The Flatlander could say it is a miracle, and start to believe, or simply ignore it as unfitting to her worldview. This second option is exactly the reaction of those who reject God and the afterlife, for it cannot fit into their physicalist worldview. They are the Flatlanders who embrace uncritically the assumptions of physicalism and reject any data that may spoil their "2D" convictions. Christianity teaches that Christ came into our (2D) world incarnated as a Flatlander and taught us things we could never have known by our limited (scientific) capacity. This is the meaning of revelation, the means by which we know that there is a further dimension of reality which includes God, non-physical beings, and the afterlife. Humans are free to accept or reject any such revelations coming from the 3D world. Lewis argues that the reason for rejecting revelation is to be found in one's assumptions:

> The sceptic's conclusion that the so called spiritual is really derived from the natural, that it is a mirage or projection or imaginary extension of the natural, is also exactly what we should expect, for, as we have seen, this is the mistake that an observer who knew only the lower medium would be bound to make in every case of Transposition. The brutal man never can by analysis find anything but lust in love; the Flatlander never can find anything but flat shapes in a picture; physiology never can find anything in thought except twitchings of the grey matter. It is no good browbeating the critic who approaches a Transposition from below. On the evidence available to him his conclusion is the only one possible.[53]

How can there be continuity between this body and the resurrection body? Think again of the Flatlander. She could easily understand what

---

52. Lewis, *The Weight of Glory*, 101.
53. Lewis, *The Weight of Glory*, 104–5.

a circle or a square is, for she can move in circles or squares. But teach her what a sphere is, or a cube, and she will say these are dreams. But for us, who are able to understand transposition from above, it is easy to understand the relationship between a circle and a sphere, or between a square and a cube. You simply rotate the circle around its diameter and get the sphere, or elevate the square to the height of its side and get the cube. Is there continuity between the circle and the sphere, and between the square and the cube? Of course there is, for the circle produced the sphere, and the square was elevated into a cube. In the same manner, the body of the resurrection will be in continuity with this body even if all its original matter is gone, for the old body is retained as an image by the non-physical soul, and based on this image God will give us a new body at the resurrection, in continuity with this one, to be the same persons in communion with him. In Lewis's words,

> How far the life of the risen man will be sensory, we do not know. But I surmise that it will differ from the sensory life we know here, not as emptiness differs from water or water from wine but as a flower differs from a bulb or a cathedral from an architect's drawing. And it is here that Transposition helps me.[54]

To accept that there will be a resurrection we need the capacity for transposition from below, as the Flatlander needs it to understand the sphere. In theological terms we call this capacity faith. It is not a complete leap into darkness against reason but a matter of trust in the One who came down from the higher reality two millennia ago. It is because Jesus Christ lived for real among humans like us, died on a cross, and was resurrected that we can look forward to our own resurrection and eternal communion with God. As converted Flatlanders we need a new body capable of integrating into that new world and we will get this new body at the resurrection.

In the next chapter we compare and contrast the Christian view of personal survival of death with those of transhumanism and reincarnation.

---

54. Lewis, *The Weight of Glory*, 109.

7

AI, Reincarnation and Resurrection as Modes of Reaching the Ultimate Fulfillment of Human Nature

IN THIS FINAL CHAPTER we can pull the threads together and summarize the differences among the three views on defeating death. The Christian view of the afterlife came to be rejected by the Western world under two influences: One was rationalist philosophy and its overemphasis of the role of science in defining human nature, which ultimately led to the emergence of transhumanism; and the other was the new religious views imported from the East, under the umbrella of New Age thought. However, the two contenders came with their own flaws, which we observed in chapters 3 and 5. In this chapter we focus on why they cannot be compatible with the Christian view of the resurrection, which is neither philosophically obsolete, nor anti-scientific.

7.1 ETERNAL LIFE ACCORDING TO TRANSHUMANISM AND CHRISTIANITY. NO DEATH VS. DEATH AND RESURRECTION

This section follows our discussion in chapters 3 and 6. As we saw in chapter 3, transhumanists consider that *Homo sapiens* is only a temporary stage of evolution and that time has come for achieving the next stage through the means provided by technology.[1] There are three ways in which they argue that we could upgrade ourselves into a new species. The first is genetic engineering, which involves manipulating the human genome. As we currently upgrade domestic animals by genetic manipulation to achieve increased productivity and resistance to diseases, in a similar way we could manipulate the human genome to prolong life and become super-humans. However, there are ethical objections to this path, so it cannot yet be pursued, at least in the West. The second imagined road is cyborg engineering. A cyborg is a combination of human organic parts and inorganic extensions. So far we see this kind of engineering at work in the lives of disabled people who get bionic limbs. The Neuralink project we discussed in section 3.5 is another example of such intended cyborg engineering. The third way demands a radical transformation of human nature into a complete non-organic being. Recall our discussion in chapter 3 on uploading the mind to an android robot and of surviving as a mindfile. However, the conclusion we reached was that such high-tech products of AI engineering cannot be conscious. They can only mimic consciousness due to the sophisticated algorithms they were endowed with.

Transhumanist scenarios for defeating death follow from a simple and often overlooked assumption: We are sophisticated machines that follow sophisticated algorithms, and nothing more. An important voice for this view, although he does not call himself a transhumanist, is the best-selling author Yuval Harari. He formulates this fundamental assumption as: "Organisms are algorithms. Every animal—including *Homo sapiens*—is an assemblage of organic algorithms shaped by natural selection over millions of years of evolution."[2] In other words, there is nothing non-physical in our nature, and we should see "giraffes, tomatoes and human beings" as "just different methods for processing data."[3] Sooner or later the algorithms that run the human being will be known well enough so that anything that can go wrong with us will be mended. Every disease and old age will cease to plague us, for they are just "technical problems" that need "technical solutions,"[4] and we will eventually attain immortality. There is nothing "divine" involved in this unstoppable

1. By technology I mean the application of scientific knowledge, including AI.
2. Harari, *Homo Deus*, 319.
3. Harari, *Homo Deus*, 368.
4. Harari, *Homo Deus*, 22.

progress, and it is all in our strength to achieve. In short, this is how the transhumanist dream can be formulated. This unlimited faith in the power of technology can be seen as the equivalent of a new religion, and Harari himself acknowledges it:

> The most interesting emerging religion is Dataism, which venerates neither gods nor man—it worships data. Dataism says that the universe consists of data flows, and the value of any phenomenon or entity is determined by its contribution to data processing.[5]

Religion belongs to the past, and there is no promise of religion that Dataism cannot achieve. Even death can be conquered with the right use of technology. Harari proudly holds that: "We don't need to wait for the Second Coming in order to overcome death. A couple of geeks in a lab can do it. If traditionally death was the speciality of priests and theologians, now the engineers are taking over."[6]

Should we follow along these lines? Is it realistic to claim that consciousness somehow arises from the sheer complexity of neural connections and that technology will eventually replicate it? Can we think of ourselves as just sophisticated physical machines? Is this assumption warranted? Science cannot prove it, for it falls outside the scientific domain. As we saw in section 1.4, physicalists are far from explaining what consciousness is and how it is (allegedly) produced by the brain. Searle has expressed his hope that a physicalist explanation of how consciousness works will be formulated in the future as a "revolution in neurobiology."[7] Since we are nowhere near to explaining consciousness in physicalist terms, the project of replicating it is even less realistic. In Searle's words, "because we are ignorant of the specific causal elements of the brain that do it, we don't know how to start making a conscious machine."[8] As for our present limitations, in section 3.7 we saw that so far scientists have not been able to create a computer simulation of the neural network of a tiny 1-millimeter-long worm with just 302 neurons. Then how realistic are hopes that the functionality of such a complex structure as the human brain, with 100 billion neurons, could be replicated as a whole brain simulation and uploaded to a machine?

5. Harari, *Homo Deus*, 366–67.
6. Harari, *Homo Deus*, 23.
7. Searle, "The Problem of Consciousness," 5.
8. Searle, *The Mystery of Consciousness*, 203.

Christianity simply rejects the physicalist line of thought by holding that consciousness is not a product of the brain, but of a non-physical part of our nature called the soul. There is nothing unscientific about this claim, for science simply cannot tell us whether non-physical things can exist or not. Science can only tell us how the physical world works, based on observation, developing hypotheses, verifying them by means of repeatable experiments, and reformulating initial hypotheses as laws of nature. It cannot tell us anything about a non-physical world. As we recall from sections 1.5 and 6.1, it is a philosophical view called scientism that leads us to reject the non-physical and God.

Since we are not machines run by algorithms, but a unity of a material body and a non-physical soul, Christians hold that immortality cannot be "engineered." It can only be a gift of God. But as any gift, it must be accepted. If we stubbornly refuse God's gift and insist on engineering immortality by our own wisdom, we are like the obstinate tin soldiers in C.S. Lewis's story who were turned into real little men, but refuse their new status and prefer to be spoilt as toys.[9] Since we are created as a unity of body and soul, we cannot become immortal if we perfect just the physical part. The soul must be restored as well, and no kind of technology can help it. Only God's grace can repair our soul, if we willingly follow the solution he has provided. This solution is called Jesus Christ. He took a human nature, dwelt among us, taught us about eternal life, and finally died on a cross to heal our soul and body from sin, so that we may conquer death in union with him.

One thing that we should clearly affirm is that Christianity does not reject technology in itself. The Christian attitude on enhancing our life and health by technological means should be similar to that on medicine, as means to *heal* the body, not to transform it into something else. Highly sophisticated prostheses which replace the function of a limb or an organ have the same role as medicine, to restore the body to its normal function, as much as possible. We praise technology for helping us improve the condition of disabled people, and for providing artificial enhancements or replacements of organs, such as cochlear implants or artificial hearts. But to use technology to transform us into different beings, or gain immortality, is quite another thing. As such, technology is used against our nature, to deform it and not to heal it. This trend is an outcome of pride, a capital sin according to Christian teaching. The ultimate "improvement"

---

9. See this illustration in C.S. Lewis, *Mere Christianity*, 179 ("The Obstinate Toy Soldiers").

of human nature is to be freed from sin, not to be brought in a position in which to claim that we no longer need God, having become ourselves masters of life and death.

When technology oversteps its proper use, it becomes religion, and one very opposed to Christianity. We can see this in the attitude of well-known transhumanists. For instance, in his anti-religious article "Transhumanism, Towards a Futurist Philosophy,"[10] Max More demands a "reengineering of our consciousness" so that it would be liberated from the false kind of certainty that is provided by religion. More thinks that humans are religious because they fear death and, to his dismay, observes that religion does not go away with technological progress: "Unfortunately, the faster technology and society changes, the greater the uncertainty in people's lives, so the greater the appeal of religion in all its forms." He considers this a very unfortunate effect of technology which must be avoided, for the same forces have generated "National Socialism and Communism at times of great upheaval." More's hope is that transhumanism will eventually do away with fears of death and extinguish religion. In his words,

> God was a primitive notion invented by primitive people, people only just beginning to step out of ignorance and unconsciousness. God was an oppressive concept, a more powerful being than we, but made in the image of our crude self-conceptions. Our own process of endless expansion into higher forms should and will replace this religious idea. (...) No more gods, no more faith, no more timid holding back. Let us blast out of our old forms, our ignorance, our weakness, and our mortality. The future is ours.[11]

Manzocco reaches an even greater level of contempt against religion, claiming that humans will themselves achieve the status of God:

> Make no mistake, though; the real purpose of religious Transhumanism is exactly this: not to simply love God or worship Him, but to be "exalted," to reach, one way or another, His level of power, knowledge and wisdom.[12]

Giulio Prisco joins this chorus and says: "I am persuaded that we will go to the stars and find Gods, build Gods, become Gods, and resurrect

---

10. Online at www.maxmore.com/transhum.htm.
11. Online at www.maxmore.com/transhum.htm.
12. Manzocco, *Transhumanism*, 272.

the dead from the past with advanced science, space-time engineering and 'time magic.'"[13]

You read it correctly, even the resurrection of the dead is a goal to be achieved by the technologies of the future. On the sci-fi means of engineering the resurrection, Prisco affirms:

> We may be copied to the future by our descendants by using time-scanning and mind uploading; or, we may already be living in a synthetic reality and the system admins may make a backup copy of interesting patterns every now and then. Hope in resurrection is, I believe, a necessary component of any effective alternative to traditional spiritualities.[14]

In contrast to the above quoted authors, who argue that technology can fulfill the highest goals of religion and thus render it obsolete, Martine Rothblatt argues that religion can fit in the new world expected by transhumanists. She expects that the world of mindclones will eventually be embraced by God:

> I do not envision the addition of mindclones as leading to an ideal or perfect spiritual state, nor to the dark night of a faithless existence. It's much more likely that most religious belief systems, but also God, will eventually accept and even embrace mindclones.[15]

Catholic clones could have their virtual Mass and confession, those of other Christian denominations their Sunday sermons, while Muslim mindclones would say their prayers in the virtual world. Buddhist mindclones will continue to meditate, while Hindu ones will follow "five principles and ten disciplines of the *sanatana dharma*."[16] All religious mindclones will have their religious leaders, and these leaders will not be confined to a particular place and time. In Rothblatt's words, "Mindclones will have no problem expressing their faith in the virtual world, and their faith will have no problem finding them there."[17]

What kind of religion can this be, but one made in the image and likeness of transhumanist expectations? Do we need a more detailed assessment of transhumanism to realize how contradictory it is to

13. Prisco, "Religion Fiction Inspires Real Religion."
14. Prisco, "Transcendent Engineering", in More, *The Transhumanist Reader*, 237.
15. Rothblatt, *Virtually Human*, 261.
16. Rothblatt, *Virtually Human*, 268.
17. Rothblatt, *Virtually Human*, 268.

Christianity? Its daring project of attaining immortality by the means provided by technology looks like an actualization of a very old project we find in the Bible, that of the Tower of Babel. In fact, Manzocco himself affirms it:

> And here we are, at the real Transhumanism; this strange hybrid movement that expressly wants to retrace the footsteps of the builders of the famous biblical tower, with the awareness that, this time, there won't be anyone to confuse the languages.[18]

We find the story of the Tower of Babel in Genesis 11,1–9. The intention of its builders was: "Come, let us build ourselves a city, and a tower with its top in the heavens, and let us make a name for ourselves; otherwise we shall be scattered abroad upon the face of the whole earth."[19]

Building the tower was an act of rebellion against God, who commanded that people scatter over the earth.[20] In saying "let us make a name for ourselves" the builders were resisting God's plan for them, intending to achieve an enduring identity (read: immortality) by means opposed to God. But since God is the real sustainer of creation, of all creatures, including humans, this is not possible. Therefore the new Tower of Babel imagined by transhumanist enthusiasts cannot be a viable project either. We are not machines, and technology is not enough to perfect our nature.

Transhumanist dreams of recent decades remind us of the similar optimism of the 1970s following the Apollo 11 landing on the moon. Popularity of sci-fi novels and films soared. Humankind believed that an age of unlimited space exploration and colonization was opening up. Those of you alive at that time remember our dreams for the year 2000. We thought we would be traveling in flying cars, or even living in lunar or Martian colonies. But in 1986 came the Challenger space shuttle explosion, and in 2003 that of the Columbia. NASA's space exploration program changed forever, and the last space shuttle (Atlantis) flew in 2011. Instead of (at least) landing on Mars, manned flights into space were limited to reaching the International Space Station. Interest and investment in space exploration decreased, and the dreams of the 1970s were put to rest.

A similar explosion of optimism as that of the 1970s has been promoted by transhumanists in the last few decades. The new ambition is to

---

18. Manzocco, *Transhumanism*, 32.
19. Gen 11,4.
20. Gen 1,28; 9,1.

attain immortality by means of technology. But in the spring of 2020 a chilling disaster slammed this optimism, this time in the form of the Covid-19 pandemic. Panic enveloped the world as a tiny little virus made us suffer lockdowns, stressful safety measures, massive job losses, and fear, a lot of fear. The economic outcome of the measures taken against this pandemic is staggering, and we have yet to discover its cost. The IMF has called it the worst economic crisis since the 1930s depression.[21] In the summer of 2020 a law enforcement incident led to unthinkable riots and violence in the US, which can hardly signal the next step in the evolution of *Homo sapiens*. Instead of unlimited progress we have witnessed the reign of hatred and fear.

Such events of the present speak volumes about the real direction in which our world is heading, proving that transhumanist projects are just empty dreams. We are not absolute masters of our destiny, but weak and scared prisoners of this virus, ready to do anything to escape its grip, even give up freedom and welcome world control in the name of health. Can we still think of ourselves as future gods, masters of life and death? Can we still think of *Homo Deus*?[22] At least one of the lessons we should learn from this pandemic is how weak we are. Covid-19 has dealt a serious blow to the optimism about the resources of technology for building an earthly paradise. Perfect earthly happiness and a perfect society are not in sight. Pandemics, famine, wars, and riots are still with us. This crisis should at least sober us up from dreams of finding "technical solutions" for every "technical problem" we face, to use Harari's words quoted above, and of attaining immortality in an earthly paradise.

Transhumanism cannot fulfill its dream of engineering immortality, for we are not machines run by algorithms. We have a non-physical part which is individually created by God to make us conscious beings. Since consciousness does not simply emerge from neural activity but is a feature of the immaterial mind, it cannot be replicated by material means. At the resurrection we will be given much more than the "third layer" envisioned by the Neuralink project, for it is not just the ability to interact

---

21. BBC News, 9 April 2020, "Coronavirus: Worst economic crisis since 1930s depression, IMF says," (www.bbc.com/news/business-52236936).

22. Recall Harari's prophecies in 2015: "Most people rarely think about it, but in the last few decades we have managed to rein in famine, plague and war. (. . .) We don't need to pray to any god or saint to rescue us from them. We know quite well what needs to be done in order to prevent famine, plague and war—and we usually succeed in doing it" (Harari, *Homo Deus*, 1).

with unlimited information that we need, but unlimited communion with our Creator. That is why we need the resurrection body, not mere technological improvements to this body, or the body of a robot. According to Christian teaching the future of humankind is not as cyborgs or as mindfiles, but as restored human beings in perfect communion with God.

As already mentioned in chapter 3, AI cannot be used to build "conscious" robots, but just to fool us into believing that strong AI is already here, or that we could survive as android robots or as mindfiles in a virtual world. Sophia has already produced such a strong impression that she was granted Saudi citizenship. Android robots of the future will mimic consciousness even better and thus reinforce the belief that we are nothing but smart machines. Even Christians may be led astray by the marvels produced by AI. It could lead many Christians into following false views, such as believing that we have a 100 percent physical nature and no immortal soul, rejecting the supernatural, and forgetting that our fundamental need is that of being saved from sin.[23] Another danger posed by AI, especially during periods of social unrest and fear, is that of becoming a powerful tool for control in the name of safety. Since AI cannot become conscious, it is not strong AI or super-strong AI that could take over the world, but those who control weak AI in times of fear.

Let me end my comments on transhumanism by retelling a fable imagined by Nick Bostrom on its great ideal, and adding some thoughts from a Christian perspective.

7.1.1 "The Fable of the Dragon-Tyrant": A Transhumanist and a Christian Reading

An ingenious defense of the transhumanist dream, while also a manifesto on the absurdity of death, is Bostrom's *Fable of the Dragon-Tyrant*.[24] It speaks of a giant dragon that demanded that every evening it must be given 10,000 men and women for dinner, otherwise it would create havoc all over the planet. All attempts to kill the dragon failed. Some tried to

---

23. At one point, some years ago, I was fascinated by a philosophical view on human nature called Nonreductive Physicalism, and believed that we have a 100 percent physical nature. So I was myself one of these Christians led astray by technology and scientism.

24. All quotes in this section, unless otherwise indicated, are taken from this article.

fight the dragon, priests and magicians used spells, chemists tried to poison it, but all they achieved was to stimulate its appetite.

The dragon obviously represents death, and the number of people sacrificed is the number of people that die each day. Some die a violent death, as in wars or accidents, while others die slowly, due to incurable diseases: "Sometimes the dragon would devour these unfortunate souls upon arrival; sometimes again it would lock them up in the mountain where they would wither away for months or years before eventually being consumed."

Religious people are depicted as individuals who "sought to comfort those who were afraid of being eaten by the dragon (. . .) by promising another life after death, a life that would be free from the dragon-scourge." They made people believe that "it was part of the very meaning of being human to end up in the dragon's stomach." This is a reference to the delusion of religion, especially to the Christian view that the road to resurrection leads through death.

A science of dragonology emerged to study the nature of the dragon, its sharp claws, impenetrable armor, its physiology and behavior, its residues; books were published, but only to conclude how invincible it was. In order to placate the dragon, humans began to organize society along its demands, and an entire economy of placating the tyrant flourished. As feeding was better organized, the dragon grew in size and requested even more humans to devour. The new figure became 80,000 people per dinner. Families had to bear more children, and the dragon-feeding industry had to modernize. They constructed a double railway track towards the mountain where the dragon lived, with a train crammed with people running every twenty minutes to it. A large administrative enterprise sprang up to collect people and have them shipped to their doom, in which real-life doctors are depicted as "comforters who would travel with the doomed on their way to the dragon, trying to ease their anguish with spirits and drugs."

However, not all lost hope that the dragon would eventually be defeated. "One of the sages, who was held in high esteem by some of the other sages but whose eccentric manners had made him a social outcast and recluse, went so far as to predict that technology would eventually make it possible to build a contraption that could kill the dragon-tyrant." This sage obviously stands for today's transhumanists who declare that death will finally be conquered by the means provided by technology.

Finally "a few iconoclastic dragonologists" (read: today's transhumanists) "began arguing for a new attack on the dragon-tyrant." They searched for a new material hard enough to pierce the dragon's armor and ways of producing a missile made of this material which would finally kill it. The world didn't pay much attention to such revolutionary ideas and kept busy with minor things, like killing the tiger who ate a farmer and eradicating a rattlesnake infestation that threatened a village. But slowly the initiative gained momentum. And as with any other revolutionary idea, the opposition grew as well. The feeding industry complained that many jobs would be lost if the dragon were to die, that it would disrupt the social order, and that the budget was already under strain. Others (read: religious leaders) argued that killing the dragon "would undermine our human dignity" and that "the nature of the dragon is to eat humans, and our own species-specified nature is truly and nobly fulfilled only by getting eaten by it . . ." Meanwhile its demand for food increased to 100,000 people per day. After many hearings and debates, the king reluctantly gave his approval for funding the new initiative. It was estimated that the new weapon would be ready in 15–20 years, and still "there could be no absolute guarantee that it would work."

We can easily identify in Bostrom's fable a sharp critique of Christian doctrines, or rather a caricature of them. In the story the dragon has no origin, while Christianity teaches that death was not God's original plan for us. It is rather the result of a revolt against the order established by God at creation, a revolt which continues to this day and thus feeds the dragon and makes it bigger by the day. God's original plan for us was that we freely choose to live in perfect communion with him. He did not create android robots like Sophia, programmed to follow precise algorithms, that could never say "No" to his love. Only free beings can respond to love with love. But freedom came with a price and with the warning that it could be used to ruin the whole plan.[25] Unfortunately this is what happened. Given our present condition, of having a nature thoroughly disrupted by sin, we are not *fulfilled* by death, but suffer it as a *cure* for sin. In other words, death is not something we seek, but something we endure while knowing that it does not end our existence.

In the fable the missile was eventually ready and the dragon was killed. All the planet celebrated and inaugurated a new dawn in human history. According to Bostrom we are "at a stage somewhere between

---

25. Gen 2,17.

that at which the lone sage predicted the dragon's eventual demise and that at which the iconoclast dragonologists convinced their peers by demonstrating a composite material that was harder than dragon scales." Christians are depicted as advocates of the dragon-feeding industry, followers of a "Deathist ideology" which demands "passive acceptance" of death and thus can no longer be "harmless sources of consolation." But as mentioned above, this is a distortion of Christian teachings.

A Christian response to this fable would state that our ultimate enemy is indeed death[26] and that two thousand years ago a man claimed to be the son of the king of the universe and that he came to deliver us from the dragon.[27] However, he did not slay it with a revolutionary new missile. Instead he let himself be swallowed by the dragon and seemed to have lost the battle. But after three days he came back telling his followers of his victory. Nobody had ever been capable of such a feat, and his disciples started preaching this good news around the world. Paradoxically, the Christian way of defeating death is by going right through it, as if passing through the dragon's belly to the other side. Christ is the ultimate ruler of the world, while the dragon is something that we ourselves have created and fed by our sins. As an ultimate test of faith, he demands that we follow him even if we are about to be chewed by the dragon. Given our present condition death is indeed inevitable, but Christ stays with us and gives us the strength to make it to the other side.[28]

If we follow the Christian view of human nature we realize that transhumanist hopes for immortality will not be met by 2029, 2045, or any other forecasted date, for human nature is not just a physical machine run by an algorithm. We cannot achieve eternal life in a human-made paradise in which we seek to "make a name for ourselves" by means of technology. Under the transhumanist project the story of the Tower of Babel repeats itself on a new scale, with new means and a new determination. What should we expect, other than a more emphatic response from God? We can reject his love all our life, for he does not force us into communion with him against our will. But he does not suspend his justice forever. What we can expect then is immortality, not in the way that he intended for us, but in the opposite way: that of hell.

26. 1 Cor 15,26.
27. John 3,16.
28. John 11,25.

In a Christian version of Bostrom's fable, the dragon has already taken a mortal blow when Christ died on the cross and it will be destroyed completely at his return. Meanwhile we live, not just waiting in resignation to be eaten by the dragon, but rather in preparing ourselves and others for life on the other side. This is a process that requires real sacrifices as a practical outcome of our faith. Just think of the priests that were infected and died during the Covid-19 pandemic while ministering to the sick. In Italy alone were more than 120 of them.[29] They died directing others how to reach the other side, not just making them believe that "it was part of the very meaning of being human to end up in the dragon's stomach," as in Bostrom's fable. Death is not an end, but a gate. Those who know it can and should help their fellow humans make it to the other side. Transhumanists would not make such sacrifices, for they haven't yet discovered the technology of immortality for themselves. They cannot comprehend the meaning of Christ's words, "No one has greater love than this, to lay down one's life for one's friends."[30]

7.2 REINCARNATION AND CHRISTIAN FAITH

Now we turn to the other challenge faced by the Christian view of defeating death, the one posed by Eastern religions and New Age Spirituality. The big questions we need to answer are: Can the Christian view of defeating death be reconciled with reincarnation? Are there hints left in the Bible that it once taught reincarnation? Were karma and reincarnation once part of Christian teachings, but removed by the clergy at some point in history? Did the early church fathers accept such views? Although these questions are answered in the positive by New Age enthusiasts, in this section we seek to understand why this cannot be, following our discussion in chapters 5 and 6.

7.2.1 Are There Hints Left in the Bible That It Once Taught Reincarnation?

Modern enthusiasts of reincarnation claim that traces of this belief can be found in the Bible itself. So let us analyze the most "convincing" texts that seem to support it and see what they really mean.

---

29. Javier Romero, "Coronavirus killed more than 120 priests in Italy."
30. John 15,13.

1. The most famous such text is related to the identity of John the Baptist as the reincarnation of the prophet Elijah. In the Gospel according to Matthew Jesus tells the apostles, "if you are willing to accept it, he (John the Baptist) is Elijah who is to come."[31] In the same gospel, answering a question on Elijah's return, Jesus tells them: "I tell you that Elijah has already come, and they did not recognize him, but they did to him whatever they pleased. So also the Son of Man is about to suffer at their hands."[32] What did the apostles make of these words? The text continues: "Then the disciples understood that he was speaking to them about John the Baptist."[33] At first sight, it seems that Jesus was speaking of the reincarnation of the prophet Elijah as John the Baptist. Can this be right?

In the Old Testament we find a prophecy about the return of the prophet Elijah which says: "I will send you the prophet Elijah before the great and terrible day of the Lord comes. He will turn the hearts of parents to their children and the hearts of children to their parents, so that I will not come and strike the land with a curse."[34] When the angel Gabriel announced to Zechariah that his son would be a great prophet, he said: "With the spirit and power of Elijah he (John, Zechariah's son) will go before him (the Messiah), to turn the hearts of parents to their children, and the disobedient to the wisdom of the righteous, to make ready a people prepared for the Lord."[35] So was John the Baptist the reincarnation of the prophet Elijah?

The exegesis of this text and its traditional interpretation in early church history suggest that the expression "with the spirit and power of Elijah" does not refer to the personal presence of Elijah as John the Baptist, but represents a case of biblical typology. By this is meant that there are people or events in the Old Testament that prefigure a special fulfillment of their role in the New Testament.[36] As Jesus is prefigured in the Old Testament by figures such as Isaac, Moses, David, and the Passover Lamb, so is John the Baptist prefigured by the prophet Elijah. Like Elijah, John the Baptist preached repentance, faced persecution from the king, and acted in times of spiritual turmoil. In this case of biblical typology

31. Matt 11,14.
32. Matt 17,12.
33. Matt 17,13, see also Mark 9,12–13.
34. Malachi 4,5–6.
35. Luke 1,17.
36. See Scott Hahn, *Consuming the Word*, or just search online for "Biblical typology."

John the Baptist had the same role as the prophet Elijah, not the same personal identity. Two other texts in the Bible which mention Elijah also point to this conclusion.

One shows that Elijah did not die a normal death, but "a chariot of fire and horses of fire separated the two of them (Elijah and Elisha), and Elijah ascended in a whirlwind into heaven."[37] To be a case of reincarnation, one must die so that the soul can be reincarnated in another body. In the case of Elijah this did not happen. Therefore, we are dealing with an exception that evades both the natural process of death and the requirements of reincarnation. Then we must recall the Transfiguration,[38] when the three apostles recognized Elijah in the vision, not John the Baptist. If Elijah and John the Baptist were the same reincarnated person, they should have recognized John in the vision, for he had just died and they were familiar with him. So, when Jesus said that "Elijah has already come," he meant that the role of his forerunner, John the Baptist, had already been fulfilled.

2. The next disputed text is that of healing the man born blind.[39] Since the apostles asked: "Rabbi, who sinned, this man or his parents, that he was born blind?,"[40] it seems that in the first case, if that man had sinned, he could have done so only in a previous life.[41] He might have been a cruel dictator who got the just reward for his deeds. In answering this question Ananda Coomaraswamy confirms that "the Indian theory replies without hesitation, *this man*."[42] The second option implies that the blind man had to pay for the sins of his parents. If Jesus had believed in reincarnation, he would surely have used this opportunity to explain to them the law of karma and its fulfillment through the blindness of that man. But his answer rejects both options: "Neither this man nor his parents sinned; he was born blind so that God's works might be revealed

---

37. 2 Kings 2,11.
38. Matt 17,1–13; Mark 9,2–13; Luke 9,28–36.
39. John 9.
40. John 9,2.

41. Another hypothesis is that the question of the apostles has nothing to do with reincarnation, but is the result of what Jesus said on the occasion of the previous miraculous healing, that of the sick man (John 5). Jesus told the sick man that his illness was a consequence of sin (5,14). In the case of the man born blind, the apostles may have been speculating how a similar causation could work in this case.

42. Coomaraswamy, *Buddha and the Gospel of Buddhism*, 108.

in him."[43] Jesus did not start a philosophical discussion about karma or punishing the sins of parents in their children, but healed that man as a sign of his compassion and as a confirmation of the words he had just said publicly: "I am the light of the world. Whoever follows me will never walk in darkness but will have the light of life."[44]

3. Another episode in the Gospel according to John recounts Jesus's discussion with Nicodemus: "Very truly, I tell you, no one can see the kingdom of God without being born from above (or "again" in other translations)."[45] Although to be "born again" may seem to suggest reincarnation, as the path to spiritual perfection, Nicodemus understood that it would be a kind of physical rebirth in this life: "How can anyone be born after having grown old? Can one enter a second time into the mother's womb and be born?"[46] But Jesus denied this interpretation and pointed to a birth of water and of the Holy Spirit, that is, of one's spiritual rebirth in this life.

4. At one point, Jesus asked the apostles what people believed about his identity. They answered, "Some say John the Baptist, but others Elijah, and still others Jeremiah or one of the prophets."[47] Since the crowd considered him one of the prophets of the Old Testament, was reincarnation a popular belief? Historically we do not find it in Judaism in the first century AD. They rather believed that one of the prophets of old had been *resurrected*. Peter gave the correct answer, Jesus was the Son of God, the Messiah expected by the Jewish people, not a resurrected (or reincarnated) prophet.

5. In the Epistle of James, according to some advocates of reincarnation, "the cycle of nature" can be taken as a reference to the cycle of reincarnation. The context, however, points to the moral damage produced by speech out of control to oneself and to others: "The tongue is placed among our members as a world of iniquity; it stains the whole body, sets on fire the cycle of nature, and is itself set on fire by hell."[48]

6. W.Y. Evans-Wentz, a figure who was very influential in popularizing Buddhism in the West, assigns a karmic interpretation to the words

---

43. John 9,3.
44. John 8,12.
45. John 3,3.
46. John 3,4.
47. Matt 16,14.
48. Jas 3,6.

of the apostle Paul: "Do not be deceived; God is not mocked, for you reap whatever you sow."[49] The following verse, however, points to the consequences of our deeds from the perspective of eternal life and not of a future physical existence dictated by karma.[50]

7. When Peter struck the high priest's servant in an attempt to prevent Jesus's arrest in Gethsemane, he was rebuked by the words: "all who take the sword will perish by the sword."[51] Neither is this text a reference to karmic justice. Although Peter's gesture was heroic, it was against God's plan. Jesus continued his rebuke: "How then would the scriptures be fulfilled, which say it must happen in this way?"[52] Peter was admonished according to the law of retaliation ("An eye for an eye", etc.) of the Old Testament, which required that the guilty be punished proportionally to their deeds.[53] However, this law referred only to the present life, not to a future one. Otherwise we arrive at the paradox mentioned in section 5.3, according to which to kill someone in this life, with a sword, would require the perpetrator to be killed in turn, with a sword, in a future life, *ad infinitum*.

As we can see, all cases of "biblical evidence" for reincarnation are distortions of the true meaning of the text.[54] We should have expected this conclusion, for karma and reincarnation were not part of first-century AD Judaism. It was only in the thirteenth century AD that the mystical school of Judaism called the Kabbalah embraced reincarnation. Medieval thinkers of the twelfth century such as Halevi and Maimonides do not mention it. Reincarnation (*gilgul*) became popular in the *Zohar*, the Kabbalistic text of the thirteenth century and even more so in the works of Rabbi Luria and his disciples in the sixteenth century.

---

49. Galatians 6,7. Evans-Wentz, *Tibetan Yoga and Secret Doctrines*, 13.
50. See Gal 6,8 and the whole chapter.
51. Matt 26,52.
52. Matt 26,54.
53. The law of retaliation demands: "If any harm follows, then you shall give life for life, eye for eye, tooth for tooth, hand for hand, foot for foot, burn for burn, wound for wound, stripe for stripe" (Exod 21,23–25). See also Lev 24,19–20, Deut 19,21.
54. Other such "hints" of reincarnation refer to the survival of the soul after death (Luke 16,22–23), or to the resurrection (John 5,28–29; 2 Cor 5,1).

7.2.2 Origen and Origenism

An often expressed belief among New Agers is that reincarnation was a common belief in early Christianity, but it was forbidden at the Second Ecumenical Council of Constantinople (AD 553). For instance Ian Stevenson argues:

> We also know that at least some Christians of southern Europe believed in reincarnation up to the sixth century. It did not then form part of official instruction, but leaders of the church appear to have tolerated it as an acceptable concept until the Council of Constantinople in A.D. 553.[55]

Shirley MacLaine affirms she was taught by a friend:

> The theory of reincarnation *is* recorded in the Bible. But the proper interpretations were struck from it during an Ecumenical Council meeting of the Catholic Church in Constantinople sometime around 553 A.D., called the Council of Nicea [sic]. The Council members voted to strike those teachings from the Bible in order to solidify Church control.[56]

Do we have real evidence that such a "purification" of the Bible text was ever done and that early church fathers believed in reincarnation?

When it comes to finding reincarnation in the writings of the early church fathers, the most frequently invoked case is Origen (AD 185–254). He is presented as an advocate of reincarnation because of the influence of Neoplatonism on his thought. However, what he took over from Neoplatonism was not a belief in reincarnation, but the pre-existence of the soul in a heavenly world, and according to deeds there, its incarnation in a human body.

One of the instances where he seems to refer to this view is his *Letter to Celsus* (*Contra Celsum*), in which he speaks of the virgin birth of Jesus. However, it is not very clear whether it is Origen's own view or that of his opponent (Celsus) that God "sends souls down into the bodies of men." In the following lines it appears clear that he refers to "the opinion of Pythagoras, and Plato, and Empedocles," who believed that the soul

---

55. Stevenson, *Children Who Remember*, 36.

56. MacLaine, *Out on a Limb*, 234–35. It was the Second Council of Constantinople, not that of Nicaea.

"is introduced into a body, and introduced according to its deserts and former actions."[57]

Even if Origen believed in the pre-existence of the soul, it did not include a belief in its successive reincarnation in other bodies. In fact, Origen himself was one of the most vehement opponents of reincarnation among the early church fathers. In his *Commentary on the Gospel According to Matthew*, written towards the end of his life, he affirms the arguments given in the previous section against the idea that John the Baptist was the reincarnation of Elijah. Origen writes: "In this place it does not appear to me that by Elijah the soul is spoken of, lest I should fall into the dogma of transmigration, which is foreign to the church of God, and not handed down by the Apostles, nor anywhere set forth in the Scriptures."[58] The next section in his commentary is entitled ""The Spirit and the Power of Elijah,"—Not the Soul—Were in the Baptist." Here Origen adds: "For, observe, he did not say in the soul of Elijah, in which case the doctrine of transmigration might have some ground, but in the spirit and power of Elijah." Therefore Origen cannot be considered a Christian advocate of reincarnation.

Belief in the pre-existence of the soul became part of a set of doctrines dubbed *Origenism*, which were rejected at the Second Ecumenical Council of Constantinople (AD 553), under the *15 Anathemas against Origen*.[59] What the church rejected at that time, of interest for our topic, is "the fabulous pre-existence of souls" before birth (anathema 1), and the idea that "the reasonable creatures in whom the divine love had grown cold have been hidden in gross bodies such as ours, and have been called men, while those who have attained the lowest degree of wickedness have shared cold and obscure bodies and are become and called demons and

---

57. The whole quote is: "And I will ask of them as Greeks, and particularly of Celsus, who either holds or not the sentiments of Plato, and at any rate quotes them, whether He who sends souls down into the bodies of men, degraded Him (Christ) who was to dare such mighty acts, and to teach so many men, and to reform so many from the mass of wickedness in the world, to a birth more disgraceful than any other, and did not rather introduce Him into the world through a lawful marriage? Or is it not more in conformity with reason, that every soul, for certain mysterious reasons (I speak now according to the opinion of Pythagoras, and Plato, and Empedocles, whom Celsus frequently names), is introduced into a body, and introduced according to its deserts and former actions?" (Origen, *Contra Celsum* I,32).

58. Origen, *Commentary on the Gospel of Matthew* 13,1.

59. See the complete text of the 15 anathemas online at: https://silouanthompson.net/2019/09/anathemas-against-origen/.

evil spirits" (anathema 4). The rejection of the pre-existence of the soul held by Origen and his disciples is thus wrongly interpreted today by believers in reincarnation as an act of erasing this doctrine from the pages of the Bible. We must be aware that between the error of Origen and reincarnation is a big difference. And since the pre-existence of the soul was considered inconsistent with traditional Christian teaching, reincarnation would have been even more so.

7.2.3 Reincarnation in the Thought of Other Church Fathers

Early Christianity spread in a world dominated by Greek philosophy and pagan religions. Many important figures of the early church had this background when they became Christians. However, to assume that they believed in reincarnation is unwarranted. Besides Origen, many other church fathers encountered reincarnation in the beliefs of pagan religions and expressly rejected it. In chronological order, the first one who spoke against reincarnationist views was Justin Martyr (AD 100–165). He rejects the doctrine of reincarnation in his *Dialogue with Trypho*, written around AD 155,[60] in which he expresses a criticism similar to one already mentioned in section 5.3. Since souls do not remember the mistakes for which they are punished by reincarnation, Justin considers it contrary to Christian ethics.

A similar rejection is expressed by Irenaeus (AD 130–202) in his *Treatise against Heresies*, in a chapter he calls "*Absurdity of the doctrine of the transmigration of souls.*"[61] He considers it absurd that the soul cannot remember anything of the previous life, the sins for which it is punished, in order to repair its deficiencies:

> For if they were sent forth with this object, that they should have experience of every kind of action, they must of necessity retain a remembrance of those things which have been previously accomplished, that they might fill up those in which they were still deficient, and not by always hovering, without intermission, round the same pursuits, spend their labour wretchedly in vain.[62]

---

60. Justin Martyr, *Dialogue with Trypho*.
61. Irenaeus, *Treatise against Heresies*, II,33.
62. Irenaeus, *Treatise against Heresies*, II,33,1.

Commenting on the *Parable of the Rich Man and Lazarus*, Irenaeus affirms that after death the soul does not pass into another body but is recognized as a unique person by other souls.[63]

Tertullian (AD 145–220), the bishop of Carthage, writes in his *Apology* that the followers of reincarnation should refrain from eating meat, since the sacrificed animal could be a distant family member.[64] He was baffled to observe that reincarnation is easily accepted by pagans, while the Christian view of the resurrection is not:

> Come now, if some philosopher affirms, as Laberius holds, following an opinion of Pythagoras, that a man may have his origin from a mule, a serpent from a woman, and with skill of speech twists every argument to prove his view, will he not gain acceptance for and work in some the conviction that, on account of this, they should even abstain from eating animal food? May anyone have the persuasion that he should so abstain, lest by chance in his beef he eats of some ancestor of his? But if a Christian promises the return of a man from a man, and the very actual Gaius from Gaius, the cry of the people will be to have him stoned; they will not even so much as grant him a hearing.[65]

Gregory of Nyssa (335–95), one of the great theologians of early Christianity, also rejected and even mocked predestination and reincarnation in his treatise *On the Making of Man*:

> They tell us that one of their sages said that he, being one and the same person, was born a man, and afterwards assumed the form of a woman, and flew about with the birds, and grew as a bush, and obtained the life of an aquatic creature—and he who said these things of himself did not, so far as I can judge, go far from the truth: for such doctrines as this of saying that one soul passed through so many changes are really fitting for the chatter of frogs or jackdaws, or the stupidity of fishes, or the insensibility of trees.[66]

Jerome (347–420), an admirer and translator of Origen's works, did not support the pre-existence of the soul. In his *Letter to Avitus*, chapters

---

63. Irenaeus, *Treatise against Heresies*, II,34,1.

64. Tertullian, *Apology*, 48.

65. Tertullian, *Apology*, 48. In his *Treatise on the Soul* Tertullian affirms that reincarnationist ideas find their origin in Pythagoras (chapter 28), and the possibility of reincarnation taking place in the body of an animal is attributed to Empedocles (ch. 32).

66. Gregory of Nyssa, *On the Making of Man* (28,3).

7 and 15, he quotes from Origen's *De Principiis*, but rejects the pre-existence of the soul.[67] In another letter (*to Demetrias*) he clearly rejects reincarnation in his characteristic temper: "This godless and wicked teaching was formerly ripe in Egypt and the East; and now it lurks secretly like a viper in its hole among many persons in those parts, defiling the purity of the faith and gradually creeping on like an inherited disease till it assails a large number."[68]

7.2.4 Has the Bible Text Been Censored?

Many authors who popularize reincarnation claim that it was removed from the Bible two centuries before the Origenist controversy, shortly after Constantine the Great converted to Christianity.[69] The reason would have been the desire of the clergy to "solidify Church control."[70] This claim is unfounded for at least four reasons. First of all, the conversion of the emperor and the Edict of Milan (AD 313) did not lead to a sudden christianization of the Roman Empire. Only persecution ceased, while pagan religions and Christianity continued to coexist. Christian clergy did not become the new leaders in society and were not in the position to suddenly change church doctrine. Second, manipulating people would have been easier by teaching them reincarnation, not by forbidding it. "Ignorant Christians" would have more easily accepted injustice if they believed that it was the result of their sins from previous lives. Third, we have no reason to believe that the biblical text was censored, either before or after Constantine the Great. We have original manuscripts of the Bible dating from before the beginning of the fourth century, and these do not differ from our present text.[71] As we saw above, the early church fathers before Constantine the Great do not confirm an existing belief in reincarnation or a removal of it from the texts of the Bible. Fourth, if the clergy had decided to erase from the Bible the "compromising" passages about reincarnation, why did they keep those mentioned above (concerning

---

67. Jerome, *Letter to Avitus* (Letter 124).

68. Jerome, *Letter 130, to Demetrias*, 16.

69. See, for instance, Prophet, *Reincarnation*, 192–223; Rosen, *The Reincarnation Controversy*, 69–86; Puryear, *Why Jesus Taught Reincarnation*, 38.

70. MacLaine, *Out on a Limb*, 235.

71. For instance, the *Chester Beatty* Papyri are dated third century. Plenty of information on the textual accuracy of the Bible can be found by searching online for "early Christian manuscripts."

the identity of John the Baptist, etc.)? Besides these four reasons it is obvious that the Bible rejects reincarnation, either explicitly or implicitly.[72] Here is a clear example from the New Testament:

> And just as it is appointed for mortals to die once, and after that the judgment, so Christ, having been offered once to bear the sins of many, will appear a second time, not to deal with sin, but to save those who are eagerly waiting for him.[73]

In other words, as the sacrifice of Christ on the cross is unique and unrepeatable, the same degree of certainty applies when we affirm that we live only once in this world, after which comes judgment and eternal life. The two elements stand or fall together. As for the judgment that follows death, to which this verse refers, it is not the judgment of the impersonal karma, but that of the personal almighty God.

Belief in reincarnation truly existed during early Christian history, but outside the church, in Gnosticism. This religious movement combined elements taken from the philosophy and pagan religions prevalent in the first and second centuries AD, and attempted to incorporate and reinterpret fundamental elements of Christianity. In other words, it was the New Age movement of that time. According to Gnosticism, the material world is the work of an evil deity (the demiurge), equated to the God of the Old Testament. Our soul is fallen into the prison of this body, from which it must escape by following the right spiritual knowledge. As long as we remain in this state of ignorance we must reincarnate. Eventually the soul will escape from the physical body and reach high spiritual realms. Jesus is a spiritual master who descended into our world to impart to us true enlightening knowledge and thus free us from ignorance, not a Savior who died on the cross for our sins. Such teachings are contained in a number of so-called Gnostic "gospels," some bearing the names of the followers of Christ, as for instance the *Gospels of Thomas, Philip*, and *Mary*, and in other writings bearing the names of the apostles, such as the *Apocryphon of John* and the *Apocalypse of Peter*. Many of them are mentioned and refuted by Irenaeus, in his *Treatise against Heresies*. Not only Irenaeus but all church fathers rejected them as heretical and unrelated

---

72. See, for instance, Job 7,9–10, Matt 25,46, Acts 17,30–31, 2 Cor 5,1–8, Rev 20,11–15.

73. Heb 9,27–28.

to traditional Christian teaching, so they cannot count as evidence for a belief in reincarnation in the early church.[74]

7.2.5 Why Is Reincarnation Incompatible with Christian Faith?

We now reach the point of summarizing the key issues that make reincarnation incompatible with Christian faith. First, reincarnation denies God's sovereignty over his creatures, turning him into a helpless spectator of human tragedies, as is the god Krishna in the Bhagavad Gita.[75] Christianity teaches that God can punish evil and reward the good, and he will do it perfectly without the need for karma and reincarnation.[76] When something evil happens to us we must remember that God allows it for our sanctification, setting it according to our strength and not letting it pass a certain limit.[77] Since he turned the most evil thing humankind has ever done, that of crucifying the Son of God, into the means of our salvation, he can surely use our present suffering for our ultimate good. As we saw in section 5.3, reincarnation cannot deliver definitive justice, but leads to an infinite series of villains and victims who exchange places, both in the past and the future. The Christian view is that full justice will be done at the resurrection. In the words of John of Damascus:

> If there is no resurrection, there is no God and no providence, and all things are being driven and carried along by mere chance. For just consider how very many just men we see in need and suffering injury, yet getting no recompense in this present life, whereas we see sinners and wicked men possessing wealth and every luxury in abundance. Who in his right mind would understand this to be the work of righteous judgment or wise providence? Therefore, there will be, there certainly will be, a resurrection. For God is just and He rewards those who await Him in patience.[78]

Second, reincarnation cannot be reconciled with Christian ethics, for it encourages passivity and undermines motivation for a virtuous

---

74. For more information of the Gnostic gospels and the Jesus of Gnosticism, see Groothuis, *Revealing the New Age Jesus*.
75. See again section 5.1.
76. See Matt 25,31–46; Rev 20,10–15.
77. 1 Cor 10,13.
78. Saint John of Damascus, *Writings*, Orthodox Faith, 4,27, 401.

life. As we saw in section 5.3, one consistent with reincarnation must consider crime, rape, theft, and other such social plagues as the result of "debts from previous lives" of their victims. The tragedy of past and present wars should also be seen as nothing more than the fulfillment of karmic justice. Any involvement in helping the "victims" of karma would only postpone its fulfillment. As we saw in section 5.1, a further issue is that reincarnation does not preserve personal identity from one life to the next. Even if we were to limit reincarnation to *human* instances of life, since it is not a conscious self that reincarnates, the one punished or rewarded for his or her deeds is not the same person, but another. As mentioned at the conclusion of chapter 5, the survival of personal identity through reincarnation and its act of universal justice do not stand, but fall together.

Third, reincarnation compromises the essence of the Christian doctrine of salvation, which emphasizes the necessity of Jesus's sacrifice for our sins.[79] If we are to pay for our sins in future lives in order to gain salvation Jesus's sacrifice was irrelevant and absurd. It can no longer be God's solution for our sins, but only a regrettable accident in history. Moreover, one would have to believe that Jesus died on the cross as a punishment for his own sins from previous lives.[80]

The Christian view on human nature adds two more arguments against reincarnation. One is that the human soul comes into existence at conception, following a special act of creation by God, so it cannot exist before the body.[81] The pre-existence of the soul was assumed by Origen under the influence of Neoplatonism, but it was never part of Christian teaching. Another aspect we should remember is that the human soul can only configure a *human* body. Since human nature is a unity of soul and body, a human soul can configure a single body, of a single human being, but by no means that of an animal. The soul and body come into existence together, at conception, separate at death and reunite at the resurrection. Therefore, Christians cannot accept a journey of the soul

---

79. Radhakrishnan confirms this contradiction with Christianity, affirming: "The past guilt cannot be wiped away by the atoning suffering of an outward substitute. Guilt cannot be transferred. It must be atoned for through the sorrow entailed by self-conquest. God cannot be bought over and sin cannot be glossed over" (*The Hindu View of Life*, 74–75).

80. To avoid this absurd conclusion, Gnostics prefer to say that it was Simon of Cyrene who died on the cross, the one that the Romans mistook for Jesus.

81. See Aquinas, *Summa contra Gentiles* 2,87,2–3 and 2,85,2.

through other bodies. Here is how Aquinas refutes reincarnation and Origen's view of the pre-existence of souls:

> If all souls existed before the bodies to which they are united, it would then seemingly follow that the same soul is united to different bodies according to the vicissitudes of time—an obvious consequence of the doctrine of the eternity of the world. For from the hypothesis of the engendering of human beings from eternity it follows that an infinite number of human bodies have come into being and passed away throughout the whole course of time. Hence, two possibilities: either an actually infinite number of souls pre-existed, if each soul is united to a single body, or, if the number of souls is finite, then the same souls are united at one time to these particular bodies and at another time to those. (. . .) That is why a number of proponents of the doctrine that souls exist before bodies espoused the theory of transmigration; which cannot possibly be true. Therefore, souls did not exist before bodies.[82]

God called us into existence by his love, as the particular human person we are right now, and thus cannot allow that we transform into other human beings, or even animals. He does not relate to beings that shift from one identity to another, or to impersonal essences, but to conscious beings able to respond to his love. In the words of Paul Williams, the Mahayana Buddhism scholar who converted to Catholicism, "Because we are infinitely valuable to God, Jesus died to save each one of us. He did not die to save chains of reincarnations, or reincarnating Selves who (as the Hindu *Bhagavad Gita* has it) put on new bodies like new garments. He died to save *us*."[83] In other words, "reincarnation is incompatible with the infinite value of the person."[84]

One that considers reincarnation consistent with Christianity must completely ignore the importance of our present physical body and consider that our ultimate fulfillment is as discarnate spirits. However, Christianity views the restoration of human nature not just as a spiritual survival of the soul, but as a complete restoration of soul *and* body, at the resurrection. Both are necessary for us to remain the same person we are now. On the one hand, if just the soul matters and is perfected across many reincarnations, the creation of human beings as soul and

---

82. Aquinas, *SCG* 2,83,33.
83. Williams, *The Unexpected Way*, 227.
84. Williams, *The Unexpected Way*, 83.

body would have been a failure. It would mean that God has changed his mind and decided to upgrade us into angels. On the other hand, our final restoration at the resurrection as a soul united to a body reminds us of the conclusion we reached in chapter 2, that *both* the bodily *and* the psychological criterion must be satisfied in order to preserve personal identity. In conclusion, the criticism addressed by Williams to the Buddhist view of reincarnation, applies to all forms of it:

> The Buddhist notion of reincarnation not only is incompatible with personal identity across lifetimes, it is incompatible with the infinite preciousness we hold as Christians for each and every individual person, and it is also incompatible with the significance of our actual human bodies in making us the persons we are.[85]

Since we are not just a soul wandering through different bodies to expiate karma and eventually dissolve into ultimate reality (as in pantheism), or a spirit evolving indefinitely to attain higher forms (as in New Age thought), but a soul united to a physical body, reincarnation does not fit in the Christian story. The Christian way of reaching the ultimate fulfillment of our nature is through the resurrection. It means receiving a new body, in continuity with this one, but adapted to a new way of being, in perfect communion with God.

---

85. Williams, *Buddhism from a Catholic Perspective*, 53.

Concluding Thoughts

I STARTED THIS BOOK by confessing the anguish the thought of death and annihilation produced in me. I found the way out of this anxiety by following the light of Christ, the one who said: "I am the light of the world. Whoever follows me will never walk in darkness but will have the light of life."[1] The final defeat of death is expressed perfectly in a famous Byzantine icon, that of the resurrection (*Anastasis*), which appears on the cover of this book. You can see it in a similar representation in almost any Eastern Orthodox church.[2]

In this icon, after Christ smashes the gates of hell under his feet, he takes Adam and Eve by the hand and snatches them out of their graves. It speaks volumes about the true source of immortality. The defeat of death and its threat of annihilation does not come from a future technological breakthrough, when science will have unraveled the mysteries of the brain, or when we are able to download our mind into the hard-disk of a robot or live as mindfiles in a virtual reality. Contrary to the expectations of transhumanists, this body cannot be made to sustain eternal life. It needs to be upgraded to a new body, in continuity with this one, but wholly transformed. Nor can reincarnation be a solution, for it not only fails to achieve justice, but also pushes one towards an impersonal end. In contrast to physicalism and Eastern religions, the Christian teaching on preserving personal identity is the resurrection of the person as a whole, body and soul. Christ redeems both from the corruption of sin because to be a human being means to have a soul united to a body, not just a soul, or just a perfected body. This is a goal we cannot achieve by technology,

---

1. John 8,12.

2. This particular painting was done in the fourteenth century and can be seen in the former Chora Church (or Kariye Museum) in Istanbul (former Constantinople).

AI, meditation, Yoga, mindfulness, or any other human initiative. It can only be the gift of God, through Christ.

Let me end this book with some thoughts on an episode in the Bible that was mentioned as evidence for reincarnation, that of the healing of the man born blind (John 9). It does not confirm reincarnation, but can teach us something very important on what the restoration of human nature in Christ means.

Its true physical dimension is probably grasped better by neuroscientists than by the average reader. What Jesus healed was not only the man's eyes, but also the optic nerve and the center of vision in the occipital lobe. The miracle appears even greater when we realize that even if all the physical parts of the visual system were healed, that man would still lack the cognitive basis on which his sense of sight could work. We know the world around us by successively adding new information to what has already been gathered and systematized by our mind. Without this cognitive basis, which is developed progressively from birth, the formerly blind person could not have comprehended anything of what he was seeing. Although his visual system was now functional, his sight would have been meaningless. His situation would have been as if he saw everywhere only symbols in Chinese. In other words, he could not have interpreted what he had just started to see because he lacked the fundamental notions in which to integrate the new visual knowledge. Therefore what Jesus healed was not just the physical part, but his whole cognitive past. Only so could he start to live like a normal human being. Otherwise he could not have started debating with the Pharisees on the identity of Jesus and behave like a normal, responsible person. This dimension of healing surpasses by far that of his eyes.

Another aspect we should consider is the means used by Jesus. He could have healed him with a single word, as he did in most of his miracles. But by using mud made of his saliva, and then spreading the mud on the man's eyes, Jesus emulated the creation of the first man "from the dust of the ground."[3] He did not just heal that man, but restored him completely to his full human dignity, physically and spiritually, as if re-creating him. This is what Jesus does when we turn to him. He heals us from our existential anxieties and gives us a whole new perspective on what it means to be human.

---

3. Gen 2,7.

In response to my anxieties, one thing I do know for sure. Like the blind man, I can say that I was blind and now I see. And in response to the first words of this book, from darkness to light, from non-being to being and from death to life, only Christ can lead us by his power and grace.

Bibliography

Abe, Masao. "Kenotic God and Dynamic Sunyata." In *The Emptying God: A Buddhist-Jewish-Christian Conversation*, by Cobb, John B. Jr., and Christopher Ives, eds. Delhi: Sri Satguru Publications, 1996.

Albrecht, Mark C. *Reincarnation: A Christian Critique of a New Age Doctrine*. Downers Grove, IL: InterVarsity Press, 1982.

Anthony, Sebastian. "Microsoft demos English-to-Chinese universal translator that keeps your voice and accent." November 9, 2012. https://www.extremetech.com/computing/139945-microsoft-demos-english-to-chinese-universal-translator-that-keeps-your-voice-and-accent.

Aquinas, Thomas. *Questions On the Soul*. Milwaukee, WI: Marquette University Press, 1984.

———. *Summa contra Gentiles*. New York: Image, 1956.

———. *Summa Theologica*. Cincinnati: Benziger Brothers, 1947, https://aquinas101.thomisticinstitute.org/st-index.

Baker, Stephen. *Final Jeopardy: Man vs. Machine and the Quest to Know Everything*. New York: Houghton Mifflin, 2011.

Behe, Michael J. *Darwin's Black Box: The Biochemical Challenge to Evolution*. New York: Free Press, 2006.

Bennett, Jonathan, ed. "Correspondence between Descartes and Princess Elisabeth." *Early modern Philosophy*. http://www.earlymoderntexts.com/assets/pdfs/descartes1643_1.pdf.

Bernstein, Morey. *The Search for Bridey Murphy*. New York: Pocket Books, 1956.

Bloom, Adam, Bear, Paul. "A Simple Task Uncovers a Postdictive Illusion of Choice." *Psychological Science*, April 28, 2016, 1–9.

Bobik, Joseph. *Aquinas on Matter and Form and the Elements: A Translation and Interpretation of the De Principiis Naturae and the De Mixtione Elementorum of St. Thomas Aquinas*, Notre Dame, IN: University of Notre Dame Press, 1998.

Bodhi, Bhikkhu, transl. *The Connected Discourses of the Buddha: A Translation of the Samyutta Nikaya*. Boston: Wisdom, 2000.

Bostrom, Nick. "The Fable of the Dragon-Tyrant." *Journal of Medical Ethics*, 31/5 (2005) 273–77, https://nickbostrom.com/fable/dragon.html.

Buddhaghosa. *The Path of Purification: Visuddhimagga*. Kandy, Sri Lanka: Buddhist Publication Society, 2010.

Butler, Joseph. "Of Personal Identity." In *Personal Identity*, by John Perry, ed., 99–106. Berkeley: University of California Press, 1975.

Cellan-Jones, Rory. "Stephen Hawking warns artificial intelligence could end mankind." *BBC News*. December 2, 2014. https://www.bbc.com/news/technology-30290540.

Chinmoy, Sri. *The Wisdom of Sri Chinmoy*. Delhi: Motilal Banarsidass, 2004.

Clarke, Desmond M. *Descartes: A Biography*. Cambridge: Cambridge University Press, 2005.

Collins, Steven. *Selfless Persons: Imagery and Thought in Theravada Buddhism*. Cambridge: Cambridge University Press, 1982.

Coomaraswamy, Ananda. *Buddha and the Gospel of Buddhism*. New York: Harper and Row, 1964.

Dalai Lama, and Howard Cutler. *The Art of Happiness: A Handbook for Living*. New York: Riverhead, 1998.

Dasgupta, Surendranath. *A History of Indian Philosophy*, vol. I-II. Delhi: Motilal Banarsidass, 1975–1991.

Descartes, René. *A Discourse on the Method of Correctly Conducting One's Reason and Seeking Truth in the Sciences*. Oxford: Oxford University Press, 2006.

———. *Meditations on First Philosophy*. Cambridge: Cambridge University Press, 1996.

———. "Objections to the Meditations and Descartes's Replies." *Early Modern Philosophy*. http://www.earlymoderntexts.com/assets/pdfs/descartes1642_2.pdf.

———. "Principles of Philosophy." *Early Modern Philosophy*. http://www.earlymoderntexts.com/assets/pdfs/descartes1644part1.pdf.

Deussen, Paul. *The Philosophy of the Upanishads*. Edinburgh: T. & T. Clark, 1906.

Doniger, Wendy. *On Hinduism*. New Delhi: Aleph, 2013.

Eccles, John. *Evolution of the Brain: Creation of the Self*. London: Routledge, 1989.

———. *The Wonder of Being Human: Our Brain and Our Mind*. London: Free Press, 1984.

Eccles, John, and Karl Popper. *The Self and Its Brain*. London: Routledge and Kegan Paul, 1977.

Edwards, Paul. *Reincarnation: A Critical Examination*. New York: Prometheus, 2002.

Eliade, Mircea. *A History of Religious Ideas*, vol I–II. Chicago: University of Chicago Press, 1978–1982.

———. *Yoga: Immortality and Freedom*. New York: Routledge & Kegan Paul, 1958.

Evans-Wentz, W.Y., ed. *Tibetan Yoga and Secret Doctrines*. Oxford: Oxford University Press, 1958.

Fodor, Jerry. "The Big Idea: Can There Be a Science of the Mind." *Times Literary Supplement*, July 3 (1992) 5–7.

Gaukroger, Stephen. *Descartes: An Intellectual Biography*. Oxford: Clarendon Press, 1995.

Gerrish, Sean. *How Smart Machines Think*. Cambridge, MA: MIT, 2018.

Gethin, Rupert. *The Foundations of Buddhism*. Oxford: Oxford University Press, 1998.

Gregory of Nyssa. "On the Making of Man." *New Advent*. www.newadvent.org/fathers/2914.htm.

Griswold, H.D. *The Religion of the Rigveda*. New Delhi: Motilal Banarsidass, 1999.

Groothuis, Douglas. *Revealing the New Age Jesus: Challenges to Orthodox Views of Christ*. Downers Grove, IL: InterVarsity, 1990.

Hahn, Scott. *Consuming the Word*. New York: Image, 2013.

Hanson Robotics. "The Making of Sophia: Facial Recognition, Expressions and the Loving AI Project." June 18, 2019. https://www.hansonrobotics.com/the-making-of-sophia-facial-recognition-expressions-and-the-loving-ai-project/.

Harari, Yuval Noah. *Homo Deus: A Brief History of Tomorrow*. London: Harvill Secker, 2015.
Harmon, Amy. "The Neuroscience of Immortality." *New York Times*, September 12, 2015.
Harvey, Peter. *An Introduction to Buddhism: Teachings, history and practices*. Cambridge: Cambridge University Press, 1990.
Head, Joseph, and S.L. Cranston, eds. *Reincarnation: The Phoenix Fire Mystery*. New York: Warner, 1979.
Heil, John. *Philosophy of Mind: A Contemporary Introduction*. New York: Routledge, 2004.
Hiriyanna, Mysore. *The Essentials of Indian Philosophy*. London: George Allen & Unwin, 1949.
Hume, David. *A Treatise of Human Nature*. Oxford: Oxford University Press, 2007.
"The Hymns of the Atharvaveda." *Internet Sacred Text Archive*. https://www.sacred-texts.com/hin/av/.
"The Hymns of the Rig Veda." *Internet Sacred Texts Archive*. https://www.sacred-texts.com/hin/rigveda.
Irenaeus. "Treatise against Heresies." *New Advent*. www.newadvent.org/fathers/0103233.htm.
Iyengar, B.K.S. *Light on Pranayama*. London: Unwin, 1983.
———. *Yoga: The Path to Holistic Health*. London: Dorlin Kindersley, 2008.
Jackson, Frank. "What Mary Didn't Know." *The Journal of Philosophy* 83/5 (1986) 291–95.
Jerome. "Letter 130, to Demetrias." *New Advent*. www.newadvent.org/fathers/3001130.htm.
———. "Letter to Avitus (Letter 124)." *New Advent*. www.newadvent.org/fathers/3001124.htm.
John of Damascus, Saint. *Writings, Orthodox Faith*. Washington, DC: Catholic University of America Press, 1981.
Justin Martyr. "Dialogue with Trypho." *New Advent*. www.newadvent.org/fathers/0128.htm.
Kampman, Reima. "Hypnotically Induced Multiple Personality: An Experimental Study." *International Journal of Clinical and Experimental Hypnosis* 24/3–4 (1976) 215–27.
Kim, Jaegwon. *Philosophy of Mind*. Boulder, Colorado: Westview, 1996.
Koch, Christof, and Giulio Tononi. "Can Machines Be Conscious?" *IEEE Spectrum*, June 2008. https://authors.library.caltech.edu/11693/1/KOCieeespec08.pdf.
Kurzweil, Ray. *The Singularity is Near*. New York: Penguin, 2005.
Leibniz, Gottfried Wilhelm. *New Essays on Human Understanding*. Cambridge: Cambridge University Press, 1996.
Lewis, C.S. *Mere Christianity*. San Francisco: HarperOne, 2015.
———. *The Weight of Glory*. New York: HarperCollins, 1980.
Libet, Benjamin. *Mind Time: The Temporal Factor in Consciousness*. Harvard: Harvard University Press, 2004.
Licona, Michael R. *The Resurrection of Jesus: A New Historiographical Approach*. Downers Grove, IL: InterVarsity, 2010.
Locke, John. *An Essay Concerning Human Understanding*. Oxford: Clarendon Press, 1975.

MacLaine, Shirley. *Out on a Limb.* New York: Bantam, 1983.

Madell, Geoffrey. *The Essence of the Self: In Defense of the Simple View of Personal Identity.* New York: Routledge, 2015.

Manzocco, Roberto. *Transhumanism—Engineering the Human Condition: History, Philosophy and Current Status.* Cham, Switzerland: Springer, 2019.

McGinn, Colin. "Can We Solve the Mind–Body Problem?" *Mind, New Series,* 98/391 (1989) 349–66.

———. *The Character of Mind: An Introduction to the Philosophy of Mind.* Oxford: Oxford University Press, 1996.

———. *The Mysterious Flame: Conscious Minds in a Material World.* New York: Perseus, 1999.

Mercer, Calvin, and Derek F. Maher, eds. *Transhumanism and the Body: World Religions Speak.* New York: Palgrave Macmillan, 2014.

Meyer, Stephen. *Signature in the Cell: DNA and the Evidence for Intelligent Design.* New York: HarperCollins, 2009.

Moore, Pete. *Enhancing Me: The Hope and the Hype of Human Enhancement.* Chichester, UK: Wiley, 2008.

More, Max, and Natasha Vita-More, eds. *The Transhumanist Reader: Classical and Contemporary Essays on the Science, Technology, and Philosophy of the Human Future.* Chichester, UK: Wiley-Blackwell, 2013.

Mossbridge, Julia, and Edward Monroe. "Team Hanson-Lia-SingularityNet: Deep-learning Assessment of Emotional Dynamics Predicts Self-Transcendent Feelings During Constrained Brief Interactions with Emotionally Responsive AI." https://www.academia.edu/40621217/Team_Hanson_Lia_SingularityNet_Deep_learning_Assessment_of_Emotional_Dynamics_Predicts_Self_Transcendent_Feelings_During_Constrained_Brief_Interactions_with_Emotionally_Responsive_AI_Embedded_in_Android_Technology.

Mozur, Paul. "Inside China's Dystopian Dreams: A.I., Shame and Lots of Cameras." *New York Times.* July 08, 2018. https://www.nytimes.com/2018/07/08/business/china-surveillance-technology.html.

Mueller, John Paul, and Luca Massaron. *Machine Learning for Dummies.* Hoboken, NJ: Wiley, 2016.

Müller, Max, transl. "The Dhammapada." In *The Sacred Books of the East,* vol. X, part I, edited by Max Müller. New Delhi: Motilal Banarsidass, 2004.

———. "The Sutta Nipata." In *Sacred Books of the East, vol X, part II,* edited by Max Müller. Delhi: Motilal Banarsidass, 2004.

Munro, Monroe P., transl. "Siva Samhita." *Internet Archive.* https://ia600304.us.archive.org/10/items/SivaSamhita/SivaSamhita.pdf.

Nagel, Thomas. *The Last Word.* New York: Oxford University Press, 1997.

———. *The View from Nowhere.* Oxford: Oxford University Press, 1986.

———. "What Is It Like to Be a Bat?" *The Philosophical Review* 83/4 (1974) 435–50.

Nanamoli, Bhikkhu, and Bhikkhu Bodhi. *The Middle Length Discourses of the Buddha: A Translation of the Majjhima Nikaya.* Boston: Wisdom, 2001.

Newton, Michael. *Life Between Lives: Hypnotherapy for Spiritual Regression.* St. Paul, MN: Llewellyn, 2004.

Noonan, Harold. *Personal Identity.* London: Routledge, 1989.

Nozick, Robert. *Philosophical Explanations.* Cambridge, MA: Harvard University Press, 1981.

O'Flaherty, Wendy Doniger. *The Rig Veda: An Anthology.* London: Penguin, 1981.
Origen. "Commentary on the Gospel of Matthew." *New Advent.* www.newadvent.org/fathers/101613.htm.
———. "Contra Celsum." *New Advent.* www.newadvent.org/fathers/04161.htm.
Parfit, Derek. *Reasons and Persons.* Oxford: Clarendon Press, 1984.
Park, Andrew Lee. "Injustice Ex Machina: Predictive Algorithms in Criminal Sentencing." *Law Meets World*, February 19, 2019: https://www.uclalawreview.org/injustice-ex-machina-predictive-algorithms-in-criminal-sentencing/.
Patel, B.N., et al. "Human–machine partnership with artificial intelligence for chest radiograph diagnosis." *NPJ Digit. Med.* 2/111 (2019). https://rdcu.be/b2y58.
Pesala, Bhikkhu, ed. *The Debate of King Milinda: An Abridgement of the Milinda Panha.* Delhi: Motilal Banarsidass, 1998.
Place, Ullin T., et al. "Is Consciousness a brain process?" *British Journal of Psychology* 47/1 (1956) 44–50.
Prabhupada, Bhaktivedanta Swami. *Bhagavad-gita As It Is.* Los Angeles: The Bhaktivedanta Book Trust, 1983.
Prasada, Rama, transl. *Patanjali's Yoga Sutras.* New Delhi: Munshiram Manoharlal, 1988.
Priest, Stephen. *Theories of the Mind.* Boston: Houghton Mifflin, 1991.
Prisco, Giulio. "Religion Fiction Inspires Real Religion." *The Transfigurist.* January 8, 2015. http://www.transfigurist.org/2015/01/religion-fiction-inspires-real-religion.html.
Prophet, Elizabeth Clare, and Erin L. Prophet. *Reincarnation: The Missing Link in Christianity.* Corwin Springs, MT: Summit University Press, 1977.
Puryear, Herbert B. *Why Jesus Taught Reincarnation: A Better News Gospel.* Scottsdale, AZ: New Paradigm, 1992.
Putnam, Hilary. "The Nature of Mental States." In *Philosophy of Mind: Classical and Contemporary Readings*, edited by David Chalmers. Oxford: Oxford University Press, 2002.
Radhakrishnan, Sarvepalli. *An Idealist View of Life.* London: Unwin, 1988.
———. *Indian Philosophy*, vol. II. London: The Muirhead Library of Philosophy, 1971.
———. *The Hindu View of Life.* New York: MacMillan, 1939.
———. *The Principal Upanishads.* London: George Allen & Unwin, 1968.
Rahula, Walpola. *What the Buddha Taught.* New York: Grove, 1974.
Reese, Byron. *The Fourth Age: Smart Robots, Conscious Computers and the Future of Humanity.* New York: Atria, 2018.
Romero, Javier. "Coronavirus killed more than 120 priests in Italy." *Rome Reports.* June 23, 2020. https://www.romereports.com/en/2020/06/23/coronavirus-killed-more-than-120-priests-in-italy/.
Rosen, Steven J. *The Reincarnation Controversy: Uncovering the Truth in the World Religions.* Badger, CA: Torchlight, 1997.
Rothblatt, Martine. *Virtually Human: The Promise-and the Peril-of Digital Immortality.* New York: St. Martin's, 2014.
Ryle, Gilbert. *The Concept of Mind, London.* London: Hutchinson, 1949.
Sandberg, A., and N. Bostrom. "Whole Brain Emulation: A Roadmap, Technical Report." *Future of Humanity Institute*, Oxford University, March, 2008. www.fhi.ox.ac.uk/reports/2008-3.pdf.

Saraswati, Satyananda, ed. *Hatha Yoga Pradipika*. Munger, India: Yoga Publications Trust, 1998.

Schumann, H.W. *The Historical Buddha*. Delhi: Motilal Banarsidass, 2004.

Searle, John R. *Mind: A Brief Introduction*. Oxford: Oxford University Press, 2004.

———. "Minds, Brains and Programs." *Behavioral and Brain Sciences*, 3/3 (1980) 417–24.

———. "The Problem of Consciousness." *Social Research*, 60/1 (1993) 3–16.

———. *The Mystery of Consciousness*. New York: New York Review, 1997.

———. *The Rediscovery of the Mind*. Cambridge, Massachusetts: MIT, 1991.

———. "Why I Am Not a Property Dualist." http://faculty.wcas.northwestern.edu/~paller/dialogue/propertydualism.pdf.

Shoemaker, Sidney. *Self-knowledge and Self-Identity*. Ithaca: Cornell University Press, 1963.

Silva, Lynn de. *Reincarnation in Buddhist and Christian Thought*. Colombo, Sri Lanka: Christian Literature Society of Ceylon, 1968.

Sivananda, Swami. *Practice of Karma Yoga*. Tehri-Garwhal, India: Divine Life Society, 1985.

Steiner, Rudolf. "Reincarnation and Karma," Lecture given at Berlin, March 5, 1912. *Rudolf Steiner Archive*. March 15, 2008. https://wn.rsarchive.org/Lectures/GA135/English/SBC1977/19120305p01.html.

———. "Yoga in East and West," Lecture given in Paris, May 1906. *Rudolf Steiner Archive*. January 15, 2001. https://wn.rsarchive.org/Lectures/GA094/English/SGP1978/19060529p01.html.

Stevenson, Ian. *Children Who Remember Previous Lives: A Question of Reincarnation*. Jefferson, NC: McFarland, 2000.

———. "The Evidence for Survival from Claimed Memories of Former Reincarnations, Part 1. Review of the Data." *Journal of the American Society for Psychical Research*, 54 (1960) 51–71.

———. *Twenty Cases of Suggestive Reincarnation*. Charlottesville: University Press of Virginia, 1974.

Strobel, Lee. *The Case for Christ: A Journalist's Personal Investigation of the Evidence for Jesus*. Grand Rapids: Zondervan, 1998.

Stump, Eleonore. *Aquinas*. New York: Routledge, 2005.

Swinburne, Richard. *Mind, Brain and Free Will*. Oxford: Oxford University Press, 2013.

Tertullian. "Apology." *New Advent*. www.newadvent.org/fathers/0301.htm.

———. "Treatise on the Soul." *New Advent*. www.newadvent.org/fathers/0310.htm.

Thaxton, Charles, et al. *The Mystery of Life's Origin*. Seattle: Discovery Institute, 2020.

Turing, Alan M. "Computing Machinery and Intelligence." *Mind*, 49 (1950) 433–60.

Valea, Ernest. *Buddhist-Christian Dialogue as Theological Exchange*. Eugene: Pickwick, 2015.

———. *The Spiritual Dimension of Alternative Medicine: A Christian Assessment*. Eugene: Resource, 2020.

Vincent, James. "Artificial intelligence can spot skin cancer as well as a trained doctor." January 26, 2017. https://www.theverge.com/2017/1/26/14396500/ai-skin-cancer-detection-stanford-university.

Vivekananda, Swami. *Raja Yoga*. New York: Brentano's, 1920.

Walshe, Maurice, transl. *The Long Discourses of the Buddha: A Translation of the Digha Nikaya*. Boston: Wisdom, 1995.

Williams, Bernard. *Problems of the Self: Philosophical Papers 1956—1972*. Cambridge: Cambridge University Press, 1973.

Williams, Paul. *Buddhism from a Catholic Perspective*. London: Catholic Truth Society, 2006.

———. "Indian Philosophy." In *Philosophy 2: Further through the Subject*, edited by A.C. Grayling. Oxford: Oxford University Press, 1998.

———. "Non-conceptuality, critical reasoning and religious experience. Some Tibetan Buddhist discussions." In *Philosophy, Religion and the Spiritual Life*, edited by Michael McGhee. Cambridge: Cambridge University Press, 1992.

———. *The Unexpected Way: On Converting from Buddhism to Catholicism*. London: T&T Clark, 2002.

Williams, Paul, and Anthony Tribe. *Buddhist Thought: A Complete Introduction to the Indian Tradition*. London: Routledge, 2000.

Wilson, Ian. *Mind Out of Time?* London: Victor Gollancz, 1981.

———. *Reincarnation? The Claims Investigated*. Bungay: Richard Clay, 1982.

Wittgenstein, Ludwig. *Philosophical Investigations*. London: Basil Blackwell, 1958.

Index

aggregates, 114–17, 119–21, 127, 171
ahimsa, 133, 155–56
algorithm, xiv, 21–24, 64–67, 69–71, 73–75, 78–80, 187, 189, 193, 196–97
AlphaGo, 69–70, 79
Amitabha (Amida), 120
angels, 3, 170–71, 180, 199, 212
Anthroposophy, 130–31
Aquinas, 163, 165, 167, 170–82, 211
Aristotle, 4, 166–67
artificial intelligence (AI), xiv, 4, 22, 24, 63–68, 70–79, 81–84, 91–94, 187, 194, 214

beatific vision, 177
behaviorism, 14–17
Bhagavad Gita, 125–26, 133, 209, 211
biological naturalism, 30, 33
Blavatsky, Helena, 130
Bostrom, Nick 82, 86–87, 93, 194, 196
Brahman, 100–101, 103–6, 113, 130, 163–64, 174
brain-machine interface (BMI), 79–81
Bridey Murphy, 135–36
Buddha, 114–18, 120–21, 128, 132, 163
Buddhahood, 118, 120
Buddhism, xiv, 96–97, 113–22, 124–29, 157, 164–65, 171, 173–74, 201, 211
Butler, Joseph, 47, 51, 145

Cartesian dualism, xiv, 4, 6–7, 9–10, 14, 17, 25, 33, 37, 52, 109, 159, 163, 166, 170, 175

chakras, 106
Chinese Room, 23, 65, 71, 74
compassion (in Buddhism), 118, 120
computationalism, 21–22, 28, 63, 65
computer avatar, xii, 76, 83, 91–93
consciousness, xii, xiv, 1, 4, 13, 26–30, 33–37, 41–47, 51–57, 59–61, 64–76, 83–84, 88, 90, 92–93, 101, 107, 109–12, 114–15, 119, 128, 131, 133–35, 138, 153–54, 159, 163, 166–67, 171, 173–74, 187–90, 193–94
cryonics, xii, 42, 87, 89

Dalai Lama, 156
Darwinian evolution, 3, 161, 165, 177
Dasgupta, Surendranath, 95, 107–8, 116, 125, 127
Deep Blue (chess program), 68, 78
Deep-learning algorithms, 66–67
DeepMind, 69
Descartes, 4, 5–9, 11–13, 30, 45, 52, 57, 95–96, 109, 163, 166
Deussen, Paul, 111, 157
dharmas, 119–20

Eccles, John, 13, 53, 56
Eliade, Mircea, 103–4, 107–9, 112, 116
Elijah (the prophet), 199–201, 204
emergentism, 25
empiricism, 57
emptiness (*shunyata*), 119, 185
enlightenment, 116–18, 120–21, 129
epiphenomenal, 26

225

Fodor, Jerry, 28
four causes (Aquinas), 176–77
free will, 30–33, 53, 69–70, 75, 165
functionalism, 20–21

Gethin, Rupert, 116–17
Gnosticism, 129, 171, 208–9
Gregory of Nyssa, 206
guna, 107

Harvey, Peter, 118
Hatha Yoga, 104–6
Hawking, Stephen, 75
Heil, John, 26
Hinduism, xiv, 95–101, 105, 112–13, 120–22, 124, 126, 130, 149, 157, 173–74
Homo sapiens, 3, 63, 82, 186–87, 193
Hume, David, 53, 57, 59–61, 91, 115
hylomorphism, 167, 171
hypnotic regression, 136–39, 141, 152

identity theory, 17–19, 25, 79–80
ignorance (*avidya*), 46, 75, 96, 102, 104, 107–9, 111–13, 116–18, 120–22, 124–26, 128–29, 131, 153, 160, 166, 174, 179, 190, 208
image and likeness, 162, 191
impermanence, 113–14, 116, 119, 164
Irenaeus, 205–6, 208
Ishvara, 108
Iyengar, B.K.S., 105–6

Jackson, Frank, 27
Jerome, 206
Jesus, 160–61, 181–83, 185, 189, 199–203, 208–11, 214
John of Damascus, 209
John the Baptist, 199–201, 204, 208

Kabbalah, 129, 202
Kampman, Reima, 140–41
karma, xiv, 102–4, 107–9, 111–13, 117, 122, 124–29, 131, 134, 151–57, 198, 200–202, 208–10, 212
karmashaya, 127
Kim, Jaegwon, 26, 35
Krishna, 125–26, 133, 209

kundalini, 106
Kurzweil, Ray, 64–65, 83, 87–88, 93

Leibniz's Law, 6, 10, 17, 28
Lewis, C.S., 162, 181, 183–84, 189
liberation, 103, 105–6, 108–13, 117, 122, 124–25, 153, 157
Libet, Benjamin, 31
Locke, John, 45–46, 95

Mahayana Buddhism, 118, 120, 122, 211
Manzocco, Roberto, 86–87, 91, 190, 192
McGinn, Colin, 29, 35, 61, 70, 74, 88, 163, 167
mind upload, 83–84, 88–90
mind-body problem, 1, 10, 13, 21, 33, 35, 53
mindclone, xii, 90, 92–93, 191
More, Max, xii, 82, 190
Musk, Elon, 75, 77, 81–82

Nagarjuna, 119–20
Nagel, Thomas, 24, 26, 28, 34, 36, 61, 163
nanotechnology, 87
Neoplatonism, 129, 203, 210
neural network, 66, 73, 90, 188
Neuralink, 79, 81, 187, 193
nirvana, 117–22
Nonreductive Physicalism, 24, 194
No-self (doctrine), 114, 116, 119
Nozick, Robert, 50

Origen, 203–5, 210
overcausation, 26, 35

pantheism, 96, 100, 106, 159, 171, 212
Parfit, Derek, 42–43, 53–56, 61, 129
Parfitian survivor, 56, 91, 129
Patanjali, 106, 108
Paul (apostle), 181–83, 202
physicalism, xiii, 3, 24–27, 30, 33, 35–38, 40, 51–53, 57, 63, 76, 81, 94–96, 101, 110, 147, 159–67, 170–74, 184, 213
Plato, 6, 11, 129, 203–4
Popper, Karl, 52
positivism, 13–14

prakriti, 107–12
prana, 101, 106, 138
property dualism, 3, 25–26
Pure Land Buddhism, 120
Pythagoras, 129, 203–4, 206

Radhakrishnan, Sarvepalli, 132, 210
Raja yoga, 105
Reese, Byron, 32, 85, 89, 91
Reid, Thomas, 51
Rig Veda, 97–99, 103
Ryle, Gilbert, 14, 17

Samkhya, 96, 106–11
samskara, 126–27, 151, 153–54
scholasticism, 4
scientism, 33–34, 36–37, 161, 189, 194
Searle, John R., 23–24, 26, 28–31, 35–37, 40, 61, 68, 75, 188
self (in Western philosophy), xii, xiv, 37, 51, 57–62, 91, 95, 154, 157, 160, 173–74
self (*atman*), 101–17, 119, 121–22, 127–29, 131–33, 153, 165, 210
Shakti, 105–6
Shanti Devi, 142, 145, 147
ship of Theseus, 39, 58
Shiva, 105–6
Shoemaker, Sydney, 42–44, 47
singularity, 65
Sivananda, Swami, 152–54, 156
Sophia (the android robot), 72–74, 82, 91, 194, 196
Steiner, Rudolf, 130–31

Stevenson, Ian, 123, 141–51, 203
Stump, Eleonore, 172, 180
supervenience, 25–26
sushumna, 106
Swinburne, Richard, 13, 53

teleportation, 45, 50, 54, 56, 63
Tertullian, 206
Theosophy, 129–30, 141
Thomistic, 163, 168–70, 174
token-token identity, 19–20
Tower of Babel, 192, 197
Trikaya, 163
type-type identity, 19
Turing Test, 21, 64

Vedanta, 96, 102, 127
Vedas, 95, 97–98, 100, 110
Vienna Circle, 14, 34
Vivekananda, Swami, 101–2

Wambach, Helen, 139
Watson (computer program), 68–69, 78, 81
whole brain emulation, xii, 43, 84, 88, 90, 188
Williams, Bernard, 44, 47–50, 146
Williams, Paul, 115, 117, 211–12
Wilson, Ian, 138, 145, 147
Wittgenstein, Ludwig, 15, 17

Yoga (*darshana*), 96, 104–9, 111–12, 126, 130, 133, 214

www.ingramcontent.com/pod-product-compliance
Lightning Source LLC
Chambersburg PA
CBHW060601230426
43670CB00011B/1918